Digital Media Worlds

Digital Media Worlds

The New Economy of Media

Edited by

Giuditta De Prato, Esteve Sanz and Jean Paul Simon

First published 2014 by
PALGRAVE MACMILLAN

Palgrave Macmillan in the UK is an imprint of Macmillan Publishers Limited, registered in England, company number 785998, of Houndmills, Basingstoke, Hampshire RG21 6XS.

Palgrave Macmillan in the US is a division of St Martin's Press LLC, 175 Fifth Avenue, New York, NY 10010.

Palgrave Macmillan is the global academic imprint of the above companies and has companies and representatives throughout the world.

Palgrave® and Macmillan® are registered trademarks in the United States, the United Kingdom, Europe and other countries.

ISBN 978–1–137–34424–3

This book is printed on paper suitable for recycling and made from fully managed and sustained forest sources. Logging, pulping and manufacturing processes are expected to conform to the environmental regulations of the country of origin.

A catalogue record for this book is available from the British Library.

A catalog record for this book is available from the Library of Congress.

Transferred to Digital Printing in 2014

The sources of our knowledge lie is what is written
on bamboo and silk, what is engraved on metal and stone,
and what is cut on vessels to be handed down to posterity.

Mozi, China, Fifth Century BC[1]

---

[1] Quoted by Tsien (1962)

Contents

Tables, Figures and Boxes

Tables

Figures

Boxes

Abbreviations

3G	third generation of mobile networks (HSPA, EV-DO)
4G	fourth generation of mobile networks (LTE, TD-LTE and WiMAX. Samsung's flagship Galaxy S3 and Apple's new iPhone)
ADSL	asymmetric digital subscriber line/ xDSL: Various technologies for DSL
APAC	the Asia-Pacific region
AVMS	audiovisual and media service directive
B2B	business-to-business
BBC	British Broadcasting Company
BBG	browser-based games
BRIC	Brazil, Russia, India, China
CAGR	compound annual growth rate
CAPEX	capital expenditure
CD	compact disk
CDMA	code division multiple access
CDN	content delivery network
CISAC	Confederation of Societies of Authors and Composers
CNN	Cable News Network
CPM	cost per mille (advertising cost)
CSA	Conseil Supérieur de l'Audiovisuel
DAT	digital audiotape
DBS	direct broadcasting services
DIY	do-it-yourself
DTT	digital terrestrial television
DVD	digital video disk
EAO	European Audiovisual Observatory
EBITDA	earning before interest, tax, depreciation and amortization
EC	European Commission
EGDF	European Game Developer Federation
EMEA	Europe–Middle East–Africa
ETSI	European Telecommunications Standards Institute
EU	European Union
Exabyte	1018 bytes

FCC	Federal Communications Commission (US telecoms and media regulator)
FDD	frequency-division duplex
FRAPA	Format Recognition and Protection Association
GB	gigabyte
GDP	gross domestic product
GERD	gross domestic expenditure on research and development
GRI	government research institution
GSA	Global Supplier Association
GSM	Global System for Mobile Communications
GVA	gross value added
HbbTV	a pan-European initiative aimed at harmonizing broadcast and broadband delivery of entertainment to the end consumer through connected TVs and set-top boxes
HBO	home box office
HD	high definition
HSPA	high speed packet access
HTC	HTC Corporation (a Taiwanese manufacturer)
HTML	hypertext markup language
HTTP	hypertext transfer protocol
IC	integrated circuits
ICT	information and communication technologies
iOS (previously iPhone OS)	a mobile operating system developed and distributed by Apple.
IP	Intellectual Property
IPR	Intellectual Property Rights
IPTV	Internet protocol television (a system that delivers television services using the Internet protocol suite over a packet-switched network)
ISP	Internet service provider
IT	information technologies
ITU	International Telecommunications Union
HW	hardware
LCD	liquid crystal display
LTE	long-term evolution
M2M	machine-to-machine
MB	megabyte

MBB	mobile broadband. Defined as CDMA2000 EV-DO, HSPA, LTE, mobile WiMAX and TD-SCDMA
Mbps	megabits per second
MCI	media and content industries
MEA	Middle East and Africa
MIT	Massachusetts Institute of Technology
MMOG	massively multiplayer online games
MMS	multimedia messaging service
mp3	a patented encoding format for digital audio
MPAA	Motion Picture Association of America
NACE/ISIC	Statistical Classification of Economic Activities in the European Community (in French: Nomenclature statistique des activités économiques dans la Communauté européenne), commonly referred to as NACE/International Standard Industrial Classification
NFC	near field communication
OECD	Organisation for Economic Co-operation and Development
Ofcom	Office of Communications (UK telecom and media regulator)
OPEX	operational expenditure
OS	operating system
OTT	over-the-top. In the fields of broadcasting and content delivery, OTT content means online delivery of video and audio without the Internet service provider being involved in the control or distribution of the content itself.
OVD	online video distributor
P2P	peer to peer (or human to human via telecommunications devices)
Petabyte	10^{15} bytes
PWC	PricewaterhouseCoopers
RTD	research, technology and development
SDK	software development kit
SME	small and medium-sized enterprise
SMS	short message service
STD	a Linux (software)-based security tool
SVOD/VOD	subscription video on demand/video on demand
SW	software
TDD	time-division duplex

TD-SCDMA	time division-synchronous code division multiple access
TSF	television without frontiers directive
UGC	user-generated content
UHF	ultra-high frequency (ITU radio frequency range of electromagnetic waves between 300 MHz and 3 GHz (3,000 MHz)). UHF radio waves are used for television broadcasting, cordless phones, walkie-talkies, satellite communication and numerous other applications.
UNCTAD	United Nations Conference on Trade and Development
VoIP	voice over IP (Internet Protocol)
WAN-IFRA	World Association of Newspapers and News Publishers
WCDMA	wideband code division multiple access
WIPO	World Intellectual Property Organization

Acknowledgements

The present work is partially based on the findings of nine pieces of research on the 'statistical, ecosystems and competitiveness analysis of the media and content industries' (MCI: 1) carried out at the JRC-IPTS, the Institute for Prospective Technological Studies, one of the seven research institutes of the European Commission's Joint Research Center (JRC).

The mission of the JRC-IPTS is to provide customer-driven support to the EU policy-making process by developing science-based responses to policy challenges that have both a socio-economic and a scientific/technological dimension.

The editors would like to gratefully acknowledge Marc Bogdanowicz (IPTS) for initiating, enabling and supporting these research projects. All MCI reports are available at: http://is.jrc.ec.europa.eu/pages/ISG/MCI.htm.

The editors would like to thank Elmer Rietveld (TNO) for carefully updating the Eurostat data for all the industries, and Andre Lange (EAO), Laurent Michaud (IDATE) and David Waterman (Indiana University) for their kind authorization to reproduce their figures and graphs. The editors are grateful to Pierre-Jean Benghozi (ARCEP, Ecole Polytechnique, Paris), Alain Busson (HEC, Paris), Claudio Feijoo (Universidad Politecnica de Madrid), Bernard Guillou (Mediawise, Paris), Augusto Preta (IT Media), David Waterman (Indiana University), Enrico Turrin (FEP, Brussels), Steve Wildman (Quello Center for Telecommunication Management and Law, Michigan State University) and Niko van Eijk (IVIR, Amsterdam) for their support. Finally, the skilful checking and editing of the text by Patricia Farrer (IPTS) is gratefully acknowledged.

The views expressed in the present work are purely those of the authors and may not under any circumstances be regarded as stating an official position of the European Commission.

Notes on Editors

Jean Paul Simon runs his own consulting company. He worked as a senior scientist at the IPTS from 2010 to 2012 on ICT in BRIC countries, as well as on the economics of the media and content industries and the impact of digitization. He has held senior positions in the telecom industry. He has written several books and articles on communications and public policy. He is a frequent speaker on telecommunications and media in Asia, Europe and the US.

Giuditta De Prato joined the Institute for Prospective Technologies (IPTS), European Commission, Directorate-General JRC, the in-house think tank of the European Commission, in January 2009 to contribute to projects on economic aspects of the information society and on the impacts of information society technologies, mainly focusing on ICT R&D, the software sector, patents and innovation dynamics in the context of the knowledge economy. She worked in the industry as a software developer and IT consultant from 1992 to 2005. From 2005 to 2009, she focused on research activities on local development, evaluation, ICT and open source at the University of Bologna.

Esteve Sanz is a Resident Fellow of the Information Society Project, Yale Law School. Previously he worked as a researcher at the IPTS. He holds a PhD in sociology from the Internet Interdisciplinary Institute of the Open University of Catalonia. He has been a postdoctoral fellow at MIT and the Sociology Department of Yale University. He has authored several publications on the information society, cultural sociology, bureaucracy, television and the Internet.

Notes on Contributors

Sophie De Vinck holds a PhD from the VUB (2011). Her research dealt with the digital challenges facing the European film industries and European-level film support. She worked as a senior researcher at iMinds-SMIT (Vrije Universiteit Brussel (VUB)) between 2005 and 2013. In October 2013, she joined the European Commission.

Andra Leurdijk is a specialist in media, innovation and policy. She works as Professor in Entrepreneurial Journalism at Windesheim University of Applied Sciences in Zwolle, the Netherlands, and as an independent consultant at forallmedia.nl. She has worked on a large variety of projects for the Dutch government, the Public Service Broadcaster, the Media Authority, the Culture Council, the Press Fund, the European Commission and the European Broadcasting Union. She is a board member of the Dutch Press Fund.

Sven Lindmark works as a senior researcher at iMinds-SMIT/VUB in Brussels, Belgium, where he researches new ICTs and media, their business models, value networks and innovation systems and their impact on industry structure, industrial competitiveness, innovation and sustainability. He holds a PhD in industrial management and economics from Chalmers University of Technology, where he also held various positions between 2002 and 2007. From 2007 to 2010, he was a senior researcher in the Information Society unit of the European Commission's Joint Research Centre IPTS.

Ottilie Nieuwenhuis is a researcher and project manager at TNO Strategies & Policy for the Information Society (S&P4IS). She conducts research on the changes in the media landscape due to digitization, Dutch and European media policy, converging markets and changing value chains, and new business models. Ottilie also coordinates and initiates research activities in the field of the Creative Industries.

Martijn Poel is a senior researcher and consultant at the Technopolis Group. Between 1999 and 2012, he worked at TNO, the Dutch organization for applied scientific knowledge. He specializes in information society policy, media policy and innovation policy. Research topics include the competitiveness of Europe's ICT sector, the influence of regulation on innovation and the impact of R&D support programmes. His PhD thesis at the Delft University of Technology (2013) explores the impact of the policy mix on service innovation. The case study is about Internet video services.

Introduction

Giuditta De Prato, Esteve Sanz and Jean Paul Simon

The objective of this book is to offer an in-depth analysis of the major economic developments of the various segments of the media and content industries: book publishing, broadcasting,[1] film, music, the newspaper industry and video games. It attempts to give an overview of the dynamics of the sector within a more global ecosystem of telecoms, media and IT. It analyses the changes that have taken place over the last decade, putting them in their historical perspective, and emphasizing the intermingling with ICTs (information and communication technologies).

The book aims to marshal the facts and document the economic relevance of the media sector, highlighting some of the specific features of each subsector. Considerations of the sociological and policy aspects, often the core of most of the literature, are dealt with only in connection with economic aspects. The media also play an acknowledged role in the ways that democracies work, and they generate further externalities for society as a whole (cultural, societal, etc.). However, though these are important issues worth dealing with in their own right, they are outside the scope of this book.

The book combines vertical views and a more synthetized horizontal approach. It describes the recent changes that have affected the telecom–media–IT ecosystem, so as to better identify some of the trends that are most likely to impact the content sector in the future. It tracks the digital evolution of the sector and focuses on core economic (weight, value added) and management issues (cost structures, value network chain, business models).

It analyses the industrial dimension, and looks at how the new ecosystem is structured and the value chains that have developed in a global market where regions like Asia are emerging. These new markets are playing a growing role in this sector. The book offers a multisector, multimarket approach that differs from the usual monosector and monomarket perspective.

About the framework

A value network chain is made up of several segments, each of which adds value in turn. 'Value chain'[2] usually describes the process of production, distribution and consumption by the various players involved in an industry. In the media and content industries, it covers specifically creation/production, publishing/aggregation, manufacturing, distribution and/or exhibition/reception/transmission, and consumption/participation of the end user through various, often sector-specific, channels or devices. The resulting value chain has traditionally been represented as a linear process; see Figure 0.1.[3]

The digital shift – that is, the digitization of information, the generalization of the Internet protocol – and the rapid take-up of these technologies (final user equipment, broadband infrastructures, etc.) is transforming the way we produce, store, distribute and consume goods and services. The different industry layers (technological infrastructures, distribution and intermediaries, and content) are being (re)articulated within a new 'ecosystem' while value chains are being restructured in a global market.

The new industrial ecosystem forces different types of companies, with different business cultures and performance, to compete and collaborate. In the 'old' world, each of these sectors focused on its core business and managed its own assets. The publisher/aggregator segment of legacy media and content industries, which was largely made up of integrated firms (production/publishing/distribution–retail), dominated the traditional value chain, and controlled distribution (wholesale and often retail). This traditional, oligopolistic and vertically integrated

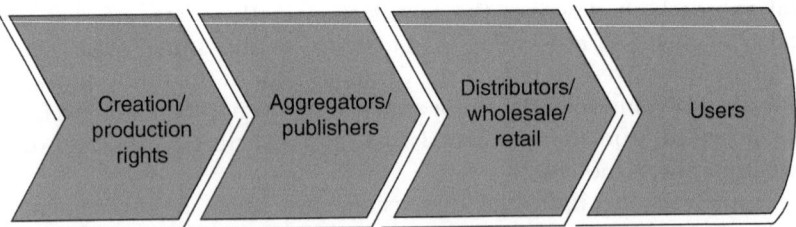

Figure 0.1   A simplified view of the traditional value chain of the sector

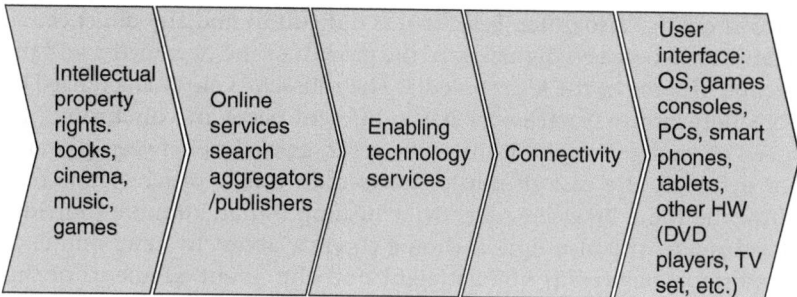

Figure 0.2 A stylized view of the Internet value chain
Source: Adapted by the authors from A.T. Kearney (2010).

market of the media industry is now being challenged, as the industry moves towards a new value chain with many different participants, some overlapping roles, shifting relations and changes in the structure and power relations within the new value chain. Figure 0.2 offers a stylized view of the new Internet value chain. Though there are some continuities with the past, disruptive innovations are taking place which are leading to innovations in business models.

The first part of this book opens with the oldest medium, the book, and ends with the newest, video games. Both of the two oldest media (books and music) have both a very sophisticated network of players (Becker, 1982) and intellectual exchanges (Grafton, 2009). For a piece of music to be played, not only are (trained) musicians obviously needed, but instruments must also be produced, stored and maintained, musical notation must be available, edited, and distributed, programmes must be printed, and rooms for concerts booked. The other media industries have also developed intricate networks of players.

All these industries have complex and evolving relationships with technologies and technological inventions. Some were born out of a technological innovation (cinema, broadcasting and video games). Others incorporate technologies at various levels and points on their value network and change accordingly (books, music). For books, the importance of technology is not new, and has always been crucial. Indeed, each segment was born and grew with a specific chain of actors around specific technologies. Digitization brings a new way to unify the entire value chain, from creation/production to consumption.

However, it does not follow that these industries will fall under some kind of strong technological determinism. Not only does interaction between the players differ from one sector to another, but the time and pace of change also differ. Besides, it is difficult to find any direct causal relationship between digitization, the growth of the new media and the decline of some of the legacy media. The subsectors are characterized by both polychrony (each sector has a different pace) and dischrony (the speed of change varies within each sector, as well as between players). For instance, the case of music shows that, unlike other sectors (e.g. film), the route between collective consumption and a more individualized mode of consumption (home cinema, access to news online or on portable devices) is not a straight one: the 'event' segment[4] of this industry has been growing.

The book follows the multiform and evolving interactions between (Section I) and within (Section II) media sectors, with a focus on the global dimension, which is not completely new. Paper and printing were invented in China centuries ago (Tsien, 1962). At the moment, Asia leads in online and mobile games. At the turn of the 20th century, the leading cinema companies were French (Gaumont, Lumière), before Hollywood took over (Segrave, 1997). Now India is the world's largest film producer, making around 1,100 films annually (UNCTAD, 2010).

Of media and technology: Short (hi)stories

The interaction between media and technologies is a complex one, involving several parameters. The drivers of adoption and change vary, as each 'world' is organized around a complex network of players and specific technologies. Some technological innovations are disruptive; others are not – though they sustain innovation. In any case, even disruptive innovations are based on some underlying continuity (Jullien, 2012): for instance, within existing trends in patterns of consumption and production. This section briefly sets the scene and gives a small vignette of the interactions between technology and the main activity of each sector.[5]

In the book publishing sector, the invention of the printing press (Eisenstein, 1980; Martin, 1997) took place in parallel with other changes. For instance, the creation of universities (studium) allowed teaching to become a real job with appropriate tools, that is, books (Frugoni, 2011: 54–55). The book business thrived, as multiple copies of the official 'exemplar' for a course were much cheaper than the expensive codex[6] (Frugoni: 60). This invention was made possible by an earlier innovation: the invention of paper some centuries before (in Spain in 1150 according to Frugoni; medieval Italy was also well known for the quality of its paper). Paper was produced in China as early as the second century BC, and in Korea and Japan around the sixth century AD (Frugoni: 80).

The printed book, as a 'new medium', initially tried to replicate as far as possible the patterns of the codex and the embellishments of the copyist. For example, the first bible printed by Gutenberg was deeply influenced by medieval habits (gothic characters, room for ornaments and colours). Time had to pass before new, more appropriate, fonts were used. The change took place in Italy, in Venetia, where Aldo Manuzio introduced new letters inspired by the *littera antiqua*. Manuzio also abandoned the traditional format and introduced a much smaller version (one-quarter the size) so that books could be made easily available. The components of the book 'chain' were in place. The book industry started to grow, together with the paper industry and other technical industries. For centuries, stationers (*librairies*; see Diderot, 2012) were at the core of the book value chain, and also acted as publishers.

This industry, being the 'oldest' (De Prato and Simon, 2014), has a long track record of public interventions, from plain censorship to the creation of ad hoc monopolies (stationers had exclusive rights to copy in the UK, for instance, from 1556 until 1695). For centuries censorship and the control of production were left to the church,[7] but, after the invention of the printing press (Eisenstein, 1980) and the creation of 'modern' states, it became a matter for the state.[8] The relationships between the players within the book value chain evolved up to the creation of copyright in the 19th century (Edelman, 2008), which was more suited to a fast-evolving book industry. Public policies have blossomed since.

Music publishing did not begin on a large scale until the mid-15th century, when mechanical techniques for printing music were first developed[9] (the earliest example was released about 1465). Prior to this, music had had to be copied out by hand. Centuries later, the progressive electrification of the guitar illustrates how innovative makers and players created a new instrument (Lemelson Center for the Study of Invention and Innovation, 2013). The electric amplification of the guitar was first introduced in the 1920s and meant that it could be heard when accompanying the brass section in big jazz bands. It paved the way for the development of the instrument from Charlie Christian through to Jimi Hendrix and rock 'n' roll. Musical performances in the 19th century were characterized by ever-larger concert settings and ensembles. Musicians needed louder and more powerful instruments, which became possible by using new materials and designs.

Cinema has had an important technological component from the start. Without a number of crucial technological breakthroughs, cinema would not have been possible. From an historical perspective, a number of prominent periods of technological change have affected the film sector more or less radically since its establishment: the introduction of sound (1920s–1930s), colour (1930s–1960s), the television screen (1950s–1960s), widescreen and 3D experiments (1950s) and home video systems (1970s–1980s).

There are a number of recurring elements in these transitions, though their nature and speed have varied. First, all of these innovations were adopted over relatively long periods of time and built upon previous technological and other changes in the sector. Important drivers of technological adoption have included transition costs, availability of technological standards, audience response and availability of content. Technology also interacts with the evolution of the aesthetics of cinema: a new handheld camera allowed J. L. Godard's chief operator (R. Coutard) to shoot *A bout de souffle* differently, giving rise to the *Nouvelle vague*. New portable devices have played a similar role in the birth of *cinema verité* (J. Rouch), and in the growth of the Canadian documentary school in the 1960s.

The evolution of television is another example of the driving role of technology in this sector (Waterman and Ji, 2012: 8–9). The mid-1970s saw the launch of geostationary satellites and a steady increase in cable system transmission capacity. The combination of satellite transmission and local cable distribution boosted the growth of the US cable industry. It allowed the birth of superstations, which could send a local signal from one area to another much further away. In 1970, a young entrepreneur from Atlanta, Ted Turner, bought an UHF station (Simon, 1991: 337). He realized quickly that the new Federal Communications Commission (FCC)[10] rules (1972) enabled him to reach distant locations. By 1976, he was serving 100 cable networks covering five states. Cable penetration went up from 10% of US households in 1972 (served by 2,841 local networks) to almost 60% in 1989 (served by 9,050 networks). As a result, channels proliferated in the US in the 1980s.

Then analogue multichannel systems were converted into digital, further expanding their capacity. Modern Direct Broadcast Satellite (DBS), launched in 1994, was digital from the start. At about the same time, cable systems began converting to digital tiers, which dramatically expanded their channel capacity. This, in turn, stimulated the entry of hundreds of new television networks. In addition, more efficient computer-based systems for controlling programme flow to consumers have contributed to a massive growth in cable TV revenue per subscriber since the mid-1990s. This was highlighted by Waterman and Ji (2012) as a less noticeable digital driving force.

In China, early government-produced news sheets, called *tipao*, circulated among court officials during the late Han Dynasty (second and third centuries AD). Between 713 and 734, the *Kaiyuan Za Bao* (Bulletin of the Court) of the Chinese Tang Dynasty published government news, handwritten on silk and read by government officials (Tsien, 1962; Gernet, 2002; McDermott, 2006; Goody, 2010).[11] Centuries later, the mechanization of printing in two waves allowed the printing press to bloom during the Industrial Revolution in the 19th century. In the first wave, flatbed printing was replaced by the rotary motion of cylinders, opening up the process of making newspapers available to a mass audience. Then, when electricity instead of steam powered the rotary printing press, the process became much quicker, and more copies with more pages could be easily produced (Charon, 1991: 37). The second wave came around 1884 with the introduction of the linotype machine, which became the industry standard for newspapers, until it was replaced in the following century by offset lithography printing and computer typesetting. The linotype brought another increase in the size of daily newspapers; up until then, newspapers had been limited to eight pages.[12] The electric telegraph contributed indirectly to the growth of information agencies, for instance in France, where Havas was granted a monopoly for its use in 1850 (Charon, 1991). This added another element to the newspaper world.

The first interactive computer game dates back to 1961, when *Spacewar!* was created by a Massachusetts Institute of Technology (MIT) student on a mainframe computer.[13] Video games, initially as 'labs games', accompanied the development of computer science (Tricot, 2012). 'First-generation' video game consoles, based on dedicated logic circuits without microprocessors, started to be distributed between 1971 and 1976. The birth of the modern video game is usually dated to 1972, with the launch of *Pong* in Sunnyvale, California, though sometimes this claim is made for the (less well known) *Odyssey* console of Magnavox (Kent, 2001; De Prato et al., 2010; Donovan, 2012). *Pong* was a machine-based game built by an engineer working for Atari, a company founded a few months earlier. The diffusion of coin-operated arcade games followed soon after, reaching a peak in 1978, largely due to the successful release of *Space Invaders*, followed by the first colour games.

Assessing the economic weight: Some figures

Accurately assessing the digital economy is a complex task in itself. Some of the most comprehensive official attempts, for instance, the Creative Economy Reports issued by UNCTAD[14] (Creative Economy Reports, 2008[15]), point out that gauging the economic weight of the media and content industries is highly complex because it raises several issues of definition and availability of data (see Box 0.1 for a summary of the main issues and Box 10.1 for some specific issues relating to the video games market). These reports often have to rely on unofficial statistics that are not compatible with official statistics and lack time series data. There is a time lag in the availability of official statistics (European Commission (EC), 2005b; Leurdijk et al., 2012). Definitions and official statistical classifications such as those adopted by the OECD,[16] UNCTAD[17] and Eurostat often differ widely from those used in academic literature or by consultancies and research institutes.

Nevertheless, it is possible to use some heterogeneous sources to document this field. Recent and disaggregated data are usually available from unofficial data sources such as trade associations and consultancies, and these have been used for the book. These sources can provide relevant data for subsectors, and contribute to an understanding of recent transformations within subsectors. They also provide qualitative analyses of trends and transformations, for instance by focusing on changes in business models, value chains, company strategies, and media and content consumption.

This section first reviews the available data on global markets and then concentrates on the EU market based on official data (Eurostat). The last part introduces another viewpoint based on World Intellectual Property Organization (WIPO)[18] data on copyrighted industries.

Box 0.1   Definition of the sectors and data availability

Official data

OECD uses the United Nations ISIC[19] classification system for categorizing economic activities, and Eurostat uses a similar system called NACE,[20] which is based on/aligned with ISIC. Categorized under the new statistical classification system for economic activities (ISIC rev.4; United Nations, 2007), the OECD defines the media and content industries broadly as:

The production (goods and services) of a candidate industry must primarily be intended to inform, educate and/or entertain humans through mass communication media. These industries are engaged in the production, publishing and/or the distribution of content (information, cultural and entertainment products), where content corresponds to an organised message intended for human beings.

(OECD, 2009)

It includes the following segments: publishing of books, periodicals and other publishing activities, motion pictures, video and television programme activities, sound recording and music publishing activities, programming and broadcasting activities, and other information service activities (news agency activities, other information service activities, etc.) (OECD, 2005).

The sectors that the OECD (2007) has identified as belonging to the industries are sometimes considered to be part of a broader sector labelled 'the creative industries', which are defined in a DCMS[21] study as 'those industries which have their origin in individual creativity, skill and talent and which have a potential for wealth and job creation through the generation and exploitation of intellectual property' (DCMS, 2001).

In other studies, the media and the entertainment sectors are grouped together. Often a clear overall definition of these sectors is lacking; they are described instead by identifying their economic activities and the kinds of products and services they produce. The media and entertainment sector, as defined by PricewaterhouseCoopers (PWC) (2013), for instance, includes filmed entertainment, TV, recorded music, radio and out-of-home advertising, Internet advertising and access spending, video games, business information, magazine publishing, newspaper publishing, book publishing, theme parks and amusement parks, casinos and other regulated gaming and sports. Again, some of these sectors, such as theme and amusement parks and sports, would fall outside the OECD's definition, because they are not distributed through mass communication media. Also, Internet access, advertising and games are not included in the underlying OECD categories, although (most) advertising and video games fit quite well with the wording of the OECD definition, as they are produced for information and entertainment and

Box 0.1 (Continued)

(often) distributed by mass communication media.[22] This example shows that not only are these media and content industries often subsumed into larger categories (creative industries, media and entertainment), but also the definitions and the identification of the (sub)sectors (categories) of the industries vary.

In addition, and more importantly, it has become increasingly difficult to allocate a company to any one particular sector of economic activities. Since the 1980s, ownership, organization and the kind of economic activities that traditional mass media communication companies are involved in have changed. The largest companies no longer specialize in one product (newspapers, films, broadcast channels, music), but have become large conglomerates (Disney, Murdoch's News Corporation, Bertelsmann, Canal+, Sanoma, etc.) that now operate internationally and across a number of different subsectors. This horizontal integration was accompanied by processes of vertical integration, whereby companies increasingly tried to control different links in the value chain. For instance, content producers are also distributing their content on international markets, and network providers look for added value by incorporating media content packagers. This can make it difficult to categorize a particular company that is active in all these sectors. Increasingly, there are many companies whose core activity has not been media and content, but which are nevertheless performing media and content activities. These emerging trends cannot be fully captured by the OECD definition of these industries, as many of the leading companies fall outside the media and content industries categorization because their prime activity still belongs to another category.

The data presented in this section (Table 0.1 and Table 0.2) comply with the ISIC rev 3.1 categorization of the media and content industries. Eurostat data are based on the European NACE classification of economic activities (commercial and non-commercial), which, in turn, is based on the international ISIC classification for economic activities of the United Nations. It comprises:

- Printing, publishing and reproduction of recorded media industry (category 221), which consists of publishing of books, brochures and other publications, publishing of newspapers, journals and periodicals, publishing of sound recordings and other publishing.

• Recreational, cultural and sporting industry (category 92), including motion picture and video activities, radio and television activities, other entertainment activities, together with news agency activities, libraries, archives, museums and other cultural activities, sporting activities and other recreational activities.

Table 0.1 EU media and content industries, value added 2010 (overall economy, Europe, constant prices 2000)[23]

Value added, absolute	Billion euro				
	EU27	EU 6	EU 9	EU15	EU new
Total EU27 economy	9,812.0	5,727.7	3,387.4	9,115.1	696.9
Total media and content industries	219.5	146.0	65.1	211.1	8.4
Publishing, printing, reproduction of recorded media	38.5	20.2	16.4	36.6	1.9
Publishing of books	9.1	4.5	4.0	8.5	0.6
Publishing of newspapers	13.0	7.3	5.2	12.5	0.5
Publishing of journals and periodicals	12.4	6.3	5.5	11.8	0.5
Publishing of sound recordings	1.8	1.0	0.7	1.7	0.1
Other publishing	2.3	1.0	1.1	2.0	0.2
Recreational, cultural and sporting activities	180.9	125.9	48.6	174.6	6.5

Source: A. Leurdijk et al. (2012), updated by authors.

Table 0.2 Distribution of value added of media and content industries and share of entire economy, 2010

	EU27	EU 6	EU 9	EU15	EU new
Total media and content industries as share of entire economy	2.2	2.5	1.9	2.3	1.2
Publishing, printing, reproduction of recorded media as share of MCI	18	14	25	17	23
Publishing of books	24	22	24	23	31
Publishing of newspapers	34	36	32	34	26
Publishing of journals and periodicals	32	31	33	32	26
Publishing of sound recordings	5	5	4	5	5
Other publishing	6	5	7	5	10
Recreational, cultural and sporting activities	82	86	75	83	77

Source: A. Leurdijk et al. (2012), updated by authors.

Box 0.1 (Continued)

Data on the recreational, cultural and sporting industry at a disaggregated level (three and four digits) are not available in the Eurostat Structural Business Statistics (SBS) database.

Availability of unofficial statistics

Investigation of data found by screening major sources from industry associations, consultancies and research institutes specialized in media and content industries has shown that it is impossible to directly compare or complement official statistics with unofficial statistics, for a number of reasons:

- There are no reports containing data on all the (sub)sectors as defined by the OECD and Eurostat. Most market reports focus on particular sub-sectors only.
- Sectoral definitions and categorizations vary, and differ from the one followed by the OECD (ISIC) and Eurostat (NACE).
- There are single country reports and some reports cover more than one country, but their geographical scope varies and there are very few sources that provide consistent and comparable country-level data over long periods of time.
- Statistics are usually confined to recent years, and sometimes include forecasts. There are hardly any publications that have appeared consistently and regularly over an extended period of time, covering the same (sub)sectors in the same countries.
- Different indicators are used for analysing (sub)sectors. Most consultancy reports contain data on market size in terms of total revenues, consumer spending, income from advertising, subscription or licence fees, or data on consumers' use of networks, services and technologies and sometimes also the number of services (Video-on-demand) or TV channels available in particular national markets. Data on the main indicators collected by Eurostat, such as value added, number of firms, number of employees and imports and exports are mostly lacking in these publications.

Source: A. Leurdijk et al. (2012).

Growing but uneven markets: Regional and sector-related differences

The industrial ecosystem, referred to in specialized literature as the global 'Telecom, Media and Technology' (TMT) ecosystem, now integrates the media and content industries (i.e. network operations, electronic components, electronic products, IT services and software, content and Internet players[24]). It has grown globally at an overall rate of 8.1%[25] from 2007 onwards, reaching US\$5,850 billion in 2011, despite a 2% decline in 2009 (Booz & Co., 2012). Within this ecosystem, the growth rate is rather unevenly distributed. Internet players have had a double-digit growth rate (over 13%), while the media and content sector as a whole has grown by 6.3%.[26] In addition, the share of revenues in relative terms of the legacy media players has dropped; for instance, it fell from 83% in 2009 to 74% in 2010 (Booz & Co., 2012: 6), and new entrants now have a share of 26%.

This overall growth is mainly due to the contribution of emerging markets (Brazil and China being the fastest-growing). They are developing at a rate of 12.6%, with an overall share of the global market that has increased from 20% to 25% between 2006 and 2011 (Booz & Co., 2011a, 2012). While emerging markets grow, mature media markets (EU, US) are declining.

Within the media and content industries, growth is even more unevenly spread, not only between regions but also between segments. Indeed, the global growth of the sector forecast by specialized consultancies is modest. PWC (2013) forecast an overall compound annual growth rate (CAGR) growth of 5.6% from 2013 to 2017. This lags behind the expected global gross domestic product (GDP) growth for the same period. Booz & Co. (2011b: 11) noted that over the period 2005–2010 these industries were split into two groups: a group benefiting by 3% on average (books, broadcasting, film, Internet advertising, video games), and a group declining by an average of 5% (out-of-home advertising, recorded music, newspapers and magazines, radio).

The video games industry is growing steadily. Broadcasting remains a profitable business. Global 'music' industry revenues rose from US\$51.2 billion to US\$74.1 billion between 1998 and 2010, but its recorded segment was badly hit: down from US\$38.7 billion in 1999 to US\$16.5 billion in 2012 (IFPI, 2013).[27] However, it increased slightly in 2012, for the first time since 1999 (IFPI, 2013). Newspaper revenues decreased over the same period, from US\$185.6 billion to US\$159.6 billion, and revenues for magazines dropped from US\$81.5 to US\$72.6

billion. The rapid decline of newspaper revenues does not appear to be slowing down.

One can assume that the figures are even more dramatic for mature markets, as the average data presented here include emerging economies. From a regional viewpoint, it is worth noting that Asia leads in terms of digital sales. About 65% of Japanese mangas[28] are on mobile. Three of the four largest world markets for video games are located in the Asia-Pacific (Japan, China and South Korea). In 2010, numbers of cinema admissions fell in mature markets such as the US (–5.2%) and the EU (–1.6%), but increased in growth markets such as India, China and Russia. India has the largest market in terms of admissions, with nearly three billion (2009), far ahead of both the US (2010: 1,341 billion) and the EU (2010: nearly one billion). Asia has a dominant position in new media (trade data: import/export; UNCTAD, 2010, 2013). Exports of new media products from China reached US$8.4 billion in 2008, or about 30% of global demand. Video games constituted the most important export (UNCTAD, 2010: 189).

The data published by PWC each year show clear growth in the digital share of global entertainment and media spending and an equally clear decline in non-digital spending. However, beyond the apparent correlation, any direct causality would be difficult to establish. Nevertheless, the US Bureau of Labor Statistics traced a nearly 30% decrease in the number of workers in 'book, periodical, and music stores'[29] between 2002 and 2009 (quoted by Wallsten, 2010: 30). The agency predicts another decrease of almost 27% between 2010 and 2020, while total employment in the US will grow by 14% (US Bureau of Labor Statistics, 2013).

Indeed, the degree of causality between the growth of new media and the decrease of some legacy media is far from obvious; numerous intertwining parameters are involved. These parameters are likely to differ from one subsector to another. For example, it is often claimed that the decline in cinema-going in the 1960s and 1970s in the EU was a direct result of the growth in broadcasting. This claim, however, is not in line with the data available. In France, for instance, box office revenues plummeted after their peak in 1957, yet in the early 1960s the household penetration rate for TV was low. The main explanatory factor (Bonnell, 1978) was not the rise of TV but the fact that many households had cars, which led to new patterns of leisure, away from cinemas. By the same token, the decline of readership (books, newspapers) started before digitization.

Although the revenue share of digital media and content industries is growing steadily, it remains modest, not to say low, for most content industries. Consequently, historically declining revenues have not been compensated for by digital revenue, and prices have fallen. Digitization is generating economic transfer from one set of players to another; there are some winners and some losers. In the EU, less than 2% of total book revenues come from e-books even in the fastest-growing European market, the UK – a far cry from the 20% of the trade market reached in the US market in 2012 (AAP, 2013). Online revenues (VOD online and SVOD) are growing, but revenues from VOD and SVOD accounted for less than 1% of the total European audiovisual market in 2010. In the US, online video streaming has become widespread since about 2000, but continues to represent less than 2% of all TV viewing (Waterman and Ji, 2012), with a revenue share of only 1.5% in 2010. Therefore, the increasing on-demand spend is not yet compensating for the ongoing decline of physical home videos.

The music industry is the exception: 34% of record companies' income in 2012 (IFPI, 2013) was generated by digital products. These products already account for most of the revenues in an increasing number of markets, such as India, Norway, Sweden, South Korea and the US. However, in spite of the rapid increase of online music revenues, they are not yet compensating for decreased sales of physical products. The music industry has claimed that over 60% of the decrease of physical sales was not compensated for between 2006 and 2010 (IFPI, quoted by Leurdijk et al., 2012). However, 'compensation' may not be the relevant economic indicator in a declining market, just as the lower number of passengers for stagecoaches was not an adequate indicator of the growth of the transport market. Some of the sectors are facing structural changes (a continuing decline in readership).

The video games industry is another exception, as it was digital from the beginning: mobile and online revenue reached nearly 50% of global revenues in 2012 (PWC, 2013). Online distribution of physical products (such as books) is not a major distribution channel: retailers (small and large) still constitute the main channel. The exception is, again, music, especially in the US and the UK, where retailers and retail chains are closing down.

These trends may change. Historically, in the US, media industries like broadcasting have benefited greatly from the introduction of new technologies over the last four decades. Revenues from the distribution of films in the US followed a similar pattern, with the introduction of each

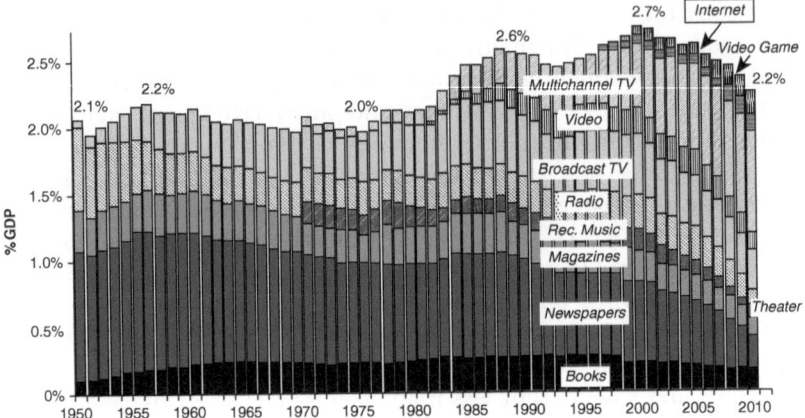

Figure 0.3   Total revenue of US commercial media as percentage of GDP, 1950–2010

Source: Waterman and Ji (2012). Figure based on US census and trade association data and authors' estimates.

new technology triggering additional streams of revenues (broadcasting, cable, pay TV, DVD, etc).

A closer look at the long-term evolution, over a 60-year period, of professionally produced commercial media revenues in the US shows that revenues measured as a percentage of the US GDP went up until 2000, when they reached a plateau. Thereafter, they decreased and only returned to their 1950 level in 2010 (Waterman, 2011). Revenues have been consistently falling (or flattening) since, especially from newspapers and music segments, and revenues from the Internet or from the newest segment of the media, video games, have so far not compensated for the decline (Figure 0.3).

The EU markets: Media and content industries are significant contributors to the EU economy

Unfortunately, no similar data are available for the EU market (Leurdijk et al., 2012). It is possible, however, to compare the average growth of value added for newspaper publishing, books and recorded music in the six largest EU markets between 1995 and 2010: a similar pattern of (recent) decline is revealed.

Over the period 1995–2010 these industries, together with cultural activities, reached a significant economic size, contributing some

219 billion euros value added in 2010 (Table 0.1), or around 2–3% of the EU GDP. Their annual average growth rate was 2.4%. Most of the value added they produced (146 of the total 219 billion euros) was in the EU 6. However, as the NACE/ISIC classification (see Box 0.1) is being used for statistical purposes, it is important to underline the dominance of the 'recreational, cultural and sporting activities' within this category over media and content-relevant activities such as film, broadcasting and video.

The media and content industry's share of the overall economy is more or less equal across Europe. Table 0.2 shows the share of 'publishing, printing and reproduction of recorded media' as a share of media and content industries, in the total EU economy, and the five subsectors' respective shares of 'publishing, printing, reproduction of recorded media'.

The economic weight of copyrighted industries

Looking at the economic weight of copyrighted industries provides another way to gauge the importance of the sector, although it underestimates some other aspects and segments. Data are available for the industries involved, although they are not always consistent. 'Copyright-based creative industries (comprising software and database production, book and newspaper publishing, music and film) contribute 3.3% to the EU GDP (2006)' (EC, 2011a: 5). Another WIPO study (2012) looked at the contribution to GDP of what they defined as the core copyright industries. Their contribution to GDP varies significantly across countries, from over 10% (US, Australia) to under 2% for Brunei. With an average of 5.4%, three-quarters of the countries surveyed (30) in the WIPO sample contribute between 4% and 6.5% (WIPO, 2012: 2). Figure 0.2 shows the average breakdown among the industry segments of the core sector. The press and literature segment contributes by far the most (40.5%) to generating added value. The software and database segment makes the second largest contribution (almost 24%) (Figure 0.4).

The contribution of copyright industries to national employment also varies significantly across countries, though the average is 5.9% (WIPO, 2012: 3). Looking at the contribution to employment, Figure 0.3 shows that almost half the labour force in the core copyright industries is employed in the press and literature segment, followed by the software and databases segment (Figure 0.5).

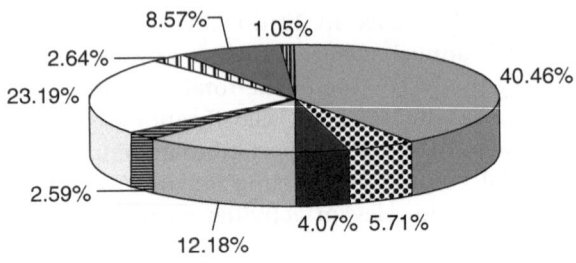

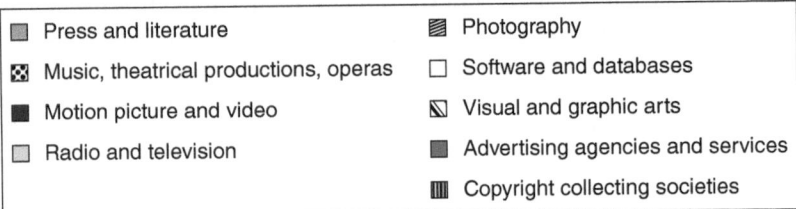

Figure 0.4   Contribution of core copyright industries to GDP by industry
Source: WIPO (2012: 13).

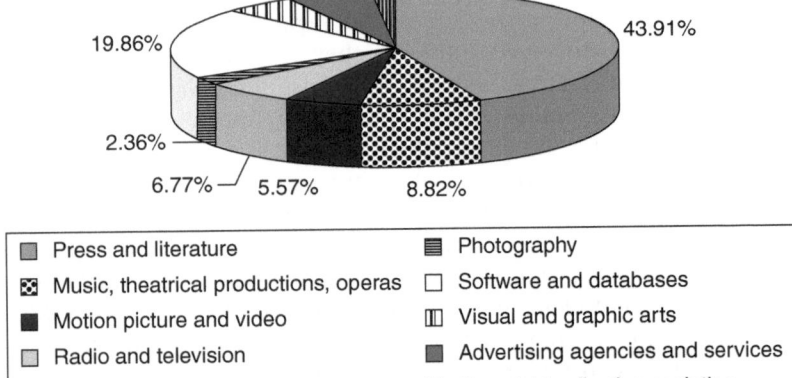

Figure 0.5   Contribution of the core copyright industries to employment by industry
Source: WIPO (2012: 14).

Towards digital media worlds

The first four chapters deal with the dynamics of the sector. They anal-
yse the move towards digital worlds, highlighting the evolution of value
networks and the changing relationships between established and new

players. Chapter 1 follows the three successive transformational waves these industries have been through. It describes the role played by new entrants (telecom companies and IT companies (search engines, e-dealers, and manufacturers)) in the upheaval of the industries. It also shows how traditional players initially reacted defensively but then adopted more proactive strategies. Chapter 2 focuses on core economic issues. It shows how changing markets and evolving cost structures are ushering in innovative business models, which offer new ways to monetize services. It shows the difficult transition away from legacy business models to new innovative ones. The changes are viewed from the perspective of other trends, such as patterns of consumption and production, and the evolution of the labour force.

Chapter 3 illustrates how sectors (such as content and media, telecommunications, information technologies) that had been separated before are progressively intermingling within a new industrial ecosystem. These changes are triggering a move towards a five-screen world: TV, PC, games consoles, connected TVs and mobile devices (smartphones or tablets). Chapter 3 focuses on the newest and fastest-growing screen: mobile devices. It highlights their fast-expanding role in the provision of content to an ever-increasing customer base.

Chapter 4, while reviewing the core economic policy issues, points out that the digital shift opens up new policy issues, novel ways to implement them, and also questions about how efficient these policies are in a digital world. It explores the tensions between initial policy goals that may still be legitimate and how to implement them in a digital world.

The following six chapters (which make up the second part of the book) set the scene for each industry, bringing further insights. They focus on specific interactions between legacy players and new entrants enabled by digitization within the new ecosystem discussed in the previous chapters. Each chapter opens with an overview of a particular industry sector (global and regional markets, with an emphasis on the EU markets), then reviews the economic characteristics of the sector, and finally studies the new relationships between the specific elements of its value network. The chapters show how, and to what extent, traditional business models are being disrupted in each case, and, further, trace the birth of some innovative business models.

Chapter 5 studies an almost stable mature book market, although the new major players in book publishing, which now account for the strongest growth, come from emerging economies (Brazil, China and India). However, this chapter stresses that, of the media and entertainment markets, the book market is the only one where EU companies (Bertelsmann, Hachette, Grupo Planeta, Pearson, Reed-Elsevier, Wolters

Kluwer) lead. Publishers are at the core of the business, but going digital (online distribution, from book to e-book) is reshuffling the value chain, with new channels of distribution (the Internet) bringing cheaper and more efficient vehicles. The chapter notes the uneven development of the e-book market: it has taken off only recently, with some regions, like the US, taking the lead, and some segments, like trade, lagging behind.

Chapter 6 describes the television sector, which has had continuous economic growth for the last 50 years, stimulated by an enormous increase of channel capacity, improvement of picture quality with high definition, and a transformation in the type of audiovisual products. It remains one of the largest media markets: a very profitable business worldwide, with viewing figures still growing. This chapter shows how access channels evolved from terrestrial TV to cable being the main access to traditional platforms in most of the regions. Analogue television platforms are now being replaced by digital ones, bringing more 'channels' through various types of distribution. These latest platforms (online video and platforms, content as applications) have experienced a significant increase in recent years. However, the industry is still finding its way among the proliferation of platforms: even though online video streaming has become widespread, its overall proportion of all TV viewing and revenue shares is still very low.

Chapter 7 looks at the historical development of the film sector, which was originally built around a cinema release. This has gradually expanded to include non-cinema delivery channels. The chapter looks at the changes that digitization has brought for the traditional organizational model. It delves into recent developments in the film industry, paying particular attention to evolution in the context of digital 'dematerialization', with an emphasis on the case of Europe. It offers a qualitative analysis centred on how digital opportunities and threats relate to the analogue strengths and weaknesses of the sector. It assesses how ongoing digital developments impact on prominent elements of the feature film value network, in particular the production, distribution and exhibition of films on different screens.

Chapter 8 addresses the roles and strategies of artists, record companies, providers of online music services, and users over the past two decades. It illustrates the transition from physical sales (CD, DVD) to increased digital sales and advertising revenues from online music services. It shows that revenue streams such as music licensing and concerts are becoming more important. Increasingly, online music services are bundled with video services and social networking. New intermediaries (Internet firms, largely US-based) are playing a major role, and are redistributing the positions of the different stakeholders in the value chain.

The newspaper publishing industry has been struggling with declining circulation, readership, sales and advertising revenues for a while. Chapter 9 looks at the newspaper industry's market structure and discusses the major changes in this industry. This chapter describes how newspaper publishers have responded in various ways to the changing market conditions over the two last decades. It reviews the value network for news production and follows the new opportunities brought by the digital shift for publishers, journalists and consumers. It shows how newspapers are now competing with the online services of many competitors, from national and large US-based news aggregators, to the initiatives of bloggers, to user-generated news sites.

The video games chapter (Chapter 10) follows the birth and growth of an industry over the last 40 years, from a mere hobby to an established form of mainstream entertainment with worldwide communities. Chapter 10 documents a series of key insights into the video games industry that allow us to understand the market and its industrial structure, including the main actors and activities. It illustrates the way the video games value chain is organized: the product, from its creation to its consumption, goes through a series of intermediaries for its commercialization, each of which plays a specific role and aims to optimize its profit and position. It sheds light on the potential transformations its existing value chain may undergo if disruptive trends are introduced, with online and mobile distribution, new platforms, and the changing role of the users. The chapter emphasizes the fact that demand has been a driving force, pushing all multimedia content towards convergence. Consumer behaviour has evolved over the past few years, unexpectedly allowing the viral diffusion of online gaming to take place.

The chapters indicate how edited media are moving towards aggregation, keeping some dimensions of the earlier world(s), such as bundling/editing, but adding others. In an online world, bundles will more and more frequently include numerous services, bringing streams of secondary and additional revenue. Some will be provided by new entrants and suppliers. App stores are offering brokerage services and indirect marketing (as newspapers used to do). New entrants such as telecommunications companies (telcos) can offer billing services. Other services will be introduced by legacy players: for instance, the video games industry is selling innovative virtual items, such as avatars, among others.

Indeed, the new players act as disintermediation agents, and provide (or will provide) content aggregation, distribution, advertising management and other additional services. The evolving business models are the outputs of two simultaneous processes: an overall trend of digital products being transformed into services, and the processes of 'disintermediation' and 'reintermediation'. This two-pronged process increases the complexity of business models, bringing some to an end and opening up new ones. Online distribution offers a new channel for distribution, much in the same way as the cinema and broadcasting industries have benefited from each technological wave (cable, pay TV, DBS, home video and now the Internet). However, 'reintermediation' through the new gatekeepers often means working under the conditions they impose on legacy players. Selling content wholesale, rather than distributing it directly to customers, creates tensions for the content industries, as they no longer control retail.

Recently, some of the media markets have been studied as two-sided markets (broadcasting, newspapers): with the entry of new players they turn into even more complex multisided markets.[30] The content markets can be described as multiaccess, multisided, multiformat (Bounie and Bourreau, 2008), providing a mechanism to bring together buyers and sellers.

This book also illustrates the changes in the way economic power is exercised along the various value chains: some players have increased their bargaining power while others are losing out. It concludes by highlighting the shift from upstream domination (production/creation) to downstream domination (distribution/marketing).

Notes

1. This book does not cover the radio industry.
2. UNESCO (2005) describes a similar value chain using the term 'value chain of cultural expression': creation, production, dissemination, exhibition/reception/ transmission, consumption/participation.
3. See chapters 1, 5, 6 and 7 for sector-specific value chains.
4. Live performances.
5. More detailed analysis of interactions can be found in the case studies.
6. Codex: block of wood, book, from Latin *caudex* tree trunk. See Grafton (2009: 288–324) 'Codex in crisis', Chapter 7 for a presentation of the book publishing industry.
7. Codified during the Renaissance with the *Index librorum prohibitorum* (1559).
8. As illustrated by France with the 'édit de 1629', and 'code la librairie' almost a century after (1723).
9. *Source*: Wikipedia, http://en.wikipedia.org/wiki/History_of_music_publishing

10. The Federal Communications Commission (FCC) is an independent agency of the US government. See Simon (1991).
11. See also: Wikipedia, newspaper http://en.wikipedia.org/wiki/Newspaper
12. *Source*: Wikipedia, Linotype machine: http://en.wikipedia.org/wiki/Linotype_machine
13. A data processing system employed mainly in large organizations for various applications.
14. The United Nations Conference on Trade and Development (UNCTAD) is the principal organ of the United Nations General Assembly dealing with trade, investment and development issues. The entity provides statistics, in conformity with the principles governing international statistical activities, to the formulation and reinforcement of which UNCTAD has contributed. See: http://unctad.org/en/Pages/Statistics/About-UNCTAD-Statistics.aspx
15. The document emphasizes the methodological issues of gathering consistent data.
16. The classification was changed in 2007, making it even more difficult to work on reliable and consistent time series.
17. UNCTAD (2013) also stresses that changes in classification can make comparison difficult. See also: UNCTAD, Creative Economy Report CER (2010) – Statistical Annex Explanatory note.
18. WIPO is another agency of the United Nations dedicated to the use of intellectual property (patents, copyright, trademarks, designs, etc.). The agency also provides economics and statistics. See: http://www.wipo.int/econ_stat/en/
19. ISIC: International Standard Industrial Classification.
20. NACE: Nomenclature statistique des activités économiques dans la Communauté Européenne.
21. DCMS stands for the UK government's Department for Culture, Media and Sport.
22. OECD itself is also not entirely consistent in separating media and content industries from, for instance, the telecom and ICT sectors in its publications. OECD studies on the information and communication economy (OECD's biannual *Information and Communication Outlook*) include broadcasting, Internet and telecommunication, but not film or publishing.
23. See Box 0.1.
24. Internet players intermediate between people, information, services and merchants, including revenues generated from online advertising. Examples are: AOL, eBay, Google, IAC/InterActiveCorp, Yahoo.
25. CAGR.
26. Growth was only 4.9% between 2006 and 2010.
27. *Source:* PWC (2011). Global retail value of 'recorded' music sales dropped from US$38.7 billion in 1999 to US$16.5 billion in 2012 (IFPI, 2013).
28. Manga are Japanese comics that have also become popular in other markets, like France, for instance.
29. Under classification 41–203: Retail Salespersons.
30. See Box 2.1, Chapter 2. Some other examples are to be found in the case studies chapters.

Section I

A Horizontal View: The Dynamics of the Sector

1
Moving to Digital Media Worlds: Three Successive Transformational Waves

Jean Paul Simon

An upheaval is taking place in media circles globally. There are new pro-gramme services, new distribution vehicles and new devices; at the same time, financing sources are being eroded, with a growing competition for advertising revenues. The companies must deal with changing expec-tations of the viewers, especially younger viewers. The legacy models, formerly based on geographic boundaries and scarcity of certain kinds of resources (i.e. spectrum) are under pressure; new services (server-based distribution of content) are location-agnostic (customers can access, for instance, YouTube or DailyMotion from any location). The ubiquity and rise of the Internet are turning upside down the legacy media logic (Busson and Pham, 2010). Media and telecommunication networks were hierarchical and had centralized architectures; the Internet has a decen-tralized architecture, open and flexible, allowing interaction at both ends (the receiver can become the transmitter), forging a major schism from that model.

This poses significant challenges for the legacy industry players, as easy access to inexpensive tools and web services not only allows new entrants to duplicate older ones with lighter-weight technologies, but also allows consumers themselves to rate, distribute, share, recommend, comment on content, receive, modify and reuse the content of oth-ers, legally and illegally. Even when duplicating familiar services, new entrants will usually provide the services at lower cost, under differ-ent business models. In turn, this stimulates another kind of media economy: disruptive, but nevertheless a continuation of progression in media.

The traditional, oligopolistic and vertically integrated market struc-ture of the media industry is being challenged, as the industry is moving toward a value chain with many participants. The traditional value chain[1] was dominated by the publisher/aggregator segment, most often with integrated firms (production/publishing/distribution–retail); some aggregators even owned the technical segments of the industry (printers in the case of newspapers and book publishers, technical industries in the cinema). The only link that was not under some kind of control by the publisher was the enabling devices (radios, TVs, recorders, CD and DVD players). The only exception[2] comes from the 'new sector' of videogames, where hardware manufacturers (consoles: Sony, Microsoft and Nintendo) dominate and also exercise a lot of power over the other segments (De Prato et al., 2010, 2012b).

Waves of change

The change came from outside the sector. It was initiated by the telecom industry, looking for new streams of revenues to mitigate the loss of its more traditional revenues from the fixed networks (voice telephony). Companies started offering other services when deploying their broadband networks (ADSL), adding to voice telecommunications and access, data and video services sold in bundles (triple or quadruple play): a move described at the end of the 1990s as 'convergence".[3] The bursting of the Internet/dot.com bubble led to some drastic readjustments, exemplified by the AOL–Time Warner merger case, initially hailed as the model of the converged media–telecom firm of the future.[4] The 'model', on the verge of bankruptcy, was partially demerged in 2009. Telcos went through similar difficulties with their ventures in the media sector and undertook a strategic repositioning as multimedia connectivity providers. Boosting non-core revenues remained an issue for telecom operators.

In a second phase, IT companies (search engines, e-dealers like Amazon and eBay, then social networks and manufacturers like Apple) took over leading the process. This second phase of digitization is disrupting the legacy model in two ways. First, the switch to digital distribution drastically cuts the need for physical logistics. A whole part of the former business has shrunk, has disappeared or will disappear: physical goods (CDs, DVDs, etc.), part of the legacy logistics (trucks, etc.), retailers (e.g. Tower records (CDs), Borders (books) and Blockbuster (DVDs) in the US filed for bankruptcy).[5]

A second major disruption is linked to the overlapping of the legacy value chain and the online value chain, thereby creating a much more complex (Chapter 3) but so far unstable market structure. This brings a significant change in the dynamics of the sector, shifting the balance of power on a global scale. The balance of the value is shifting downstream, and some consider that value is not only shifted but destroyed in the old media by the capture of consumers and traffic. It can no longer be regained, as was once the case. This is a drastic move, as it stands in sharp contrast to the local/domestic aspect of legacy media markets (entrenched services), with the limited exception of music. Transitioning away from homogeneous media to a variety of content, mixing global and local content, distributed by an array of players, is not easy.

Toward the third wave

This section takes a closer look at the current initiative coming from the legacy players; it deals with the fast-evolving relationships between 'old' and 'new' players. It also underlines the recent changes in the behaviour of the legacy players, and their more proactive attitudes, the new modes of cooperation. In 2011, Yahoo, the number one US online news site (with 39 million monthly unique visitors) (Pew, 2012a), partnered with ABC news (owned by Disney). YouTube commissioned Reuters, as a leading news organization, to develop original content on the video-sharing site (Pew, 2012a) and entered into numerous partnerships with content providers (FCC, 2012: 125). Netflix reached an agreement with Disney to stream its films from 2016, only seven to nine months after the cinema release. The *Wall Street Journal* and the *Guardian* entered partnerships with Facebook.

The new players are giving access to their platforms under their own conditions (sharing of revenues, prescribed retail prices, type of sales) but also managing the direct relationship with customers. As of 2011, Apple imposed upon the news publishers the exclusive use of its App Store to distribute their content; users of the iPad could not access the content publishers' services directly. Regarding retail prices, Apple 'invented' the US$0.99 per song uniform price[6]; however, in 2007 Apple was making US$8 billion of revenues from the sales of its iPod, but only US$1.7 billion from songs (Waldfogel, 2011a). In 2003, Apple convinced the music industry to open up its catalogues for digital music downloads in the iTunes online music store, and this became the first significant step toward the emergence of a legal digital online music market. Notwithstanding the fear of piracy voiced by legacy players, in 2007 Apple heralded the end of digital right management (DRM), a technological protection device that the rights holders were asking for as a tool against piracy. Amazon did the same in 2007, forcing Universal and Warner to come into line (Cooper, 2008).

Distributing news online: Trials and errors

Although the new intermediaries are circumventing publishers through their direct access to the consumer, their role is compelling: bringing 'oxygen'[7] to some declining media. In 2010 the regional French newspaper *Ouest France* was receiving 40% of its consultations through Google,[8] making it difficult to avoid this intermediation. The same newspaper, when opening up its Internet service as early as 1995,[9] imported the press/news content from the newspaper, quickly finding that consumers were unwilling to pay. When moving toward free content online, the newspaper industry suffered, but, as BCG (2011) points out, mostly from self-inflicted injuries, failing to understand the impact of the Internet on its business, the foreseeable acceleration of the decline of readership and accompanying falling advertising revenues. Newspaper are now trying to introduce some kinds of pay packages, to renegotiate the sharing agreements with the search engines and social networks, or are attempting to set up territorial copyright licence fees again, for instance in the EU. They also lobbied governments to mandate a special tax ('Google tax'; see Chapter 10) on new entrants.

So far, only the *Wall Street Journal* and *New York Times* have managed to have some success with a paying online customer base, an experience not easy to duplicate. When the *Times* and the *Sunday Times* moved their online site to a fully paid service in 2010, the audience plummeted from 22 million to fewer than 200,000. However, a more limited audience does not necessarily equate to a collapse or to losses, as there is room for a niche supplier, such as Mediapart in France[10] (60,000 online subscribers[11]), known for the quality of its analysis and investigation. In 2012 the website turned profitable.[12] Its Canadian equivalent, Rue Frontenac, another online pioneer, even started offering a printed version (Lafrance, 2013: 71).

Nevertheless, newspaper companies seem eager to move from the free 'online age' to what appears to be a more attractive 'app age' (BCG, 2011) with paid-for applications, even if this means (re)negotiating with the dominant providers. Moving from the public Internet to proprietary platforms (Apple iStore and the mobile operators) is bringing opportunities and threats to the media sector.

According to C. Beckett (2010), moving from products to services is bringing a huge awareness of value within the existing newspaper organizations, but these organizations are often failing to understand what is happening. Journalists are adapting quickly, as nearly 50% of the permanent positions will disappear with the restructuration of the sector, and they may not have many other options, according to Beckett. Much of the content will come from amateurs or from companies not considered as media companies: what he called the 'end of fortress journalism' and moving toward 'networked journalism', 'now an integral part of British mainstream journalism' (Beckett, 2010).

One of the key issues, in any case, seems to be the difficulty of monetizing news. Hal Varian, a well-known information economist and now Google's chief economist, noted that 'online world reflects offline: news, narrowly defined, is hard to monetize' (Varian, 2010: 20). Newspapers are another well-known example of two-sided markets, with readers on one side and advertisers on the other. The former subsidy scheme for news (Waldman, 2011: 17) seems to be broken, as customers do not appear to value edited news (the most expensive to produce) as they used to. According to Waterman (2011), the Internet revealed the 'analytic'[13] part of news to be far less attractive than the news industry thought it was for consumers now accessing a huge sample of information.

Retaining full control of all commercial aspects of their digital sales channels is key for newspaper publishers, to keep their grip on their main asset, the content. However, the online news audience is enormous and growing: the top 25 news sites in the US recorded 624 million average unique monthly visitors in 2012 – up 17% over the prior year, according to comScore (Pew, 2013a). According to the same Pew annual survey, brands matter, as 'the traditional players remain the most popular sources for digital news'.

In France, the newspaper trade association (Syndicat de la Presse Quotidienne Nationale: SPQN) launched the French consortium ePresse. On June 30th, 2011 its digital kiosk opened. ePresse brought up eight titles: five dailies (*Le Figaro*, *Le Parisien* and its national edition, *Libération*, the sports daily *l'Equipe* and the business paper *Les Echos*), and three newsweeklies (*L'Express*, *Le Point*, *Le Nouvel Observateur*) (Filloux, 2011). ePresse is competing with Lagardère's Relay.com, offering their magazines under mostly monthly bundles, but also with Apple's Newstand (25 titles, eight thematic), in France.

In Spain, 30 dailies (including the leading Spanish papers *ABC*, *AS*, *Cinco Dias*, *El Pais* and *La Vanguardia*), 60 magazines (*Lecturas*, *Muy Interesante*, *Saber Vivir*), 252 journals and over 700 other publications can be downloaded on a tablet. Kioskoymas[14] supplies services for mobiles and PCs with monthly subscription fees from €9.99 (*El Pais*,

ABC) to €23.99 (*La Vanguardia*). The service was opened in July 2011 and set up by a consortium of companies: PRISA, Vocento, Heraldo, La Información, La Voz, Intereconomía, Godó, Zeta, Última Hora, Axel Springer, RBA, América Ibérica and G+J. A minimum discount of 30% is offered for the online format. During 2012, sales increased four-fold.[15] A new generation of online news sites is blossoming in Latin America ('Plaza Publica', Guatemala, 'Idl reporteros', Peru, 'Puercoespin', 'Chequeando', Argentina, 'Animal Politico', Mexico) (Quesada, 2013).

In the US, publishers announced tablet-based apps throughout 2011. Time Inc. announced tablet versions of all 21 of its publications (Pew, 2012a. *The Huffington Post*, a digital native, strongly benefited from its social media strategy, with the adoption of Facebook Connect generating big traffic gains starting in 2009. The online paper announced the creation of its own 24-hour online news channel modelled on CNN. Some US newspaper companies are now taking a much more aggressive approach to digital transition: for instance, Digital First Media[16] is pursuing a 'digital-first' strategy at the Journal Register and MediaNews Group papers; digital revenues went up from 5% of the revenues in 2010 to 30% in 2012.[17] Pew (2012b) followed this search for new business models and identified some 'revenue' success stories (Pew, 2013b).

In the book sector, the leading French book publisher Hachette signed a deal with Google for e-books in August 2011 to put a large number of out-of-print books on its Google Editions eBook store. The company has been leading with innovative applications for its magazines.[18] Lagardère Active is the leading media group in mobile Internet in France, with 18 brands[19]; mobile audiences are equivalent to web audiences, pioneering on tablets.[20] Lagardère Active Digital, the digital business unit,[21] was generating 7% of the company's revenues in 2009, with over 100 websites worldwide aggregating an audience of 80 million unique visitors (vs. ten million in 2006). Hachette Book Publishing was already deriving 23% of its US revenues from e-books in 2012.

Broadcasting on the move

Traditional broadcasters are trying to reinvent themselves in a way that is reminiscent of what Telcos went through over a decade ago when telecom markets were opened up in the EU. The move of traditional broadcasters toward media organizations is enabled by the mix of broadcasting and broadband. This hybrid is blending networks[22] (broadcast/broadband hotspot and BC overlay networks, offloading of broadband traffic to broadcast networks, data broadcasting solutions), devices (connected TV sets, hybrid radio sets) and services (HbbTV,[23] connected TV, VOD, second screen interactivity and personalization). Players are different, coming from different horizons, but all competing to own the screen/the user, and the redistribution is having a huge impact on the value chain.

Until fairly recently, because of the physical limitations (scarcity) of the broadcast spectrum, and the expense of physical storage medium devices required to play the media types, these constraints worked to the benefit of the digital models based on scarcity, for advertising dollars or production dollars. Scarcity drove production budgets and selection of content in a certain direction; this is eroding today. The technical obstacles preventing distribution of the media via the Internet and local networks onto multiple devices are gone, and as an output the role of the distributor is being redefined, with different players along the value chain competing for this enhanced role under different business models (see next chapter).

Connected TV is now growing fast (Preta, 2011; IDATE, 2012, 2013). Connected TV (or smart TV[24]) refers to the delivery of broadcast and broadband content to the consumer through connected TVs (direct access) or Blu-Ray players, set-top boxes and game consoles (indirect access). It allows consumers to access, on a single television set, traditional linear broadcasting programmes as well as catch-up and on-demand services, content and applications (social networks, widgets,[25] webmail, etc.) that are available on the Internet. The difference with IPTV is that the content is delivered via an unmanaged Internet connection and not through a managed network with controlled quality of service.

Over-the-top (OTT) television of all kinds is becoming a real alternative to the linear distribution of video (cable or satellite subscriptions), as illustrated by the growth of Netflix in the US (20% of the traffic, 20 million subscribers, a market share of 36% for SVOD) (IDATE, 2012), or catch-up TV in the same market (Hulu, funded by advertising, is ranking no. 2 after YouTube: one billion videos watched). Preta (2011) forecasts a big boost to the OTT market that will take it from €300 million in 2011 to €3 billion over just three years. An Informa Telecom & Media report (2013) states that OTT TV viewers will outnumber IPTV viewers by 2013 (Sony ConnTV: 10% connected, Sony PS3: 30% connected). The report claims that, by 2015, 380 million people globally will view online video via connected devices such as TVs, games consoles or set-top boxes from the likes of Apple and Google. In 2011, some 5% of UK households owned an Internet-connected smart TV (Ofcom, 2012a). Other connected TVs are provided by TV set manufacturers like Samsung and Sony. The market is booming: the development of connected and hybrid TV devices (including connected TV sets, games consoles and stand-alone TV set-top boxes) in the EU was estimated to reach 47 million active connected in-home devices at the end of 2011 in the EC's first report on the AVMS directive application (EC, 2012: 9).

However, some observers note that sale of a 'connected' TV does not equate to connecting the set to the Internet, especially for sets with such direct access (Fontaine, 2011; FCC, 2012; Ofcom, 2012b), and that linear TV and the 'lean-back experience' remain at the core of viewers' behaviour. The AVMS report notes as well the limited use of connected TV: only 20–30% of connectable TVs sold are actually online (EC, 2012). A number of parameters are likely to interfere, including the absence of unique standards, the lack of proper interface with the viewer (such as programme search, interaction between broadcast/Internet content, proprietary systems and operating systems, billing system, pre-installed apps) and the quality of services ('best effort' over the Internet). In other words, an increase in equipment is not equivalent to a full use of all functionalities.

Online distribution is offering new avenues. This is being recognized by the mainstream broadcasters as well as by a growing number of players, as noted by the FCC (2012: 111).[26] The Internet is not seen as a threat any more by broadcasters, but as an opportunity (Biggam, 2011). The broadcasting industry sees more clearly the role of this distribution channel in creating a wholesale demand for their content. However, moving to the position of wholesaler of content, rather than distributing it directly to customers, creates tensions, as control of retail is being lost.

Nevertheless, TV companies are adapting to the new world, distributing through different platforms to different devices (multiscreen strategy: see Figure 1.1). The BBC launched its online news service in the 1990s (Cohen-Tanugi, 1999); its iPlayer has been a major success, and the public broadcaster is involved in the creation of eView. The Spanish channel Antena 3 is offering live streaming services.[27] Most private broadcasters are moving in that direction. News Corp is now licensing all kind of content (e-books, movies, TV shows, papers, etc.) to all platforms. However, the company is still trying to turn these new channels into a profitable business; so far, they have not compensated for the loss of offline revenues. Like telecom operators before them, broadcasters are looking for a new pay model, such as, for instance, pay-per-click.

BskyB launched Sky Player (five million live streams in 2011) but also developed apps on mobile as companion services. The RTL group

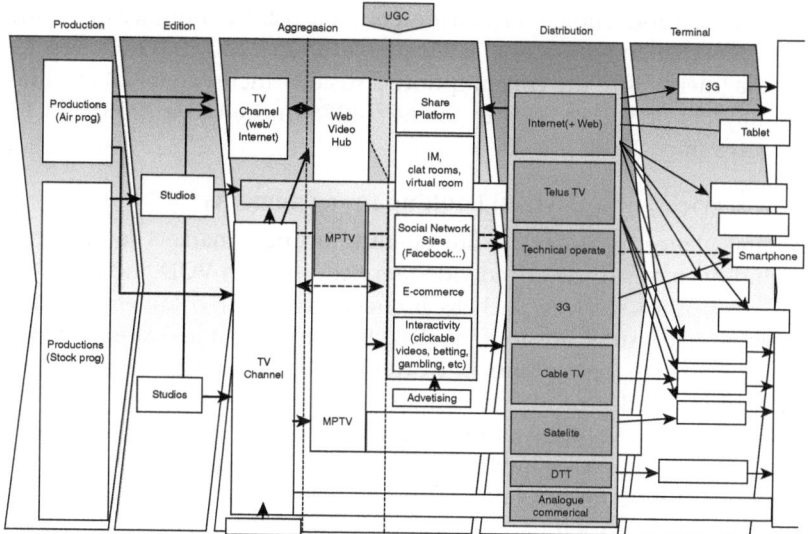

Figure 1.1   An example of a complex value chain[28]: Broadcasting in a digital world
Source: Busson and Landau (2011).

reacted with the creation of a family of channels, which can be customized (from 'mass to niche'), and diversification of its activities (38% of RTL Group revenue originates from a broad range of non-advertising activities). The German group Prosieben provides another example of diversification with online video, with online games accounting for a growing proportion of the revenues. Its online games publishing subsidiary ProSiebenSat.1 Games launched a new mobile app on the iOS platform in 2013 and announced a partnership with Kabam,[29] the leading provider of F2P (see Chapter 6) games for mobile devices (gamesindustryblog, 2013). One of their leading shows has already generated 18 million video views, 4.5 million interactions online and 199,000 mobile downloads. The Canadian audiovisual firm, TVA, based its growth on the integration of the various channels (Lafrance, 2009: 194). On May 2011, Warner Bros. acquired the social networking site Flixster, a movie discovery service that owns the film review website Rotten Tomatoes (Sanz, 2012). These evolutions point to the interaction of old and new television logics tied up in complex relationships.

There is growing competition in the EU: the number of channels has increased from 47 to 7,200 in the last 20 years; quite an amazing leap, generating more choice for consumers. In 2012, the number of online video on-demand services was estimated at 251 (EC, 2012).[30] Despite the fragmentation, the consumption is steadily increasing: 222 minutes per day/per person in 2009 in the EU[31] (275 in the US), a growth of 19 minutes since 2000.

New services, new devices: Looking for agreements

At first glance, new devices are opening up new markets for viewers, including access to advanced video services (such as VOD and catch-up TV) and other services, such as interactivity and e-commerce, which enrich broadcasters' linear offers (BskyB strategy) and increase the value of the main asset: programmes. However, this comes with some threats, increasing the degree of fragmentation that has been one of the main features of the evolution of broadcasting over the last decade (Missika, 2007). Nevertheless, even with a high degree of fragmentation and the amazing number of available channels, the main legacy channels are still dominant in each national market (Sanz, 2012).[32]

Acting as disintermediation agents, the new players provide, or will provide, content aggregation and distribution or advertising management. This opens up a window of opportunity for studios to directly distribute their content on the market (via a worldwide VOD provider, for example, such as Netflix), depriving the channels of the content they need or just increasing the costs of the programmes because of an increased demand. Studios are clearly benefiting from online distribution with increased margins. Waterman (2011) showed that the studio share increased from 33% (out of a retail price of US$3.25 for a DVD in 2002) to 70% (out of an 'online' rental of US$4.41 in 2010).

This is one of the reasons why, for instance, in November 2010, the 19 available French digital terrestrial channels signed a charter[33] announcing that they will not make available their content and online services to manufacturers who do not allow full control by the broadcasters of the way online services appear on their programmes. Likewise, in the US, ABC, CBS, NBC, Fox, Hulu and Viacom refused to grant Google TV access to their online content. Therefore, manufacturers are striving to strike deals with broadcasters to allow access to their digital content, especially the more 'localized' content. Sony has secured access to HBO content for its Playstation in the US, while Canal + is available on the Xbox in France, and Bsky in the UK. Sony, Samsung and Panasonic have struck deals with domestic content providers in EU countries. For instance, in Germany Sony (Bravia TV) connected TVs allow access to

ARD/ZDF, Pro7/Sat 1 and eurosport under such an agreement. In Spain, LG partnered with Antena 3.

However, the willingness of content providers to strike deals with the new players cannot be taken for granted, and search engine providers will be more and more challenged by rights holders. For instance, Google Music, introduced in November 2011, has struck deals with Sony, Universal and EMI but not Warner Music.[34] By the same token, the *Financial Times* and *Boston Globe* have created mobile pages using HTML 5,[35] thereby avoiding the 'app' worlds controlled by Apple or Google (Pew, 2012) and maintaining direct relationships with their customers. The *New York Times* and *Guardian* did the same in 2012b (Pew, 2013b). In Brazil, as of 2012, 150 newspapers (about 90% of the circulation) also decided to opt out of Google News: the decision triggered a 5% decrease in traffic (Mora, 2013).

At the same time, the dominant position of such players is allowing others to act as some kind of 'White Knight', offering better options to content holders: Telcos may take this opportunity to intervene as a trusted middleman under more favourable commercial agreements. For instance, in November 2010, Orange signed a deal with the ePresse consortium integrating their content into Orange's digital kiosk. In contrast to Google, Orange was willing to pay for the content under a 'fair deal' sharing agreement. For book publishing, the company is proposing a similar deal to counter OTT players under an open model (like the Internet or GSM), maintaining each player in his (legacy) role: publisher, bookshop and transmitter. Nevertheless, in Germany, France, Italy and Spain, some major digital platforms, bringing together several national companies, were launched in 2010 in the book publishing sector (Chapter 1). Scientific, technical and medical (STM) publishing is already in digital format (90%).

Established relationships and the related expertise in the field are another asset for legacy players (De Prato and Simon 2012a). On the other hand, Telcos, when buying audiovisual players, an activity quite far away from their core businesses, seem to have historically had some trouble integrating the newcomer. Telefonica bought one of the leading European audiovisuals, the Dutch company Endemol, and sold it some years later. Orange-France Telecom went through similar zigzags: creation of the satellite distributors TPS in the 1980s, then exit from the company, and various attempts in the content sector; the most recent attempt was investing in the French video-sharing service Dailymotion,[36] with an acquisition of 49% of the shares, in 2011.

Conclusion

The traditionally integrated structure of the media markets is being challenged as these sectors are progressively becoming a component of a broader ecosystem, where they may lose most of their power positions. Retaining control of their commercial assets remains a key aspect of their strategy, as they are under threat of being circumvented by new entrants and powerful distributors acting as disintermediation agents.

Nevertheless, after a period of trial and error, of necessary readjustments of strategy, legacy players are becoming more and more active players in a digital world, offering an array of new options to meet the fast-evolving consumer demand, to cope with new patterns of consumption enabled by the last wave of new devices (tablets). New modes of cooperation are also emerging after an often painful learning process. For the legacy players, benefiting from strong brands, striking deals with new entrants (Disney/Netflix, ABC/Yahoo, YouTube/Reuter, Facebook/*Wall Street Journal*) offers avenues for growth and an improved management of the digital channels. For broadcasters, online distribution is adding new streams of revenues.

This does not mean that some of the structural issues (decline of the audience) faced by some of the sectors will go away; monetizing news has been an issue and will remain an issue, while former trade-offs and cross-subsidy mechanisms need to be replaced by updated ones.

The value chains are changing; some parts may even disappear (logistics). The power relationships between players are evolving; they may take some time to stabilize. However, if legacy players lack the technical expertise brought by new entrants, they can still build on their own. For instance, the track record of the telecom operators in the media sector may not be particularly convincing; the new IT leaders may encounter similar issues, as already shown by the missed merger of AOL and Time Warner.

Notes

1. UNESCO (2005) describes a similar value chain under the term 'value chain of cultural expression': creation, production, dissemination, exhibition/reception/ transmission, consumption/participation.
2. Although historically, when radio was introduced, manufacturers were subsidizing content to sell their devices. Later, the role shifted to advertisers (soap manufacturers) – the notorious 'soap operas'. Sony Paramount is another exception, but the content/devices synergy is far from obvious.

3. The move was accurately summarized in the EC 1997 Green Paper.
4. Acquisition of Time Warner by AOL for US$350 billion, January 10, 2000.
5. In the UK, in 2009, 1,000 outlets closed down (Leurdijk et al., 2011).
6. This figure is not fully set by the market, but by the record labels charging a wholesale price of around 65 cents per track.
7. The chairman of the *New York Times* compared Google with oxygen; quoted by Ramonet (2011).
8. A. De Tarlé, chairman of the newspaper publishing company *Ouest France* at the 'économie de la culture' conference, Paris, February 2011.
9. *Ouest France*, a leading French regional newspaper, is a well-known pioneer of the electronic distribution of news. The company was an established leader for *télématique* in the 1980s.
10. Founded in 2008 by the former editor in chief of *Le Monde* (1996–2004), E. Plenel. *Source*: GQ, no. 49, March 2012: 168.
11. The news service broke even in 2010. *Source*: Wikipedia. http://fr.wikipedia.org/wiki/Mediapart.
12. Other examples in France, Baksheesh (founded 2006) and Street 89 (founded 2007), are in the same niche (Busson and Pham, 2010).
13. He considered news to have two parts: one telling what happened and the other offering an analysis.
14. http://www.kioskoymas.com/epaper/viewer.aspx.
15. *El Pais*, December 22, 2012: 62.
16. Digital First Media owns three companies and an 800 multiproduct platform reaching 57 million Americans each month across 18 states. Journal Register Company offers local news and information in ten US states to 21 million consumers. MediaNews Group is the second largest newspaper company by circulation in the US. http://www.digitalfirstmedia.com/.
17. *Source*: http://meta-media.fr/2012/06/03/le-numerique-d%e2%80%99abord-seul-moyen-de-sauver-les-vieux-medias/.
18. In pdf, enriched pdf or reformatted format.
19. *Source*: Company from Q3 2010 Mediametrie. Emmanuel Vacher, Lagardère Active Digital, Executive Vice President Development & Corporate Alliance, presentation at Digital Content Monetization, London, January 2011.
20. Introduced as of Spring 2010.
21. Created after major acquisitions in 2007–2008: two online publishers in France (Newsweb, Doctissimo), one in the UK (Digital Spy) and one US ad network (Jumpstart automotive). *Source*: E. Vacher.
22. For instance, SES, a leading satellite distribution TV company (5,500 channels worldwide to 276 million households), combines broadcasting and Internet. Vodafone offers a similar option in Germany.
23. HbbTV is a pan-European initiative aimed at harmonizing broadcast and broadband delivery of entertainment to the end consumer through connected TVs and set-top boxes. In 2010, ETSI approved the HbbTV specification.
24. A TV with a full web browser and/or access to an app store.
25. Widget: An applet intended to be used within web pages.
26. They include stand-alone distributors, programmers, content producers/owners (including broadcasters) and subsidiaries of the largest hardware, software and online delivery companies per se.

27. www.antena3.com/directo
28. See, for the audiovisual sector, Figure 7.1: The traditional film sector value chain.
29. Including the successful 'Kingdoms of Camelot' and 'The Hobbit: Kingdoms of Middle Earth'.
30. This figure does not include catch-up TV, news-only services, adult programmes, films trailers, home shopping programmes and branded services such as YouTube, Dailymotion and iTunes; at 2.
31. 228 minutes per day in 2010 according to P. Delusinne.
32. This was already the case in the US when cable was growing fast in the 70s and 80s, an offer of around a hundred channels did not prevent consumers from watching mostly the networks and some very popular channels like the sport channel ESPN. Channels allocated in ranking above 50 were described as 'Alaska' (Charon and Simon, 1989).
33. 'TV connectées: les chaînes de la TNT fixent leurs conditions', Guillaume Deleurence, 01net, 24/11/10: http://www.01net.com/editorial/523929/tv-connectees-les-chaines-de-la-tnt-fixent-leurs-conditions/
34. Offering a library of some 13 million songs. *'Google Music goes live; takes on iTunes'*, Mobile Business Briefing, November 17, 2011.
35. As HTML5 apps work across mobile devices, there is no need to develop separate apps for each platform. HTML5 is the fifth revision of the HTML standard created in 1990. HTML: Hypertext Markup Language.
36. Reaching 110 millions users (CSA, 2011). Services available in 19 countries and 12 languages. In 2013, Yahoo tried to buy the company but the deal was blocked by the French government.

2
Production, Consumption and Innovative Business Models

Jean Paul Simon

Digital technologies unlocked marketing and distribution channels for music, digital animation, films, news, advertising, and so on. Prices of media distribution are decreasing at an amazing order of magnitude, for instance, from a price of media information per Gbit/capita of $0.21 for a book down to $0.00001 for broadband and $0.0000001 for ultra-high broadband in 2015 (Noam, 2010). One can assume with Waterman (2011) that these new technologies will bring further broad gains through flexible pricing, low delivery costs and virtually unlimited capacity (server-based and cloud applications lower costs of capacity as opposed to traditional multichannel video programming distribution such as cable or satellite), as well as higher efficiency.

The transformational waves triggered changes in market structures, ushering in new business models. In turn, transformations are taking place within existing trends in patterns of consumption and production.

Changing patterns of consumption

Changes in the patterns of consumption paved the way for the use of digital technologies, which, in turn, have reinforced and facilitated further changes in consumption patterns. As summed up in a prospective study commissioned by the French minister of culture: 'A retrospective analysis suggests that most of the cultural and media practices traditionally measured since the early 1970s will, with the exception of listening to recorded music, experience a more or less marked decline over the coming years'[1] (Donnat and Lévy, 2007). The growing momentum of audiovisual media compared with print media, for example, can be traced back to 30 years ago, with a drop in newspaper reading and a decline in book reading but a continuing increase in time spent watching television under an ever-diversifying audiovisual scene. The generation of digital natives is likely to have a further negative impact on the previous cultural and media practices. At the same time, this generation is also bringing in new practices that ought to be better understood, as changes in these areas are explained, by and large, by a 'generational factor'; that is, a particular generation originates a practice that will be continued and expanded by succeeding generations.

With a shift from products to services, toward more 'dematerialization', it is all the more important to take into account the evolution of patterns of consumption. Typically, the glorious days of the album format in music may be over. Younger customers are listening to music in a more itemized way, creating their own repositories. Patterns of consumption are changing, and customers are given new muscle and 'a new found ability to self-supply or engage in collaborative production' (Cooper, 2008), on an unprecedented scale.

Customers are moving away from the physical product as long as they have ways to access the product as a service anywhere, anytime, as illustrated by the example of browser games in the video game industry (Chapter 10). The huge memory of portable devices (mobile, USB key, hard disk) enables consumers to plug in their playlist wherever they go (at home, at work, travelling, etc.). New forms of interaction between devices and platforms pave the way for ubiquitous consumption.

The status of ownership of a media product is transformed. More broadly, consumers are looking for/accessing items rather than a legacy bundle: an article rather than a newspaper, a tune rather than a DVD,[2] a film rather than a cable network (growth of Netflix), catch-up TV rather than linear TV. Consumers have a wider range of consuming patterns, and, depending, for instance, on the quality and kind of music, they may or may not still use bundles (Elberse, 2010). New technologies are opening new, more immersive forms of experience (watching video games and films in 3D), leading to a shift in the forms of consumption to experience/performance. Experience has always been a part of music, and the music industry business is moving from selling CDs toward the performance process. Artists will concentrate on tours rather than touring to promote CDs as they used to (Page and Carey, 2010; Rogers and Preston, 2011). Different consuming patterns generate different streams of revenues. Consumers have also created a new revenue stream for music companies by uploading their favourite music video clips or remixed versions to platforms such as YouTube, which now pay royalties to the music companies holding the rights to these songs.

However, customers may be facing several challenges, one of which being interoperability of devices. There are other uncertainties: customers do not know what to expect from an e-book, or an MP3 file, or a game. Such uncertainty about the main characteristics or normal functioning of digital content is common to all the new digital services. A survey published by *Consumer Focus* in February 2010 found that 73% of consumers do not know what they are allowed to copy or record (Hargreaves, 2011). This can lead to a 'clash of culture' (Helberger and Guibault, 2012) between two different notions of property. Physical objects (books) as goods are sold and become the property of their buyers, but digital contents are 'licensed' and remained managed by the rights owner under various layers of intellectual property rights (IPR) (Helberger and Guibault, 2012: 15). Customers may have concerns about access (interoperability, etc.), lack of information (functionality, redress and support) and presentation of information (terms of use, etc.), functionality (watching, copying, printing and forwarding) and privacy (profiling, tracking and sharing).

Willingness to pay is still a question mark, especially online after a period of 'free' culture opened by the Internet. However, in the media sector there is a trend toward paying rather than free (including advertising-based), according to Waterman (2011), who notes a shift toward direct pay support since 2000 in the US media markets, including online media as a whole.

Changing patterns of production

On the production side, a richer content also means a more expensive content. This is also a continuation of trends for Noam (2010). It requires creativity, many programmers, lots of alpha and beta testing, and many new versions. However, such expensive content exhibits strong economies of scale on the content production side, and network externalities on the demand side. Both favour content providers with big budgets that can diversify risk, can distribute over other platforms, have a strong brand and can coordinate the specialized inputs of the various segments involved. The major media firms then become mainly coordinators, integrators and financiers of the specialist firms, and the branders of the final products in a global market.

Some authors stress that the new situation and its potential growth create room for a second model: the community model, in which modules of media creation and play modules will be created by decentralized peers, collaborating loosely with each other. This involves another, less mainstream, form of creativity, 'but it's not likely to be the main way to create new content' (Noam, 2010). It may help to reach a critical mass, as was the case for radio in the 1920s and Internet in the 1980s, as Noam sums up: 'grassroots created the market then they are dismissed' (Noam, 2005). Wu offers similar views (Wu, 2010). The role of user-generated content (UGC) should not be overstated; it will probably not become the main source for the provision of content. As noted by Cameron and Bazelon (2011: 36):

> With a major film costing over $200 million on average, of which $39 million is spent just on marketing the film, it is hard to imagine that selling credits or garnering attention in social media sites will ever be able to cover the costs or inspire investors to back such a large undertaking.

If crowdsourcing cannot support a whole industry, it adds another source, thereby increasing diversity and offering some novel avenues for creativity: the DIY (do it yourself) model (Bacache-Beauvallet et al., 2011). Nevertheless, companies like Yahoo are using some form of crowdsourcing to fill the gap between edited content and amateur content, to track unmet demand. Crowdsourced curated websites such as Freshscouts or Recordscout help consumers discover new artists (Cameron and Bazelon, 2011: 5). Even in the broadcasting industry, sites such as Kickstarted, Lanzanos and Quirki have contributed to the funding of television shows. Crowfunding takes several forms: donation-based (JustGiving), reward-based (Kickstarter), equity (My Major Company) and lending-based (Kiva) (Salmon, 2013: 32).

In the book sector, Editeursauteursassociés, Les NouveauxAuteurs, Crowdbook and Manolosantis are using the funding scheme (Benhamou, 2012: 93). The 'vanity' presses may evolve quickly and allow some direct access and sales, but, again, it may not be sufficient to move to self-editing. The low barriers to entry allowed by service tools (for instance, by Amazon with its Amazon Digital Text Platform to self-publish) are not equivalent to a new form of pervasive online publishing; the expertise of the publisher may be more crucial in that case (not to mention the marketing/promotion of the product). For unknown authors, their lack of popularity is likely to be a major obstacle, even if anecdotal evidence of success stories of some unknown authors can be found (Cameron and Bazelon: 49).[3] The case of music tells a similar story, according to a 2010 study (Bastard et al., 2012) showing that, despite strong online self-promotion conducted by little-known artists, online promotion by fans and online success still benefit artists who have already achieved success offline.

Flichy stresses the blurring of the borders between professionals and amateurs (Flichy, 2010), resulting from the dramatic fall of the prices audiovisual production tools, for instance. This leads to the consumption on the same device or in the same room of new blends of more varied types of content, truly 'edited' content, user-generated content ranging from almost professional production to content provided by 'friends' (an average of 130 'friends' on Facebook) and transaction (utilitarian audiovisual, such as tele-shopping, tele-transaction, interactive advertising, etc.) (Busson and Landau, 2011). The blend is likely to change over time, but new entrants, especially social networks, are the engines of these changes toward multitasking, multiscreening behaviours, with consumers moving from the 'wisdom of the crowd' (recommendations on web 1.0) to the 'wisdom of the friends' (their trusted network on web 2.0). Media consumption is gliding from push to pull. New forms of interpersonal communication (instant messaging, chatting, etc.) are emerging, with new kinds of content being added to the legacy ones.

New sources of distributed labour? Creative worker or unpaid labour?

Another aspect of this blurring of the borders hinges on new ways to distribute, outsource and remunerate labour. The success story of online newspapers seems to suggest that appearing on the online service delivers sufficient status to compensate for the lack of real payment: the *Huffington Post* does not pay its writers. Blog publishing companies such as Gawker Media[4] or Spreeblick Verlag[5] combine a number of blogs and pay the authors who write for them, or at least provide them with a platform to raise their profile. The French online news website *Le Post* (a subsidiary of the firm *Le Monde interactif*) also relies on voluntary contributions. For their online editions, most newspapers frequently rely on their readers' contributions.

These various forms of crowdsourcing in the media can obviously be perceived as an easy option to reduce the overall costs of labour and to better adjust to the sea of changes. However, the fear that this flexible form of outsourcing will 'drain jobs from the regular work force' is not justified, according to Bughin, who stresses that what he described as co-creation is, indeed, an entirely new type of work, much along the lines of Benkler. He gives two examples in the video game industry. The first example is about professional gamers in South Korea who manage to make a living by competing in multiplayer games such as *StarCraft* because they are broadcast to a large audience. The second, also in Asia, is the case of so-called gold 'farmers'[6] with online games in China, paid to dig up virtual treasures (Bughin, 2010: 37) and making revenues through the sales of virtual items.

Nevertheless, the question of whether this trend will lead to a substitution of current work is still pending. However, distributed labour may open up opportunities in segments where most of the workforce is not employed on a permanent basis (like authors in literature[7] or music). This does not mean that it offers a panacea for all 'creative workers', not having to be allocated permanent positions, or for 'knowledge workers'. The idea, which has been around for some time, that creative/knowledge workers were the single model for the future of work is questionable and will require some additional evidence to be sustained.

Menger (2003, 2010) analysed the cultural industries and other creative industries[8] as being characterized by uncertainty and behaviour specifically taking into account an uncertain horizon, and therefore over-producing, as illustrated, for instance, by the over-production of films in the EU.[9] These are social processes and organizations that are dynamically unpredictable, so as to produce innovation as well as mainstream works. However, he strongly questioned the idea that creative workers are anticipating the face of future capitalism,[10] and that they represent the *avant-garde* of the world of labour, offering a combination of autonomy, pressure and competition in a world with, once again, blurred borders between independence and permanent positions. Firms and workers need a long-term relationship, and, according to Menger, few employers would be ready to shift their entire workforce to a 'pay by the task' status. Increased pressure and competition can also act as a counterincentive for creativity.

Business models: A moving target?

With digitization, costs are being reallocated, altering the cost structure. Some costs disappear: manufacturing of the physical good/production (in the case of newspaper printing/production this accounted for 39% of the total costs in 1994, according to Waterman, 2011), physical transportation and storage. Some costs remain unaffected (creation/ development, the editorial process, marketing and sales[11]), while others are shifted (part of the production in some cases, like music with 'home studios'[12] and promotion with the coming of blogs and other tools; but they may decrease, as, for instance, in music[13]) (Waldfogel,

2011b). New costs are appearing mostly on the software side (security, right management, etc.), with the development of a growing segment of enabling technology providers (web hosting, content delivery networks and billing). Bringing fixed costs down will facilitate creation (Waldfogel, 2011a) and even boost quality (Waldfogel, 2011c). A radically changed cost structure paves the way for different business models (Ha et al., 2008; Wildman and Ting, 2009).

Disintermediation/reintermediation

The evolving business models are an output of two simultaneous processes: the overall trend of transformation of digital products into services, and the processes of disintermediation and reintermediation. This two-pronged process is increasing the complexity of the business models, bringing some to an end and opening up others.

On the disintermediation side, direct sales from the producer/creator/ developer become possible. In the case of video games, a developer can sell to the consumer with an increased return and a lower price for the consumer (see Chapter 6). In the film industry, for independent filmmakers, direct sales (e.g. theatre, exhibitors or even the audience) appear as an attractive option (De Vinck and Lindmark, 2011). The growth of the blogosphere is another well-known example, although the ways to monetize do vary. Because of her fame, J. K. Rowling, the author of Harry Potter, is able to sell her e-books directly on her site, Pottermore, even imposing conditions on Amazon and other retailers for rerouting their customers to Pottermore.[14] This may turn out to be another threat for publishers.

On the reintermediation side, app shops are bringing new streams of secured revenues through their large customer base, but they handle the relationship with the customers and set retail prices, although under an agency model[15] this is achieved through an agreement with the content providers (Apple), or wholesaling in the case of Amazon. The position of legacy providers is all the more uncertain as the new entrants can offer contents in various kinds of bundles, pushing their own products or services first, as Amazon did with e-readers, thereby reducing publishers' already narrow margins. Even though content is clearly a strategic asset for new entrants, it does not provide the bulk of their revenues. For example, Apple's revenue from 'net sales of other music related products and services'[16] accounted for a mere 6% of the company's 2011 net sales (FCC, 2012: 116).

Part of the complexity has to do with the number of streams of revenues that could now be added to the retail (physical) models. In that

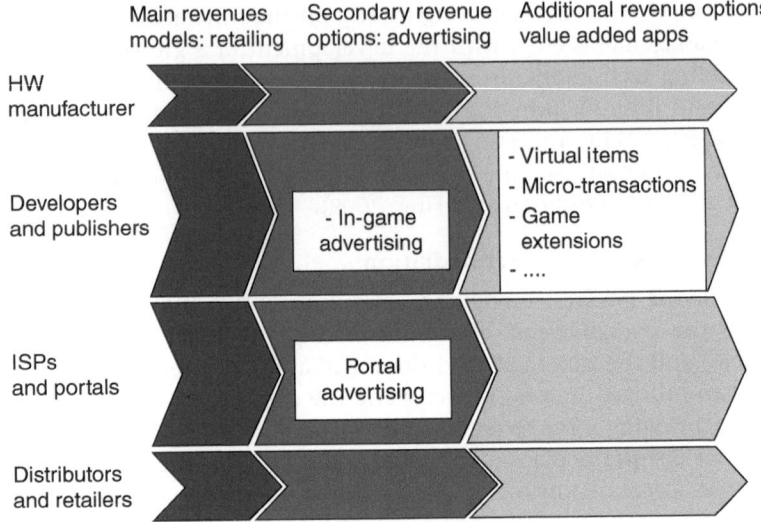

Figure 2.1   Business models in (re)construction
Source: De Prato et al. (2010).

complex interexchange some main revenues are likely to become secondary and vice versa. The video games industry offers a good example of these hybrid business models, as illustrated by Figure 2.1.

Figure 2.1 shows, for instance, how it becomes possible to introduce new forms of advertising for magazines, e-books or music online. It illustrates the path toward a service model where the consumer is buying a service linked to some editorial content rather than simply the media per se. The video games industry saw the birth of the virtual item model, and basically any item can be sold as virtual. Players can use virtual money and buy 'powers' or 'characters' features, together with various types of extension to the gaming experience: soundtracks, scenarios and textures. This paves the way for a creative way to leave the 'doom of free'; under this modified 'economics of free' model, free content is used to lure the customer into buying some elements, to access other models. Online distribution offers novel ways to monetize content and to test consumers' willingness to pay.

New entrants like telecom operators, hardware and app stores are de facto updating for the digital world the sharing models that existed with offline distribution. The landscape is characterized by an array of competing business models; some of them will turn out to be sustainable, others will not. There are two main categories: the paid models and the free model, which used to be based on advertising but is now seeing novel approaches enabled by innovative use of multisided markets. In between, one will find intermediate categories granting a new flexibility and creating room for innovation.

The pay models

Pay as you go: online transactions allow a variety of pay-per-transaction model according to the kind of content that is being bought, with a clear trend toward more itemized sales (song, article, pages of books, avatars). Users pay a separate fee for every piece of content they download, listen/watch or play with. They can pay by download on a temporary (equivalent to rental) basis or on a perennial basis (sale).

An example of temporary pay-per-download is Apple's iTunes Store. Pay-per-listen/view services are mainly streaming-based services that prevent users from storing content. This model, pioneered by iTunes, remains the largest revenue source in the online sector. Benkler (2011) claims that experiments with pay-as-you-wish pricing in the music industry reveal that fans will voluntarily pay far more for their favourite music than economic models would ever predict. Salmon (2013) stresses, in a similar way, that consumers can decide how to pay.

The French e-presse kiosk charges per issue or through a pre-paid credit (€5–25). The *New York Times* introduced a successful metered model in early 2011. According to Pew (2013), a tipping point was reached in 2012 in the US, with 450 of the nation's 1,380 dailies starting or announcing plans for some kind of paid content subscription or pay wall plan. The metered model allows some free access before requiring users to pay.

Subscription model: users pay a periodic flat fee and receive the right to download or listen to/watch content (un)limitedly for a certain period of time. This is the standard model for cable and satellite TV, often marketed through bundles (tiered offers), and also for VOD (S-VOD).

Examples are Spotify, an EU firm, and Last.fm., streaming platforms in the music sector. Virgin Media UK launched a mobile music store based on the book club model: for a monthly fee (€3.36) subscribers can download five tracks per month (PWC, 2011). In the case of video games, this model can be boosted by the use of the community of gamers. For instance, members of the 11 million-strong *World of Warcraft* gamer community typically pay close to $170 annually to play, on top of an initial investment in software and upgrades ranging from $50 to $195 per player (Hadida and Ryan, 2010).

Services (secondary and additional revenue options): in an online world, bundles will more and more include numerous services. App stores are offering brokerage services and indirect marketing (as newspapers used to do). New entrants such as Telcos and e-commerce platforms such as Amazon can offer billing services. Classified ads are a well-known source of revenues that shifted online.

The free models

Advertising-supported service model: in a typical two-side market arrangement, the aggregator charges advertisers to reach consumers (economies of scale). Streaming takes the place of over-the-air distribution. On Pandora, customers specify what artists or songs they enjoy listening to, and similar music is then streamed to them (Cameron and Bazelon: 8).[17] In the book sector, the French Leroutard.com and the Spanish 24 Symbols.are advertisement-based. InLibro Veritas offers a free digital copy of e-books, but hard copies must be ordered and paid for (Benhamou, 2012: 98).

UGC plays a major role in social networks (Ala-Mutka, 2008; Punie et al., 2009), and, for sites like YouTube, it is a vital component of their advertising-based business model. YouTube was launched in 2005 and then bought by Google in 2006 for $1.65 billion. By June 2010, this video distribution platform had more than 100 million different visitors per month (Busson and Pham, 2010).

Online distribution allowed new forms such as in-stream or in-page ads with various sharing agreements with the rights holders (per click, per hit, etc.) and, especially, more focused advertising, as well as viral marketing. It raised new questions about the kinds of metrics to use to charge advertisers (per click, video view, engagement, etc.) rather than the standard cost per mille (CPM).[18] Free online video providers are nevertheless trying to move toward pay models (Leborgne, 2010): YouTube opened a video rental store in April 2010; Hulu offers a paid version on the iPad. Pandora also offers a premium pay version without commercials.

Freemium: the content is made available for free online (with free basic features: free trial period, full version for a fee). Some customers may be willing to buy items, as illustrated by the example of the Free-to-Play model for video games. The model is built on economies of scale. This is an innovative use of a two-sided market with a segmented pricing (or non-pricing) scheme; most customers will get free services supported by those who are willing to pay. According to research by NPD Group, around 40% of freemium game players make in-app payments.[19]

The hit video game-maker firm, Zynga, sums up this approach nicely: 'Games should be free. Free games are more social because they're more accessible to everyone. We've also found them to be more profitable. We have created a new kind of customer relationship with new economics – free first, high satisfaction, pay optional' (Zynga, 2011). Pandora (music online) and Flickr (online storage of photos) are other examples. Zynga (Chapter 10) introduced virtual currency (zcoins), and Amazon announced the launch of its own virtual currency in April 2013 (Costello, 2013a), given to customers for free to spend on Kindle Fire apps, games and in-app items (on the same sharing model).

Non-commercial models: maintained by a community (Wikipedia being the best known) or sponsored, 'patronism'[20] is based on voluntary contribution from music fans to connect to artists (Cameron and Bazelon: 14), stressing that 'patronage is the oldest form of arts funding'.[21] Probublica is another interesting US example of 'philanthropically sponsored investigative journalism' (Katz, 2011), as it was founded with a large private grant.[22] Public service, of course, is another well-known example (the BBC iPlayer is a notorious model). The public service is not totally free, as it is funded through a specific tax (licence fees in the case of public broadcasting). Public subsidies (often indirect through various funds) are also found in the case of cinema, newspapers or books.

Box 2.1 Media and multisided markets

The traditional media products are characterized by high fixed costs and low marginal costs (Waldfogel, 2011b). Digitization is bringing both costs down (marginal cost of distribution is almost nil), and, with falling marginal cost, the consumer surplus is increasing. The network effect generates 'preferences externalities' which are likely to yield more focused products. It allows market enlargement and wider product availability; for instance CNN.com and NYTimes.com are available, in the US, in every local newspaper market; US music and movies are available everywhere.

The content markets can be described as multiaccess, multisided and multiformat (Bounie and Bourreau, 2008), providing

---

Box 2.1 (Continued)

a mechanism to bring together buyers and sellers. Media provide content to consumers, often at a subscription price below marginal cost for print media or zero for over-the-air broadcasting, giving the advertiser access to the consumer. The multisided market approach may shed some light on the issues. If we follow Julien (Julien, 2011), there was a need for a new theoretical model to better understand competition between 'platforms'; hence the concept of two-sided markets emerged in the 2000s as a reaction to the evolution of the markets and issues faced by anti-trust and researchers: dematerialization of the exchanges (Internet, e-trade), the importance of services (financial, intermediation, etc.) and the rise of the content industry/media (new business models, free newspapers, services online, etc.).

Platforms organize/facilitate the exchanges between agents; such an activity requires taking into account the externalities between actors of the platform, and the complementarities between products or services. The prices play a more complex role than in the case of firms selling a standard consumption good or input. The general level is used for generating revenues, but the structure shapes the behaviour of users and affects the quality of service. There are other important dimensions (design, choice of the services, control information, etc.).

Julien defines two-sided markets in the following way. A two-sided market combines three elements:

1. The existence of two or more groups using the service, with different prices (asymmetric pricing).
2. The existence of crossed network externalities between these groups (a group being all the more attracted by the platform that the participation of the other group is important).
3. The importance of the price structure, that is, not only the total sum paid by the two groups but also the decomposition of this sum between the two groups. One side of the market becomes an input for the other side, as stressed by Wauthy (Wauthy, 2011).

The main examples are: dating clubs, credit cards, Business-to-Consumer (BtoC), Business-to-Business (BtoB) intermediaries, search engines, operating systems, smartphones, newspapers, TV, video games, Yellow Pages and shopping malls. A media bundles content and advertising; the consumers will pay (or not) for the content, the advertisers pay for the attention of the consumers. The Internet evolved from two-sided markets (search engine, directories, online press) to multisided platforms (social networks, e-commerce, portals, news aggregators), where the content is diverse and complex.

In such a market structure, the price structure of the platform takes some specific form. Pricing rules must be adapted to the presence of cross-externalities between groups. Attracting a customer on one side of the market allows raising the price on the other side of the market (e.g. an advertiser). The platform can thus sacrifice profit on one side to increase its profit on the other side. There is an implicit cross-subsidy between the two sides. The stronger the externality generated by one side, the lower is the price charged on this side.

The video game industry provides a good illustration. A game platform sets its prices on both sides of the market (players and game publishers) through an assessment of the expected network effects generated by each user group, not only by taking into account its production costs (Bourreau and Davidovici-Nora, 2012). It is then optimal to subsidize the side of the market that generates most network effects. According to the economic literature applied to game consoles, subsidies should fall on the players' side; hence the very aggressive pricing strategies of consoles. Microsoft sold its Xbox 360 at least $125 under its marginal costs, according to industry sources (Bourreau and Davidovici-Nora, 2012).

The activity of two-sided platforms implies leverage effects between sides, which may create an impression of excessive exploitation of market power. In two-sided markets, pricing at marginal cost does not constitute a good benchmark. A price above marginal cost is not always a sign of market power, just as price below cost is not always predatory. Cross-subsidies can be pro-competitive in that particular case.

The economic principles for two-sided markets are different from those which apply in the standard markets (Evans and Schmalensee, 2013[23]). The prices do not reflect simply the costs, but the costs adjusted for the cross-externalities. Price-skewness

---

Box 2.1 (Continued)

and some cross-subsidies are socially beneficial in general, and are exacerbated by competition. Multihoming[24] reduces competition on one side but increases it on the other side. Some practices that are harmful within a standard framework (monopoly prices, rationing, bundling, etc.) can be pro-competitive and socially beneficial. Besides, some apparent 'inefficiencies' may help the overall performance (Caillaud and Jullien, 2003).

Source: Julien (2011) and Wauthy (2011).

Conclusion

On one side of the equation, the dramatic decrease of the prices of media distribution is likely to bring some further broad gains through flexible pricing, low delivery costs and virtually unlimited capacity. Declining (production) cost may boost creativity. On the other side of the equation, for the specific cost structure of each subsector, the global output may not that easy to establish. Some costs are disappearing (logistics, some elements of manufacturing), while others are appearing, or remain (like the core expertise of each industry: creation/development, the editorial process), but may increase, like marketing in a highly competitive environment. In some sectors, like film or broadcasting, 'quality' is often correlated with higher costs.

In any case, a radically changed cost structure paves the way for different business models. The evolving business models are an output of two simultaneous processes: the overall trend of transformation of digital products into services, and the processes of disintermediation and reintermediation. Moving to a service (online) model allows the consumer to buy additional services linked to some editorial content rather than simply the media per se, as illustrated by the sales of virtual items pioneered by the video games industry.

Disintermediation allows direct sales from the creators (books, films, video games). Reintermediation opens up the availability of sales channels, but often comes with some kind of power position exerted by the new intermediary. The two main categories of business models, the paid models and the advertising 'free' business models, have now developed into various categories, bringing new streams of revenues linked to different kinds of services.

The increase of value brought by digitization seems to benefit more digital consumers. Consumer consumption has a wider scope with the exponential growth of available contents and access capacities. As consumers become prosumers, they can play a new role in the creative processes (for news, video games, music, etc.). However, this role should not be overestimated, and existing industries may have to rely on stable existing relationships with creators.

Notes

1. Based on the findings of the four waves of enquiries into the cultural practices of the French (1973, 1981, 1988 and 1997). EC (2005b: 22) stressed the same ongoing structural decline for newspapers over the last two decades.
2. Although Page and Carey (2010) added a note of caution about this trend, stressing an upward trend for digital albums in 2009 in the UK, reaching the same value as digital download.
3. Other publishing systems are available such as Lulu, or Barnes & Noble's PubIt!, FastPencil, Publish Green, Scribd, or Smashwords.
4. http://www.gawker.com/about.
5. http://www.spreeblick.com/impressum.
6. *Source*: Gold farming. Wikipedia.
7. In the publishing industry, the author appears to be more in the position of a supplier working under various contractual arrangements (Chapter 1).
8. For some other views, see Busson and Evrard (2013); Miège et al. (2013: 18).
9. Bonnell (2011), former director of Studio Canal, the film production branch of Canal Plus and a well-known economist of the cinema industry: 260 films in France with a peak in 1957 v. 260 in 2010.
10. Wikipedia 'Gold farming' notes: 'Academic studies of gold farming reveal that the social networks of gold farmers are similar to those of drug dealers'. Retrieved July 23, 2010.
11. In the case of music, marketing and promotion also have a large share in the total costs: 28% in 2009.
12. Traditional studios are closing,.
13. Old days, promotion on the radio: $60 million payments to radio in 1985, when recording industry profits were $200 million, $150,000 to promote hit single. *Source*: Waldfogel (2011b).
14. 'A Too-Cosy World?', *The Economist*, April 14, 2012, p. 62.
15. The contract for an agency model includes 'most favoured nation' clauses; publishers are prevented from selling books to other buyers at a cheaper rate. Publishers set the final price of the books, and distributors, like Apple, get a fee from the publishers on every book sold (about 30%). Under the wholesale model (used by Amazon), the publisher sells books to the distributor at a set price (usually 50% of retail) and the distributor sells the books to the public at whatever price the distributor chooses.
16. Segment covering, among other things, online video and music sales.
17. Other sites offering the same service are available: Grooveshark (http://grooveshark.com), Musicovery (http://musicovery.com/) and Slacker (http://www.slacker.com/).

18. Advert cost per thousand views.
19. 36% for mobile app. NPD Group's *Insights into the Freemium Games Market* report. Quoted by *Mobile Business Briefing*, April 26, 2012. http://www.mobilebusinessbriefing.com/articles/survey-almost-half-of-freemium-gamers-make-in-app-payments/23624?elq=c7e01fe0e5d2433d8c56e290da0965c3.
20. 'Become a patron of your favourite band': http://patronism.com/.
21. *Source*: website. http://patronism.com/.
22. By Herbert Sandler, http:/www.propublica.org.
23. The paper provides a comprehensive overview of the literature up to 2012 (Evans and Schmalensee, 2013: 47–73) as a 26 pp. appendix.
24. An agent is 'single-home' if he is active only on one platform, or 'multihome' if he is active on several platforms.

3
Media in the Changing Media–IT–Telecom Ecosystem

Jean Paul Simon

The second section (case studies) documents the growth of the online and wireless media market, driven by the increase in the number of broadband subscribers and the innovation in handheld devices such as iPods or tablets. The other side of the coin is that content is often seen as a major incentive to roll down networks; to improve transmission for upgraded content so as to provide customers with attractive applications and services for the new devices. Drastic changes have taken place over the last decade in the telecom services and equipment subsectors (Simon, 2011a, 2011b). They have been driven by the entry of players from other sectors of ICT (e.g. Apple, Microsoft, Google and Yahoo).

The blurring of previously distinct sectors has been described accurately as 'the new ICT ecosystem'[1] (Arlandis and Ciriani, 2010; Fransman, 2010; Booz & Co., 2011a). The role of telecommunications operators goes far beyond the mere provision of networks and services: for example, as enablers of innovation for the other players, backing the creation of new market opportunities such as applications on smartphones[2] (Lombard, 2011). The telecom subsectors play a crucial role at the very core of this ICT ecosystem, creating the conditions to boost the innovative capacity of the whole (the development of smartphones and mobile apps). Figure 3.1 shows the worldwide adoption of ICT up to 2010 (ITU, 2012).

The deployment of broadband networks and the diffusion of new devices (smartphones, tablets) have been identified as major enablers of the growth of new services and markets. Telecommunications and other kinds of infrastructures are the prerequisite for advanced use of the Internet and subsequent services. Their availability conditions both the type of content and patterns of its creation, sharing and use over the network. According to the ITU (2013), in 2013, 41% of the world's households

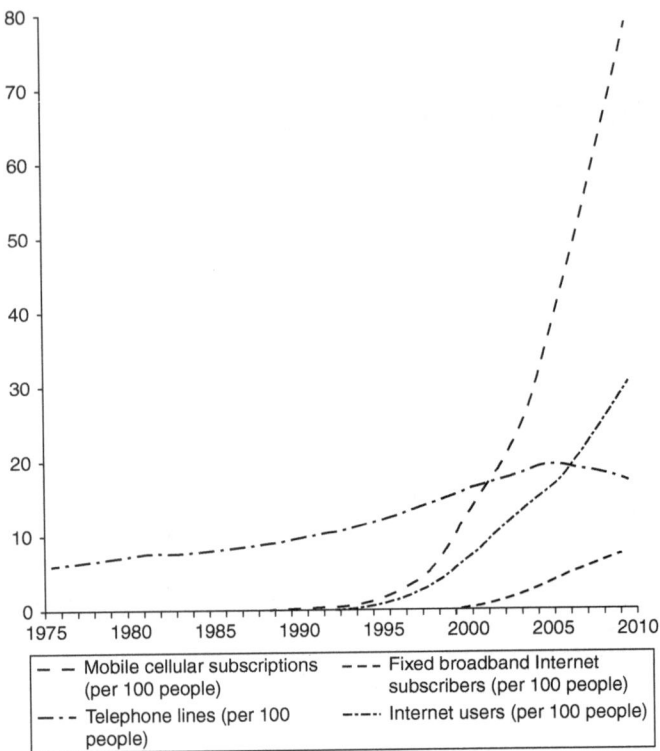

Figure 3.1 Worldwide adoption of ICT: The current digital age (ITU, 2012)
Source: Katz (2012).

are connected to the Internet: half of them are in the developing world, where household Internet penetration has reached 28%, while 78% of all households are connected in the developed world (see Figure 3.1).

Accordingly, broadband networks became top priorities for policy makers under initiatives such as the US national broadband plan (FCC, 2009; Simon, 2010), the EU digital agenda (EC, 2010a), various broadband plans in Latin America (Katz, 2013a) and the ITU Broadband Commission target.[3] Internet and broadband ('digitization') are often perceived[4] as general-purpose technology with the potential to alter the nature of the economy, bringing productivity gains. Their transformative power is seen as a driver of economic and social growth. The spread of broadband networks (and ultra-broadband in the future) represents one of the critical factors for the distribution of digital content over Internet Protocol (IP). This process is usually perceived as bringing great benefits to the economic growth of firms and markets (Katz, 2012, 2013b)[5] and, above all, to the creation of an environment that is socially advanced, more competitive, reducing the social divide. The contribution to GDP is considered of major importance.

Cloud computing[6] is expected to yield further substantial benefits, as fixed costs become variable costs (or CAPEX/OPEX), offering on demand highly elastic self-service with increased IT flexibility, reduced IT costs and improved process efficiency. Amazon (Amazon Web Services: AWS), Google (Gmail, Google Docs, Google App Engine) and Microsoft (Windows Azure) are pioneering companies in this field.

In the US, more than three-quarters of adults own laptop or desktop computers, and, as of December 2012, about 45% of adults owned a smartphone (Pew, 2013); the number of tablet owners has grown by about 50% since the summer of 2011, to 18% of adult Americans (Pew, 2012): 62% of smartphone owners, and 64% of tablet owners, said they consume news on their device weekly (Pew, 2013). According to Nielsen, approximately 48% of Americans now watch video online and 10% watch mobile video (FCC, 2012: 111). We are moving toward a five-screens world: TVs, PCs, game consoles, connected TVs and mobile devices (smartphones or tablets). The screens are usually used sequentially, but more and more often simultaneously (multitasking, complementary activities). Based on a US-only survey, a Google study claims that, in 2012, 90% of media interactions were screen-based, 4.4 h per day (38% of media interactions were on smartphones, 9% on tablets; Google, 2012: 8), and only 10% non-screen-based (radio, newspapers and magazines).

PCs remain the primary access but are almost stable, as mobile is growing fast. Smartphones are expected to overtake PCs in 2016 (Verwaayen, 2012). Forrester is predicting that tablet ownership in Western Europe will quadruple by 2017 to over 50% (Lomas, 2013). Besides, as noted by the Pew 2012 report: 'Smartphone owners are even more likely than others to be digital omnivores.' It is, then, worth considering the perspective brought by mobile for the distribution of content, as noted by the Google study (2012: 45): 'Going mobile has become a business imperative.'

Going mobile[7]

Wireless-mobile technology is, indeed, a major driver of economic value in the world economy (EU: $\approx$€250 billion, or 2–3% of GDP, and rising). ITU (2013: 1) counted, in 2013, almost as many mobile-cellular subscriptions as people in the world, with more than half in the Asia-Pacific region (3.5 billion out of 6.8 billion total subscriptions). Wireless Intelligence (2012a) estimated the total number of unique (eliminating subscribers with multiple SIM cards) mobile subscribers worldwide at 3.2 billion in 2012. Wireless Intelligence (2012b) forecasts 8.5 billion connections by 2017, with 50% from the new generation of mobile networks (3G[8]: 40%, 4G[9]: 10%).

The number of smartphones in use worldwide topped one billion in 2012. The release of the Apple iPhone in 2007 played a major role in triggering this migration, while mitigating the expected negative impact of the financial crisis, as data growth in mature markets accelerates. The consultancy Deloitte found a positive correlation between mobile data growth and economic growth (Deloitte-Cisco, 2012: 7).

The smartphone phenomenon has not only contributed to the upgrading of devices. It has also changed the way customers are using their mobile phones, among other things by shifting the patterns of use toward the Internet world and allowing access to all kinds of content. This phenomenon is only the most visible indication of the changes taking place in the ICT ecosystem. It paved the way for the creation of an array of new applications whose number has skyrocketed. Mobile became a significant way to distribute news and music. and is certainly one of the fastest-growing platforms to provide such content and assorted services. Cloud applications allow mobile users to overcome the memory capacity and processing power limitations of mobile devices, and reliance on cloud computing increases demand for the quantity of bandwidth as well. The mobile revolution is changing the lives of millions of people in the developing world (UNCTAD, 2010: 26).

The growth of traffic is now mainly driven by consumers (as opposed to business, as previously), with consumers becoming more and more active as 'prosumers'. Looking at the composition of the traffic growth, this growth is mainly driven by media, video being the driver (over 50% of the traffic) (Cisco Visual Networking Index, 2013). Video streaming and communications applications such as YouTube, Hulu and Netflix rank highest on both smartphones and tablets (Cisco Visual Networking Index, 2013: 21). Indeed, the shift to digital information is scaling up by several orders of magnitude (exabytes) in data volume every couple of years. The Asia-Pacific region (APAC) will generate 47% of all mobile data by 2017 (Cisco Visual Networking Index, 2013).

Notably, China and India are the fastest-growing mobile markets in the world. The 3G market started growing with China and India (De Prato et al., 2013). China as a whole surpassed the one billion milestone earlier in 2012, with three companies in the top ten mobile operators and China Mobile ranking first (nearly 700 million connections and revenues of US$22 billion in 2012) (Abbot, 2012). Sixty-nine per cent of India's Internet users access the Internet via their mobiles (McClelland, 2012). China is a front runner in mobile Internet. India's Bharti Airtel ranked fourth. Among the ten top-ranking companies, six are from BRIC countries, seven with the addition of Telenor, a Norwegian operator with revenues coming mostly from Asia. Smartphone penetration in South Korea reached 63% in 2012 (KISDI, 2012: 22).

In 2012, mobile operators' revenues in BRIC countries (over US$250 billion out of US$1.16 trillion in 2012; Wireless Intelligence, 2013a) represented almost 22% of total global mobile revenue (up from 16% four years ago), having already surpassed North America in terms of sales during 2011 (Wireless Intelligence, 2013b). They will be the primary engine of growth, contributing over 40% of global revenues by 2012.[10] Indonesia is the largest smartphone market in South Asia and is estimated to have 37 million Facebook users, second only to the US, according to web statisticians Socialbakers (Ranjini Mei Hua and Melissa, 2012: 15).

The centre of user-driven innovation is shifting to emerging economies. They create more content over the Internet and are more creative, according to an online survey[11] conducted by the Oxford Internet Institute and INSEAD[12] (WEF, 2011: 35). One of the authors states that Chinese users are leading in online entertainment, leisure and commerce (Dutton, 2013). Figure 3.2 depicts the dimensions of mobile content: from processed information to creative content and the degree of specificity to the mobile environment, including some examples of mobile content market segments. The resulting mobile content

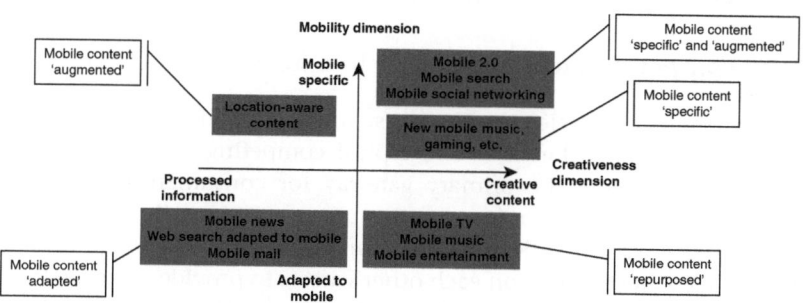

Figure 3.2 Dimensions of mobile content
Source: Feijoo et al. (2009).

space can then be categorized into four broad classes, not mutually exclusive:

- 'adapted' from available information (coming from a different medium), adjusted to be displayed and used in a mobile environment, for example, 'mobisodes',[13]
- 'repurposed': content reused and adapted to mobility,
- 'original' or 'specific': designed with mobility in mind, mobile games being a good example (casual games),
- 'augmented': content (of any type) that uses additional and specific properties of mobile systems (such as location-awareness with the expected growth of location-based services) to increase its value and interest for users.

On the edited side of the markets, there are four main vertical segments: mobile music, mobile television/mobile video, mobile gaming, and others such as mobile media, m-books, education, and so on. Each segment tells a different story, with failures (mobile TV[14]) and outstanding successes such as the game *Angry Birds* from Rovio. The Finnish start-up hit one billion downloads of *Angry Birds* in May 2012. Mobile games are no longer a delayed-in-time 'poor brother' of console and PC games, but a distinct and exciting experience, part of a new wide ecosystem with wide demographics. The mobile news segment is also growing fast: in the US half of smartphone owners (51%) and a majority of tablet owners (56%) use the devices for news. 'Fifty six percent of all mobile device users, and 47 percent of the population, now use such devices to get local news via an Internet connection' (Waldman, 2011: 17). According to the Pew 2012 survey, mobile is adding to and expanding rather than replacing news behaviour. In 2012, US consumers spent 5 hours 26 minutes per month on mobile video (Nielsen, 2013).

New competing business models in a new value network

Within this Media–Telecom–IT ecosystem, the consultancy BCG (BCG, 2011) distinguishes between five typical competing business models, battling to become the primary gateway for consumers for content navigation, to control access to consumers and to collect consumer data (cross-platform collection and monetization). The companies but nevertheless have to rely on each other's assets to provide their services.

The first business model, the distribution-centred model, provides the largest segment of the total, accounting for over €260 billion in 2008

(A. T. Kearney, 2010), and is built upon an infrastructure capacity (cable network, telecom networks and satellite operators). This infrastructure (performance and capacity), together with its billing capacity, constitutes its main strategic asset. This sector has been declining, and is not expected to grow. New networks are being deployed nevertheless, and new services offered with a higher quality of service (Hutchins, 2011). Specific specialized subnetworks, such as content delivery networks (for example, Akamai, Limelight networks and Level 3), are being deployed to offer enhanced services to content providers, placing content on the 'network edge' closer to the customer (instead of a central server) to reduce the latency for video delivery.

Box 3.1   Content Delivery Networks (CDN)

A content delivery network is designed to distribute content over a network and maximize bandwidth. Its purpose is to improve quality of service by taking data traffic off the major backbone of the Internet.

These specific specialized subnetworks (like Akamai, Limelight networks or Level 3) are being deployed to offer enhanced services to content providers, placing content on the 'network edge' closer to the customer (instead of a central server) to reduce the latency for video delivery. Strategically placed edge servers decrease the load on interconnects, public peers, private peers and backbones, freeing up capacity and lowering delivery costs. Instead of loading all traffic on a backbone or peer link, a CDN can offload these by redirecting traffic to edge servers. CDN technologies give more control of asset delivery and network load.

Due to the rapid growth of streaming video traffic, telecommunications service providers have begun to launch their own CDNs as a means to lessen the demands on the network backbone and to reduce infrastructure investments.

Source: IDATE (2013) and IT Media (2011).

The second business model, the aggregation-centred model, is based on the marketing of its valuable contents (application software, games, film, music, video, etc.) under its own brand (Sky, BBC, RTL, Hachette, etc.). Platforms may be linear (TV, cable) or non-linear (online). The third model, the search-centred model (Google, Bing, Yahoo) is built on research algorithms offering navigation through the available content and being an entry point to the Web. Grounded in network effects (direct and indirect), it requires the creation of platforms of multisided markets, 'Google economics' (Perrot, 2011), to drive traffic to its ads monetization engine (97% of Google's revenues; BCG, 2011).

The fourth model, the device-centred model, tries to circumvent the other players by luring customers into its closed ecosystem, like Apple with iTunes and, above all, the Apple apps, but also Nintendo, Microsoft, Sony with games, and now TV manufacturers with connected TV. It gives birth to a new form of vertical integration, 'Apple economics' (Perrot, 2011). Within its ecosystem, Apple is able to design and manage the customer experience, which also raises concerns among regulators and consumer associations. They point to the lack of interoperability and the limitations of the potential uses compared with the physical/analogue world.

Content providers (and applications providers) also have to abide by the conditions imposed upon them, including specific technological requirements. Besides, as noted, some of these players already have a stake in the production of content (console games or phone apps). This model was initially introduced by Apple for the music business for the launch of its iPod, but also by Sony, Microsoft and Nintendo for games. It was successfully reintroduced by Apple for mobile apps. Recently, the launch of the iPad opened up the e-book market (PWC, 2011). Apple appears to act as the game changer in these digital markets.

The device-centric model is now appearing tentatively in the TV market. Manufacturers of TV (Samsung, Sony) and other type of access devices (hybrid receivers, set-top boxes, digital media players) are now trying to replicate the success story of Apple within the realm of broadcasting with the introduction of connected TV.

The fifth business model, the community-centred model (YouTube, Twitter, Facebook), derives its strength from economies of scale and scope (networks effect) on a global scale as well, aggregating contents produced by users and others (prominently for social network sites), generating interuser communication (comments, posts and sharing), while building their core strategic asset, data gathering. The scale is central, too, for this business model: in 2013, Facebook claims 751 million mobile users monthly (from a total user base of 1.1 billion) (Costello, 2013c).

Players from the IT sector operating as aggregators, search-engine providers, manufacturers and social networks are also often introduced as 'Over-the-top' (OTT) providers in the industry jargon.[15] Their growing role and influence have raised concern from both media players and infrastructure providers. Telecom operators and other infrastructure providers fear becoming 'dumb pipes' carrying (in the EU) US contents and services. Telecom operators have lost their value for services to various kinds of applications providers. OTT messaging services such as Apple iMessage, Viber, WhatsApp and KakaoTalk have had a negative impact on the revenues of telecom operators (short message service, SMS: a high margin segment[16]). At the same time, this 'commodization' of telecommunication may just be the output of more competitive markets with reduced margins and decreasing prices. Customers benefit from more communication services and applications.

Besides, both sets of players (media, telecom) share the view that OTT players do not share a fair part of the funding (of contents, of infrastructure). They claim that these new entrants do not play by the same rules and are by and large unregulated, which is not the case for the two other kinds of players under content regulation (media) or economic regulation (telecom). They will usually plead for similar conditions in the name of 'levelling the playing field'. As Williamson (2013) sums it up, they tend to argue that OTT applications are undermining the capacity of network operators to invest and are free-riding. However, as he stresses, this is more linked to reliance on legacy voice and text revenues, and therefore suggests a telecom industry adjustment: an option explored in the next section.

Funding new networks under increased competition

The current data explosion calling for the deployment of new networks is taking place at a difficult economic time. However, the market is reaching saturation, and infrastructures will plateau as about 92% of US households have access to at least one wired broadband platform (adoption stands at about 65%), and about 90% of the population are covered by 3G mobile wireless broadband. Therefore, the telecom industry and the IT sector are facing several challenges; huge investments are needed for the deployment of new fixed (ultra-fast broadband) and mobile networks (3G, 4G), under uncertain economic returns. Indeed, the funding of such deployments, at least in some areas (medium and low density), appears somewhat problematic. Unless the sector is able to show some revenue growth and provide adequate returns, it is unlikely that investors will show commitment to the additional CAPEX[17] that the industry requires for rolling out the new networks, as the telecoms sector index has underperformed the general index by 29.3% over the last ten years (Minerva, 2010).

Tensions and disconnect in the Internet value chain

Whatever its role, the telecom industry as an enabler of the distribution of content and services is facing some paradoxical challenges. Traffic is increasing, even exploding in the case of mobile networks, making the deployment of new networks unavoidable, but at the same time revenues are declining. Customers generate vast amounts of traffic but show low willingness to pay for additional traffic. Besides, there seems to be a lack of demand for massive fixed additional bandwidth.

The telecom industry claims that there is misalignment between prices and costs, making the existing business models unsustainable. Other experts claim that the largest transfer of value is not taking place between telecom companies and IT companies but from companies to users; hence this 'mispricing' (i.e. 'unlimited' undifferentiated Internet access) is turning into a major challenge for the industry searching for the right pricing model for both retail and wholesale, to find a better way of encouraging willingness to pay.

Unlimited flat rate has allowed a faster adoption of the Internet, but may have reached its limit from an economic viewpoint, especially, as stressed by Bonneau (2010), in the case of limited resources like spectrum for mobile. Bughin (2010: 62–66) acknowledged that the 'web produces extraordinary value' but also that most of it benefits digital users. He gauged a value net (US, Europe) of €250 billion, shared 40% by online advertisers and 60% by consumers.

A study by A.T. Kearney[18] (2011: 1) stresses the difficulty of solving all the structural issues of a disconnect in the Internet value chain:

> those who benefit from higher traffic volumes are those who generate traffic (typically content sites) and those who consume it (typically end users). Those who have to build and operate the networks required to carry these traffic volumes earn almost no revenues and are often locked into flat rate price schemes with the latter group, continually decreasing because of competition.

US ISP[19]s have begun to impose data caps or shift back to usage-based billing (Comcast in 2008, AT&T in 2011) (FCC, 2012: 123). As noted by Cisco Visual Networking Index (2013: 4), many operators across the globe have eliminated unlimited data plans. Swisscom maintained unlimited access but under various price plans. Vodafone introduced a mobile broadband tariff in Spain with time-of-day elements, off-peak usage not included in traffic caps and the acceptance of traffic throttling[20] during periods of congestion in exchange for lower fees.

However, these attempts are triggering concerns about discriminatory treatment of players. Another option, considered by some players, is offering a more segmented choice (often limited by the regulators fearing price squeezes) and avoiding unlimited flat rate (as with the peering agreements), as traffic looks very unbalanced. Some companies, like SoftBank, the number three Japanese mobile operator, are looking at a two-sided business model, combining a charge for the communication and one for the content charge, alongside its tiered flat-rate model.

However, growth is to be expected, with mobile data services as the main driver of future revenue growth (ITU, 2012: 162); consumers will generate still more traffic, and then the issue becomes: how to monetize this growth? This may call for innovative approaches, such as morphing into an access business under different rules, and finding appropriate charging schemes other than volume and metered charges; new interconnection schemes, performance-based quality of service and traffic wholesale for OTT providers, pay per use, per quality and new bundles of traffic and services for end users.

Besides, paradoxically, part of the perceived reluctance of the telecom industry to deploy ultra-fast broadband is linked to the signals received from the market of a lack of demand for massive fixed additional bandwidth: there are no significant signals of consumer demand, a major difference from Asian markets (online gaming). The take-up is very low. This reluctance was noted in the Digital Agenda Scoreboard 2011 (EC, 2011a), but the report claimed that it 'will lessen gradually as new services requiring higher speeds become available', quoting, for instance, what happened with online games (Digital Agenda, 2011: 20). However, the case of Denmark, a leading country in the deployment of ultra-fast broadband, does confirm the wide gap between availability and take-up: the deployment rate went up to 65% of the population in 2012 having access to 100 megabits (fast Ethernet), while the take-up rate was only 0.8% (Andersen, 2012, 2013). Customers do not appear to grasp what they can get from this increased bandwidth because of a lack of attractive applications; without an increased value proposition, consumer uptake will remain at a suboptimal level (Katz, 2013b). Marcus notes that in countries with an impressive deployment of ultra-fast broadband, like Japan and South Korea, usage is not significantly higher (Marcus and Elixmann, 2012, 2014). He concludes that ' "too much" bandwidth availability cannot promote bandwidth consumption' (Marcus and Elixmann, 2014: 1).This may point toward some demand-side policies, not only supply-side policies.

Conclusion

Telecommunications and other kinds of infrastructures are the prerequisite for advanced use of the Internet and subsequent services. Their availability conditions both the type of content and the patterns of its creation, sharing and use over the network. The deployment of broadband networks and the diffusion of new devices (smartphones, tablets) have, therefore, been identified as major enablers of the growth of new services and markets. These deployments have been at the core of the creation of the new ecosystem.

Wireless-mobile technology has become a major driver of economic value in the world economy. Indeed, the mobile revolution is changing the lives of millions of people in the developing world. The growth of traffic is driven by consumers (opposed to businesses, as before). Looking at the composition of the traffic growth reveals a growth mainly driven by media, with video being the driver (over 50% of the traffic). Video streaming and communications applications such as YouTube, Hulu and Netflix rank highest on both smartphones and tablets.

Within this Media–Telecom–IT ecosystem, each segment is now competing with the players of the other segments. Five different business models can be distinguished, each one building upon its respective assets: the distribution-centred model is built upon an infrastructure capacity (cable network, telecom networks and satellite operators), the aggregation-centred model is based on the marketing of its valuable content (application software, games, film, music, video, etc.), the search-centred model uses its research algorithm to offer navigation through the available content, the device-centred model bets on its own closed ecosystem, and the community-centred model derives its strength from economies of scale and scope (networks effect) aggregating contents produced by others.

However, the infrastructure providers (telecom operators) are facing a dilemma. Traffic is increasing, even exploding in the case of mobile networks, making the deployment of new networks unavoidable, but at same the time revenues are declining. The issue, in a way similar to the one faced by content providers (Chapter 2), becomes how to monetize this growth in a sustainable way for infrastructure providers, service providers and end customers.

Notes

1. This notion refers to symbiotic relationships (financial, informational and material flows between the actors) and synergies.

2. There is no precise definition of a smartphone. It is usually considered as a mobile phone offering advanced capabilities, PC-like. It typically includes a complete operating system and a platform for the development of applications.
3. The Broadband Commission for Digital Development was launched in 2010 by ITU and UNESCO. See: 'Measuring the Information Society 2012' (ITU, 2012: 9).
4. However, the impact is difficult to assess (Wallsten, 2010: 28).
5. Katz (2012: 3), while being cautious about the evidence needed to establish the economic impact of broadband, considers five areas: contribution to economic growth ('positive externalities'), contribution to productivity gains, contribution to employment and output of broadband deployment ('countercyclical effect'), creation of consumer surplus, and improvement of firm efficiencies.
6. Usually an end user runs applications on data stored locally on his or her computer's hard disk. Cloud computing moves the data to the network, the data being accessed on demand. Cloud is leveraged in conjunction with mobile technologies, sensor networks and 'big data'. For the types of cloud computing services, see 'The NIST Definition of Cloud Computing' (NIST, 2010).
7. This section builds on the work of Feijoo et al. (2009), De Prato & al (2010), Feijoo (2011a), Feijoo and Gomez-Barroso (2012).
8. 3G: HSPA, EV-DO.
9. 4G: LTE, TD-LTE and WiMAX. Samsung's flagship Galaxy S3 and Apple's new iPhone 5 are LTE-enabled devices.
10. GSMA, *The Global Cellular Industry Balance Sheet*, 2012.
11. 5,400 adult Internet users from 13 different countries.
12. Global Business School with campuses in France, Singapore and Abu Dhabi.
13. Short TV format.
14. See Chapter 2 for an overview.
15. OTT is a general term for the delivery of web-based video services that can be utilized via a broadband connection over the open Internet, on different devices such as connected TVs, games consoles, hybrid receivers and digital media players, supplied by players such as search-engine providers, manufacturers (Apple, Samsung) and social networks.
16. 'KPN effect': in May 2011 KPN became the first mobile operator to report that subscriber use of OTT voice and messaging applications triggered a decline in voice and messaging traffic and revenues. Clark-Dickson (2013: 148).
17. CAPEX: capital expenditures.
18. A study commissioned from A. T. Kearney by the four leading EU telecom operators.
19. ISP: Internet service provider.
20. Traffic or bandwidth throttling: managing the traffic, an industry euphemism for the intentional slowing down of Internet service by an Internet service provider, in other words limiting or cutting the traffic of heavy users.

4
Toward Enabling Policies

Jean Paul Simon

Public intervention and public policies are historical features of the media industries (with public support, IPR regulation, freedom of expression, cultural diversity, etc.) as the production of these merit goods generates further externalities for society at large (cultural, societal, etc.). The digital shift opens up new questions about such policies, about novel ways to implement them and about their effectiveness in a digital world. At the same time, it creates space for policies to ease the transition toward these digital media world(s). This chapter emphasizes the main issues and engines of public intervention; in line with the previous chapters, it analyses the challenges policy makers are facing with the digital shift, but it does not comprehensively review all the policies.[1] It concentrates on the issues of funding creation, and of copyright.

Public intervention in a digital world

The standard view in favour of regulation and public intervention[2] is built on the understanding that books, films, videos and CDs are not just commodities, but have a special value to society as cultural goods, and, as such, deserve to be treated differently from other tradable commodities. The production of these merit goods generates further externalities for society at large (cultural, societal, etc.) (UNESCO, 2005). Besides, the media have an acknowledged role in the functioning of democracies, triggering consequent rights and responsibilities with respect to human rights, democracy, freedom of information and cultural diversity (EC, 2010b). Rules and regulations[3] have been set in place to ensure these policy goals. An array of existing policies aims to foster these goals: governments often interfere directly (subsidies in the case of cinema in France, or zero VAT on books in the UK, for instance) or indirectly (various tax breaks, reduced postal rates for the distribution of newspapers or books).

From an economic viewpoint, the relevant question is: are we facing market failures and, consequently, is public intervention needed? To take the example of the fixed retail price of books, meant to ensure the persistence of networks of independent bookshops, opponents to the measures (see Chapter 5) argued that any regulatory interference artificially increases the prices of books. In the US, such an agreement would be held to be illegal as a mandated retail price. It worked, nevertheless, in the sense that under 'normal' market conditions most of the retail points would have disappeared. In Japan, according to Kamata (2011), the most influential factor in publishers' reluctance to embrace e-books has been the willingness to maintain a unique book distribution system. Publishers are trying to keep an alternative to Amazon's streamlined supply chain. The example of movie theatres in the late 1950s and 1960s, when cinema-going started to decline sharply,[4] has shown that when supply was reduced (with theatres closing) the demand dropped (Bonnell, 1978).

However, some may question the relevance of the policy of propping up legacy players, as the distribution in a digital world is very different from the physical distribution of cinema in the 1950s. For instance, in the debate in France about the extension of the fixed price to the e-book, the French authority (*conseil de la concurrence*) questioned the transferability of the former policy goals (Perrot, 2010).[5] The 'long tail' is taking care of the rotation issue. Bookshops are not the main access point for e-books. According to Perrot, in an emerging market, it would be unwise to freeze the market. The French authority took a similar position for connected TV.

Whatever the policy choices, it is clear that, as the book market moves away from the former integrated value chain with the publisher at the centre, a growing disconnect is happening, between distribution and creation, between the economics of distribution and the economics of creation. In other words, some forms of integrated cross-subsidization between lines of bundled products are no longer possible. The distribution side may not use its revenues to fund more content. At the same time, other forms of cross-subsidization become possible in two-sided markets, as seen in the case of video games (games/consoles) or distributors (Amazon with readers and e-books).

Funding of creation

The benefits of the shifts described are clearly unevenly distributed; hence, the question of how to support production in a sustainable way appears crucial. There is a sharp contrast between legacy players experiencing varying degrees of challenge to survive in the last couple of years and new entrants thriving.

Therefore it is not surprising that the usual view among content holders (broadcasters, producers, rights holders) is that all other (new) players (irrespective of their country of origin or delivery mode) should participate in the 'financing of creation'. This was one of the main rationales for the introduction of quotas in the Television without Frontiers (TSF) in the 1980s (EC, 1989), mostly under pressure from some EU Member States. The directive was designed to take into account new developments such as cable and pay TV, program sponsorship and teleshopping. The promotion of European content and Europe's diversity of cultures was added. When the directive was reviewed, becoming the Audiovisual Media Services (AVMS) directive, the potential extension of the quota mechanisms to the non-linear media triggered hot debates. Some EU Member States, like France, mandated further obligations on Internet access providers after the implementation of the revised directive. The same debates are taking place, in the EU, around connected TV or Over-the-Top about the need to review the same directive or to adopt policies (CSA, 2011; EC, 2013).[6]

Nobody will question the urge to fund creation and the legitimate concerns it triggers, but it may not be the most relevant approach from an economic viewpoint. The core question is: do these new forms of distribution contribute to increased media production, more diversity, and enhanced consumer and producer surplus? Another difficult side of the issue is how to find the proper indicators to answer these questions; without robust evidence they can lead to endless debate between entrenched positions.

New media and new players (search engines, social networks and manufacturers) are usually exempt from the regulations mandated upon legacy players; hence the debate that took place for the AVMS directive and the current debate about the rules for connected TV entrants. The standard incumbent argument claims that such an unequal regulatory regime will place incumbents under a competitive disadvantage. The strategy to deal with the new competitors using regulatory means may vary, from trying to stifle this competition, as the US broadcasters did with cable,[7] or simply to seize the opportunity to receive more flexibility (this was the case with advertising in the new audiovisual directive), asking for a 'level playing field'.[8]

Legacy players will argue, understandably, for some measures to compensate for lost revenues. This was at the core of the 2012 debates throughout Europe about the need to mandate a payment from distributors like Google that were benefiting from the content produced without contributing, similar to the argument, noted in the previous chapter, made by the telecom companies for the funding of the networks. They will argue that fundamental principles should apply to non-linear services. Therefore, some EU Member States have mandated or plan to mandate financial contributions upon such players' distributing or 'packaging' of audiovisual works (ISPs, mobile operators, etc.). This has been the French approach for the funding of creation (an obligation to invest 3% of the turnover). The principle adopted was that 'each company making money from the use of work should contribute to the funding of the creation' (Gabla, 2012). Other EU regulators agree on that principle. Such a principle may sound nice and (almost) fair, but leaves open the much more tricky issue of the 'how'. Its implementation would require some robust evidence and a clear basis to quantify the contribution, as most of the revenues derived from content are indirect revenues (advertising) and not from direct sales to customers. Indeed, the case is far more complex, as we are facing sophisticated multisided markets (see Box 2.1).

In 2010, a report for the French government (Zelnick & al, *Création et Internet*, 2010) came up with the idea of a tax on advertising online revenues, called 'universal cultural contribution', quickly translated more harshly into 'Google tax'.[9] In 2012, in the field of newspaper publishing, the debate bounced back on the 'Google tax'. A bill was put forward by one of the French newspaper trade associations,[10] but dissenting voices were heard within the newspaper industry, stressing that propping up a declining business model was not an appropriate way to tackle the challenges newspapers are facing. In January 2013, under the threat of a possible legislative act, Google signed an agreement with the French government to grant 60 million Euros[11] to a special fund designed to help newspapers transitioning to digital media (Mora, 2013). A legal action was initiated in 2006, in Belgium, which ended with an undisclosed agreement in December 2012. In March 2013, the German government adopted legislation, put forward by the German Trade Association (BDZV, 2013), creating an ancillary copyright for press publishers requiring search engines to pay fees for the display of news extracts. The act grants a right, but the fees are open to negotiations. Lastly, another report commissioned by the French government (Lescure, 2013) suggested a (low) tax on devices, in the wake of existing taxes on recording media (cassettes, CDs, USB keys).

In a well-functioning market the production of such goods should attract adequate financial resources. The growth of the US cable markets illustrates the link between the development of the market and investments in programmes: to maintain its growth ratio, the US cable industry tripled its investment in programmes between 1984 and 1989 (Simon, 1991: 336). TBS, the US pioneer company for 'superstations', created two of the most innovative channels in the early 1980s: Cable News Network (CNN) and CNN-Headline News. Similarly, in 2012, US VOD companies Netflix and Hulu started offering original TV series on their platforms.[12] There are no reasons to assume that new entrants are not potential investors in the field, although their means of intervention may differ from those of legacy players, and their agendas may not be in line with other players' agendas. Mandating funding obligations upon new entrants, especially through additional taxes, may freeze the market and prevent innovation.

Asking for the participation of the distributor is like asking logistics players, like truck services,[13] to contribute to the production of the wares they transport. It departs from the standard business approach, whereby a supplier will normally charge for its services and not the other way round. It even departs from the current transportation model used to transmit the signal of over-the-air TV; broadcasters pay the transmission companies (tower companies). Some cable companies did indeed try to come back to this standard business logic and to charge the channels they were distributing, at least the less popular ones[14] that were not under any 'must carry' obligations. This was also the business model of channels of teleshopping in the US; cable networks gained a share of the revenues (an average of 5%; Simon, 1991). The model is similar for e-commerce companies taking a commission on online transactions. Hence, the claim is representative of the change of power relations between producers/aggregators and distributors, the former losing their prominent position over the legacy value chain.

Content holders stress that, nevertheless, radios airing music are paying to that end through royalties. Indeed, CISAC (2011) data show that radio, TV, cable and satellite generate most of the performing rights (56%). Television is the medium that contributes the most to creators' revenues (more than €1 billion).

Copyright[15]

The invention of copyright

The concept of musical copyright had its beginnings in 1575, when a 21-year patent monopoly on the printing and publishing of polyphonic music was granted. The earliest attempt at a printed musical copyright notice appeared in the 'Shir Hashirim' of Salomone Rossi (Venice, 1623), which included the first anti-piracy tool: a rabbinical curse on those pirating the text.

The first modern copyright law was the Statute of Anne (1710), which protected all published works for a fixed period of time. The US copyright clause was introduced later in the US constitution (1787) and the US Copyright Act passed in 1790. The developing book industry gave birth to the concept of intellectual property (copyright/*droit d'auteur*). The concept of *droit d'auteur* was coined under the influence of the French Enlightenment philosophers (Beaumarchais[16] (Edelman, 2008)). The *droit d'auteur* values the link between the author and his or her creation, while the notion of copyright stresses the link with the market, the protection of the investments. Historically, the notion of copyright was influenced by the utilitarian theory of Bentham, rather than by the approach of Locke, whose notion of natural property was closer to that of the French philosophers (Benhamou and Farchy, 2009: 5). Both *droit d'auteur* and copyright are harmonized and enshrined in the Berne convention of 1886 (Simon, 2012b).[17]

Once the work has been produced, it can be easily duplicated if not legally protected. From an economic viewpoint, copyright is a form of legal protection designed to correct a market failure linked to the very nature of creative goods as public goods characterized by high fixed production costs but low reproduction costs. Therefore intellectual property provides an exception to competition law, affording not only creators but most often owners of the exploitation rights (licences)[18] of intellectual innovations and products (publishers) legal protection from copying, with a limited monopoly on permission to reuse material. Intellectual property provides a strong management tool for this category of asset, allowing the holder of the right to strategically use exclusivity, windowing,[19] versioning,[20] and bundling,[21] and to price discriminate.

The role of copyright in business models

Legacy industries link the process of creation with the use of copyright to protect and fund back creation; to recoup their investments in creation. The role of copyright within the business model of each industry does vary, from some rather simple cases, as with books or even newspapers, to a complex intermingling of rights, as in the audiovisual sector, or combined with other means of managing assets, as in the video game industry. Each industry will blend different kinds of revenues. The role of copyrighted contents differs, then, from an industry relying more on advertising revenues than on direct sales (retailing), such as, for instance, broadcasting, but even in that case copyright is important to ensure other streams of revenues, and from a marketing or symbolic strategies (exclusivity) viewpoint as well, so as to boost the legitimacy of the product. In the case of cinema, the pre-negotiation of rights may contribute to the funding of a film (up to 65%); such pre-sales will usually come with some territorial rights attached.

However, clearing territorial rights, country by country, may raise the transaction costs artificially in a digital age, particularly in the case of music rights (Ranavoson et al., 2013). A KEA/CERNA study (2010) stated that, if international licensing could foster the availability of audiovisual works across borders, it remained difficult to predict whether this would increase the demand for non-national audiovisual works in the Member States. They found that so far VOD had not led to more circulation of European audiovisual works in the EU, since local distributors remained very important for the success of an audiovisual work (e.g. through a marketing strategy targeted at the national market). A study by Plum for the EC reached similar conclusions about a low level of domestic demand for TV or video originating from other EU markets (Plum, 2012).

Besides, copyright is not just a protective tool; it is a powerful marketing device, deeply grounded in the business models of these industries, and accordingly should be studied carefully. Waterman showed how the US movie industry made the most of it with successful market segmentation (Waterman, 2005: 118), 'maintaining pecking order and timing in sequence'. It is understandable, then, that these industries would display caution before leaving a well-established and functioning business model for an unproven one. Adding a new business line is a complex operation, especially within the existing tight release windows[22] (Chapter 3). There is fear of the new product cannibalizing the existing segments, especially, as stressed by Waterman (2005), as the video window is 'by far the most important in economic terms'.[23] In the 1980s the introduction of videotape (to be replaced later by DVD) gave birth to an internal debate about the right marketing strategy: rental, sales or a combination of the two. It took some time to stabilize and for the video window to become the main source of revenues.

The shortcomings of the economic case of copyright

If the business case looks robust from a policy viewpoint, so far the research remains inconclusive and evidence may be lacking about its economic role (Landes and Posner, 2003: 422), especially seen from the user's interest viewpoint and not only from the rights holder's revenues perspective (Handke, 2011: 41). 'Similar to the literature on patents, research on copyright has not produced conclusive empirical evidence whether unauthorized use of copyright works decreases social welfare, or what type of copyright policy would solve such a problem without excessive unintended consequences' (Handke, 2011: 41). The first attempts date back to the 1930s, when Plant was exploring the issue, asking how the absence of copyright would affect the book industry: 'Would books be written in such circumstances, and would they be published?' (Plant, 1934). The answer was positive, pointing to the lack of a strong relationship between the supposed incentive and the output. Some 30 years later, Thomas (1967) combined Coase's[24] very critical[25] approach to media (Coase, 1950) 'with Plant's skepticism about IP[26]' (Johns, 2009a: 53, 2009b). Cultural goods, information goods and knowledge are public goods whose consumption is non-rivalrous and non-excludable (Stiglitz, 2008: 1700). Digitization is further increasing these features, rejigging the balance that copyright is supposed to strike.

Cooper (2006, 2008) and Lessig (2004),[27] suggest that copyright may well be the suppressor of radical potential. These scholars, and others like Benkler (2006, 2011), argue that legal regimes and technology are often out of phase, as in the case of many uses of collaborative software. When such incompatibilities are proven to exist, they usually suggest that the copyright regime should be reinterpreted or adapted to knowledge society/information society goals. Along much the same lines, others are wondering about the costs of safeguarding copyright, and predicting that copyright reform will happen sooner or later.

Besides, if copyright is a central element to generate revenues for managers of rights, it does not appear to play the same role for creators or artists. Benhamou and Sagot-Duvauroux (2007) stressed the tension between copyright as a way to protect the work and the rights of creators and copyright as a means to remunerate authors. They note that artists draw only a relatively minor and rapidly decreasing portion of their income from copyright. Music is a typical case (Coleman and Bazelon, 2011) of an historical upturn where revenues are coming from performances[28] and related rights rather than from royalties redistributed by music companies. The sales of cultural goods generate only a very small fraction of revenues for the creators, with the notable exception of the book industry.[29] Often creative workers obtain revenues from other financial resources, from other professional occupations (teaching, journalism, etc.) or even, in some cases, from public subsidies, as with performers (musicians and players) in France. Copyright, at least for the creator, may not be the core source of revenues.

In such an uncertain context the ways to pay the authors/creators are moving targets (neither the level nor the bases are to be taken for granted).[30] It is understandable that legal theory and policy makers struggle to evaluate the claims of rights holders, especially as they also have to balance these claims against other main policy goals, such as freedom of expression or consumer rights (Helberger and Guilbaut., 2012; Maxwell, 2012). However, most of the goals of the copyright regime can remain and still be perceived as legitimate: to enable creation and innovation. The means to achieve these goals can change over time, as can the guidelines to implement them (Coene and Dumortier, 2012). Reviewing copyright law may offer an opportunity to strengthen the position of authors, but at the same time it may render the exploitation more complex.

Box 4.1   Updating treaties and policies

The World Intellectual Property Organization (WIPO) adopted in Geneva on December 20, 1996 the WIPO Performances and Phonograms Treaty ('the Performances and Phonograms Treaty') and the WIPO Copyright Treaty ('the Copyright Treaty'). The adoption of these treaties triggered the passing of legislation on both sides of the Atlantic.[31]

The EC has been very active in that field, trying to come up with solutions to streamline the process of copyright licensing. The Information Society Directive (EC, 2000) was adopted after several years of enquiry and discussions at the European Commission on the challenges brought about for the information society by the emergence of the digital networked environment (see EC, 1995). The EC displayed a strong willingness to intervene in order to correct what are considered as major inefficiencies for the internal market. The focus of (DG MARKT)[32] shifted from harmonization (copyright directive, EC, 2001) toward the management of rights with a view to facilitating the acquisition of multiterritorial licences, more suited to the Internet age. The accessibility of digital content is also a prime target on the EU Lisbon Agenda.

The 2011 document on the strategy for IPR calls again for the creation of a comprehensive framework for a digital single market (EC, 2011c). 'One-stop shops' are still seen as a way to facilitate rights acquisition. The creation of European 'rights brokers' is being considered, for instance, for the musical repertoire. At the same time, the Commission is trying to improve the licensing processes, perceived as lengthy and costly (Barnier, 2012: 2), and paying attention to the governing structure of collective societies. In July 2012, the EC adopted a proposal for a directive to facilitate the pan-European licensing of music on the Internet and to promote greater transparency and governance of collecting rights management companies.

However, from a competition angle, the DG Comp[33] took a harsher approach. On April 29, 2004, the Commission issued a statement of objections to collecting societies because of the anti-competitive effects of the territorial exclusivity clauses of the agreements. After two years of consultations, the DG Competition issued a decision in July 2008 alleging that the 24 EEA societies involved had violated European competition laws (CISAC was not included in the list).[34] Furthermore, in 2011, the European Court of Justice's Advocate General took the position that existing territorial content licensing models contravene the goal of a single open market.[35]

WIPO: references of main treaties and convention (WIPO manages 24 treaties):

http://www.wipo.int/treaties/es/ip/berne/trtdocs_wo001.html
http://www.wipo.int/treaties/es/ip/paris/trtdocs_wo020.html
http://www.wipo.int/treaties/es/ip/rome/trtdocs_wo024.html
http://www.wipo.int/treaties/es/ip/wct/trtdocs_wo033.html
http://www.wipo.int/treaties/es/ip/wppt/trtdocs_wo034.html

Source: Simon (2012b).

Conclusion

Public intervention and specific public policies are fairly common in the media sphere to achieve some highly legitimate policy goals. However, changing conditions may require changing policies, even if the policy goals are maintained as such. In a well-functioning market, the production of such goods should obtain adequate financial resources. Therefore, from an economic viewpoint, the relevant question for policy makers is: are we facing market failures and, consequently, is public intervention needed? For instance, under 'normal' market conditions most of the book retail points would have disappeared; therefore, keeping access to an extended network of retailers was deemed useful in some countries to maintain such an access network.

The benefits of the digital shift are clearly unevenly distributed; therefore, the question of how to support production in a sustainable way appears crucial. Mandating funding obligations upon new entrants is the standard approach to 'compensate' for losses or changing revenues, especially through additional taxes. However, it is clear that, as such approaches may freeze the market and prevent innovation, they require some robust evidence on a case-by-case basis, as the track record for propping up legacy players may not appear over-convincing from an economic viewpoint. The core question is: do these new forms of distribution contribute to an increased media production, more diversity, and enhanced consumer and producer surplus?

Copyright is another form of legal protection to correct a market failure linked to the very nature of creative goods as public goods (high fixed production costs but low reproduction costs). Therefore, intellectual property provides an exception to competition law, affording not only creators but most often owners of the exploitation rights (licences) of intellectual innovations and products (publishers) legal protection from copying, with a limited monopoly on permission to reuse material.

Copyright is a major element of most media existing business models, and needs to be properly taken into account. Besides, copyright is not just a protective tool; it is a powerful marketing device for these industries. If the business case looks robust from a policy viewpoint, so far the research remains inconclusive, and evidence may be lacking about its real economic role. The economic case of copyright is far from being obvious from an economic viewpoint. It is difficult to assess properly whether, absent such legal protection, innovation will decrease. The core question, about the contribution to media production, diversity and consumer surplus, remains the same. Copyright, at least for the creator, may not be the core source of its revenues, and is turning out to be less and less adapted to new collective or collaborative works, as well as novel ways to monetize these works.

Policy makers struggle to evaluate the claims put forward by rights holders, especially as they also have to balance these claims against other main policy goals, such as freedom of expression or consumer rights. However, most of the goals of the copyright regime can remain and still be perceived as legitimate: to enable creation and innovation.

In both cases at hand (funding, copyright) the means to achieve the policy goals can change over time, as well as the guidelines for implementing them to accommodate change in the markets and other policy goals. For policy makers, evidence may still be needed to choose maintaining an historical regulatory regime or opting for changes. Legacy policies should not act as a barrier to innovation and economic opportunity; there is a need to better understand the different aspects and to find the appropriate balance between conflicting goals.

Notes

1. Other policies, such as competition, privacy and data protection, are reviewed in Simon (2012a, b). For the issue of net neutrality, see Marsden (2010), Simon (2012a).
2. For a critical view on leaving media regulation to the 'hegemony of market forces', see, for instance, Feintuck and Varney (2006), focusing on access, stewardship and diversity. The body of academic literature in that field has been significant since, for instance, Dahlgren (1995).
3. There is an important body of regulation that is outside the scope of this chapter.
4. In France a peak was reached in 1957.
5. For the relation between regulation and competition in the media sector, see, for instance, Perrot et al. (2008).
6. The EC launched a consultation at the end of 2012 and released a Green Paper in 2013 (EC, 2013). The European Parliament published a report with a focus on media pluralism and adopted an opinion in January 2013, suggesting that the following issues should be included in the Green Paper: standardization, technology neutrality, personalized services and accessibility for disabled people, security of cloud computing, protection of minors and human dignity.
7. A short-term tactic, as the broadcasters eventually lost their case; on the other hand, the nascent cable industry managed to be granted some protection and privileges in the US in the 1970s (Simon, 1991). As reported by Waldman, newspaper executives tried to undermine competition from radio as the latter grew in popularity in the 1930s.
8. Or 'treat like as like', one of the eight solutions advocated by the EU Media Futures Forum, together with 'reward creators and creation of content'. The EU Media Futures Forum was established in December 2011 by the EC (see http://ec.europa.eu/information_society/media_taskforce/doc/pluralism/forum/exec_sum.pdf). The forum released a report in 2012.
9. A bill was prepared, but the article was removed during the debate in parliament, in 2011.

10. *Association de la presse d'information politique et générale* (IPG), founded in 2012.
11. Not really an impressive amount of money, especially compared with the amount of money that the French tax administration is claiming from Google: €1 billion. The firm from Mountain View is supposed to have circumvented the French taxes, claiming its commercial operations were generated from Ireland. Other governments showed concern about the leading IT companies escaping most of the taxes by headquartering in the countries with the lowest taxes: Luxemburg with VAT at 15% (Amazon, eBay, Netflix, PayPal, etc.) and Ireland at 12% (Apple, Facebook, Google, Twitter, Zynga, etc.). However, while Member States can question the tax strategies of other Member States, for companies there is nothing illegal in such tax shopping. The issue was nevertheless flagged by the EC (2011b).
12. *Lilyhammer*, a US–Norway production for Netflix, already a hit in Norway, and *Battleground* (a total investment of US$500 million) for Hulu. http://meta-media.fr/tag/hulu/, February 20, 2012.
13. Spain (Andalusia), where the authors live, is a major producer of strawberries that are distributed throughout the EU, mostly by truck. Truckers are making money by charging for the transport, and most likely it is a key business for their companies. However, it does not follow that truckers should contribute to the production of strawberries. The argument seems an oversimplification of business relations and value chains.
14. *Numéricâble* in France in the early 2000s.
15. This section builds on Simon (2012a, b).
16. The French writer Beaumarchais was the founder of the first French authors' society in 1777.
17. The US did not sign the Berne Convention until 1989.
18. From a legal perspective, publishers do not 'own' the copyright, but they have the exploitation rights (licences). In practice, the difference is often minimal; from a legal perspective, ownership and exploitation rights are two different concepts.
19. Staggered sales, for instance the practice of releasing some book formats first (hardcopies) and others (paperbacks), video releases.
20. Discrimination through quality.
21. Combined sales.
22. The usual chronology after the showing in theatres is video/DVD sale, video/DVD rental, VOD, pay TV and free-to-air television.
23. In 2008, the distribution of North American revenues was as follows: theatrical box-office distribution US$9.6 billion and home video US$25.8 billion, while online distribution accounted for only US$227 million (Coleman and Bazelon, 2011: 22).
24. Ronald Coase, future Nobel Prize winner for economics, was an ex-assistant of Plant.
25. Johns (2009a: 49) described the book *British Broadcasting: A Study in Monopoly* as "devastating".
26. IP: Intellectual Property. IPR: Intellectual Property Right.
27. His famous book *Free Culture* was released on the Internet under the Creative Commons Attribution/Non-commercial license on March 25, 2004.

28. In 2007, Madonna left Warner Music to sign a so-called '360 degree' deal with the live entertainment company Live Nation, sharing revenues from music sales, performances, merchandise and the right to her name. Coleman and Bazelon (2011: 13).

29. In France, the amount of royalties peaked in 2006 at nearly 500 million Euros (Minidata, 2011: 9); in 2010 it reached 435 million Euros out of a publishers' turnover of 2.8 billion Euros (Minidata, 2012). Robin (2007: 5) notes that the real amounts for sole authors are probably lower, as this amount covers other contributors (editors, for instance).

30. The French government passed a law on March 1, 2012 to offer a new mode of collective management of rights.

31. The main international obligations arising from the two treaties on copyright and related rights needed to be transposed. The US adopted the DMCA in 1998.

32. Directorate-General for Internal Market and Services (DG MARKT) is a Directorate-General of the European Commission.

33. Directorate-General for Competition (DG Comp) is a Directorate-General of the European Commission.

34. 'Antitrust: The European Commission prohibits practices which prevent European collecting societies offering choice to music authors and users', press release July 16, 2008. http://europa.eu/rapid/pressReleasesAction.do?reference=IP/08/1165&format=HTML&aged=1&language=EN&guiLanguage=fr.

35. Cases C-403/08 and C-429/08 Football Association Premier League Ltd and Media Protection Services Ltd. On October 4, 2011 the European Court of Justice adopted a ruling in a case involving the use in the UK of decoder cards intended to gain access in other Member States to satellite retransmissions of live English football matches.

Section II
Case Studies

5
The Book Publishing Industry

Giuditta De Prato

This industry can be dated back to the introduction of the format used for modern books (the codex: block of wood, book)[1] around the first century[2]: a bound book with pages. The codex gradually replaced the scroll (roll of papyrus, parchment or paper). This new format/technology allowed random access, whereas scrolls could only be accessed sequentially. This is considered as the most important 'technological change' before the invention of printing,[3] after the invention of writing as a cognitive technology (Goody, 1977).

The seminal work of Elizabeth Eisenstein (1980) on the printing press as an agent of change described its profound effect on society when Europe was transitioning away from the medieval to the modern world. Eisenstein compared this invention with the advent of computers, stating: 'until the recent advent of computers, has there been any other invention which saved so many man-hours for learned men' (Eisenstein, 1980: 521). She showed that, if the printing press did not create the book, it contributed to redefining it. She stressed that a cultural change of that magnitude took quite some time to unfold, as the effects were not seen clearly for more than a hundred years; in other words, if the technological change spread quickly, the cultural changes did not. The printed book as a 'new medium' initially tried to replicate as much as possible the patterns of the codex.

From a more modest viewpoint, this chapter highlights some of the changes taking place within the industry and its 'book chain' with digitization. The first section introduces the markets at a global, regional level and describes some of the major EU markets (France, Germany, Italy, Spain and the UK). The second section analyses the value network of the European book publishing industry, identifying the transformations taking place in the value network and in business models as a result of the ongoing digitalization process. The third section concludes with an assessment of the power relationship in the new digital environment.

The book publishing markets

For 2012, the global book market revenue estimated by the consultancy PricewaterhouseCoopers (PWC) was US$101.6 billion for the consumer and educational book publishing market[4] (PWC, 2013).[5] In the media and entertainment markets, the book market is the only one where EU companies (Bertelsmann, Hachette, Grupo Planeta, Pearson, Reed-Elsevier, Wolters Kluwer) lead, with seven companies among the top ten (*Publishers Weekly*, 2012). The ten largest publishers accounted for about 47% of all revenue generated by the 54 leading world companies (*Publishers Weekly*, 2012). Scientific/technical/medical (STM) publishers generated the largest share of sales among the top ten publishers, but trade sales fell in the 2008–2010 period, representing 31% of revenue in 2011 (*Publishers Weekly*, 2011). Pearson remains the world's largest book publisher by far (*Publishers Weekly*, 2011). In July 2013, Bertelsmann and Pearson have merged their trade book-based publication arms, Random House and Penguin, operating in five continents, to create the world-leading trade publisher, Penguin Random House[6].

The global market

The book market is a mature market and appears almost stable. China ranked number 2 in 2011, right after the US, with revenues of €10.6 billion, ahead of Germany that year. In 2012, China was the largest publisher of books and ranked second for electronic publishing (Baozhong, 2013). India ranked tenth in 2011 with a market value of €2.50 billion, right behind Brazil (€2.54 billion euros). The new major players in book publishing are companies from China, Brazil and South Korea specializing in educational books fuelling a stronger growth as well as much of the expected growth. In China, Higher Education Press merged with China Education and Media Group[7] to create a €320 million company (US$445 million in 2011). However, if these firms are quickly climbing in the global ranking of publishing firms, the first South Korean company, Woongjin ThinkBig (established in 1980 as Woongjin Publications), ranks only 29th; the first Chinese company, Higher Education, 37th; and the first Brazilian company, Abril Educacão,[8] 40th (IPA, 2012).

The US market

In 2012, the entire publishing business was estimated at 27.1 billion and overall trade publisher revenues at US$15.05 billion (*Publishers Lunch*, May 15, 2013).[9] The US market is highly concentrated, with leading firms including McGraw Hill, Random House, Penguin and Scholastic. The presence of EU companies is significant: Random House is owned by the German media group Bertelsmann, Penguin by the UK publishing house Pearson. Hachette Book Group (Lagardère, France) is a major player (Thompson, 2010: 116).

In 2012, e-books stood at 20% of trade sales (US$3 billion). In 2011, e-books became, for the first time, the number 1 individual format for adult fiction (AAP, 2012a). Internet access and the rise of e-books contributed positively to the growth of exports by volume (AAP, 2012b),[10] as illustrated by the case of exports to the UK: a 1,316.8% increase in e-books but only 10.4% for printed books. Leadership of e-books followed a major increase in ownership of e-book reading devices and tablet computers[11] (Pew, 2012): in all, 29% of Americans aged 18 and older own at least one specialized device for e-book reading, either a tablet or an e-book reader.

Nevertheless, this growth does not offset the losses of revenues over a longer period of time, as illustrated by Figure 5.1. Figure 5.1 shows that the relative strength of the book sector vis-à-vis GDP is declining and that this level plateaued between 1995 and 2000.

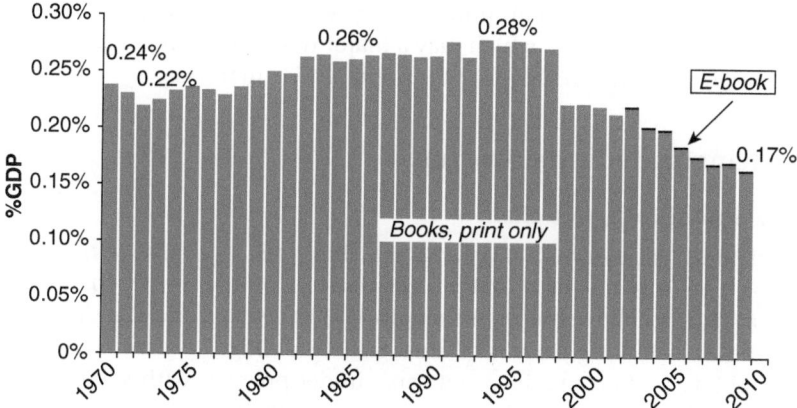

Figure 5.1 Books: Total revenue by category as a percentage of GDP, 1970–2009
Source: Waterman and Ji (2012).[12]

The EU market

Book publishing is a significant market in the EU, with a turnover of €22.8 billion in 2011 (FEP, 2012). Book publishing is the largest cultural industry in Europe, according to the same source. Table 5.1 introduces the core data for turnover, sales, number of titles and level of employment, and the distribution across categories. These figures show a relative stability over the period 2004–2011, though employment level has decreased (by nearly 7% between 2004 and 2011), and numbers of published titles have increased, as well as the size of the catalogue (up 50% since 2004). The revenues of the different categories also remain stable: trade is the largest segment, fluctuating around 50% in 2011.

Notwithstanding the importance of the leading publishing EU firms, the fragmentation of the market is a well-known feature. It is first fragmented along linguistic lines, but its industrial structure and the size and role of the different players (the revenue stream composition) varies as well. The patterns of consumption differ from one country to another, as do the policies (for instance, the regulation of the retail price).

The main EU markets

The major EU markets share some features, as shown in Table 5.2. The major EU markets are highly concentrated, although with some variations in the degree of concentration: in France's oligopolistic market, for instance, 4.3% of the firms bring in 65.3% of the revenues, while in Spain 19 top publishers reach 30% of the titles.

The EU benefits from an important network of retailers (a significant number of bookshops), which play a major role as a leading distribution channel, as shown in Table 5.2 for the main EU markets.

A changing industry structure

The publishing value chain

Publishing is perceived as a long-term business, as profit margins are slim. This has meant a stable organization of the value chain (see Figure 5.2) to allow the publishers to build the portfolio they need to sell books over long periods of time. Such a catalogue is indeed a source of stability and profitability, but came under pressure with some developments in the 1980s and 1990s (Thompson, 2010) with the increasing role of large corporations pushing for more speed. Nevertheless, the core business involves a well-functioning relationship between the different parts of the value chain.

Table 5.1 Turnover (€ billion), number of titles and employment, 2004–2011[13]

	2011	2010	2009	2008	2007	2006	2004
Publishers' revenue from sales of books	22.8	23.5	23	23.75	24.5	23.25	22.2
Educational (school) books	18.7%	17.9%	17.6%	15.9%	18.9%	14.8%	
Academic/professional books	19.5%	20.5%	20%	21.5%	22.5%	29.4%	
Consumer (trade) books	49.8%	49.6%	50.5%	50.6%	48.9%	47.7%	
Children's books	12.1%	12%	11.9%	12%	9.7%	8.3%	
Sales by area							
Sales in the domestic market	80.5%	81.5%	84.4%	83%	82.7%		
Exports	19.5%	18.5%	15.6%	17%	17.3%		
Sales by distribution channels							
Trade (retail and wholesale)	80.9%	78%	79.5%	77.5%	78.3%		
Book clubs	6%	5.7%	5.6%	5.9%	6.9%		
Direct	13.1%	16.3%	14.9%	16.6%	14.8%		
Number of titles published in period							
New titles	530,000	525,000	515,000	510,000	490,000	475,000	455,000
Number of titles in print (active catalogue)	8,500,000	7,400,000	6,400,000	6,100,000	5,600,000		
Number of persons in full-time employment in book publishing	135,000	135,000	135,000	135,000	140,000	140,000	145,000

Source: FEP (2012), Estimates, all figures rounded.[14]

Table 5.2 The main EU markets in 2011

	Germany	France	Italy	Spain (2010)	UK
Size of the market (billion euros, based on sales)	9.6	4.3[15]	3.3	2.89	£3.2
Number of publishers	1,850	305[16]	2,225[17]	2,994	2,200[18]
Number of retailers	3,800			1,432	3,683 (2009)
Channels of sales (based on value)					
Retail[19]	49.7%	29.6%	37.9%	35.5%	5%
Direct	19.1%	14%[22]	15%[24]		
Mail order	17.8 % online included[20]				
Internet		17%	9.7%	4.1%	35%
Specialized stores		27.6%	41.3%	16.3%	33%
Department stores	1.8%				
Non-specialized superstores (including hypermarkets)		16.7%	17.9%		9%
Book clubs	2%				6%
Other	9.5%[21]	4%[23]			12%[25]
Number of titles released		72,139	63,800	114,205[26]	149,800
E-books					
As % of the total market	1%[27]	1.2%	0.9%	1%,2.4% in STM	8%
As % of the publisher revenues (average)	6.2%	2%			
Titles available	25,000	22,000	31,416		933,330[28]

Source: Compiled by the author from AIE (2012), Booksellers Association (2008), Börsenverein des Deutschen Buchhandels (2012), Cegal (2011), FGEE (2011), lemotif.fr (2012), Minidata Ministère de la Culture (2012), Publishers Association (2012), SNE (2013). As the data comes from heterogeneous sources, the total in % may not sum up to 100%.

Figure 5.2   The traditional value chain of the sector

The content is supplied by the author, who provides the work directly to the publisher or indirectly through the mediation of an agent. According to Thomson (2010), this kind of middleman saw his power growing in English-language trade publishing, what he described as a *'proliferation of agents'*.

As in other creative industries, a major feature of this creative workforce is that it is not usually supported directly, at least on a regular basis, by its main customer, the publisher. The author appears more in the position of a supplier working under various contractual arrangements, and will receive in most cases royalties within the range of 7–15% of the list price set for the physical book. However, the book sector is the only sector in which authors derive a significant amount from royalties (Benhamou and Sagot-Duvauroux, 2007: 11).

Publishers are at the core of the business. Their functions include the aggregation, presentation (reading, editing and designing), pricing and marketing of books and dealing with other parties in the value chain, including the technical intermediaries (printers, phototypesetting, binders, etc.) and a specialized workforce, in-house or outsourced (proofreading).[29] They are also responsible for the 'quality' of the edited product and, even if they may not have to finance the initial content creation, their funding role nevertheless grants them a pivotal position.

Publishers have become all the more central as other segments have been considerably weakened: for example, printers, retailers (especially the smaller bookshops) and also, in the case of the US markets, the large retail chains that used to dominate the market (Borders, the second largest bookstore chain, filed for bankruptcy protection in February 2011).[30] Now, with the rapid development of online distribution, distributors are also under threat.

Going digital: From books to e-books

This industry went through various technological developments. The first commercial application of e-paper (also referred to as 'e-ink') was launched in Japan in 2004 (Forge and Blackman, 2009). Audio books began to be developed and distributed by retailers in the late 1980s, though spoken word albums existed before the age of videocassettes, DVDs and compact discs. In 2002, Random House and Harper Collins started selling digital copies. In October 2004, at the Frankfurt book fair, Google launched its 'Google print' project, which later became Google books (12 million references).

New channels of distribution (the Internet) are bringing cheaper and more efficient vehicles and a strong pressure to get rid of intermediaries while, at the same time, new aggregators/distributors are appearing. Created in 1995, Amazon.com has come to dominate the online book sales market. It has had one of the fastest growth rates in the Internet's history, even as compared with eBay and Google. Amazon has since become an e-commerce platform for others, thanks to its pioneering retail e-commerce/e-shopping business in many product categories, not just books. Amazon launched its eReader Kindle late in 2007.[31] In 2008, the online retail giant emerged as the leader in the stand-alone eReader market with its Kindle line-up, and the company maintained its lead despite an array of competitors entering the space. In the two leading markets (US and UK), in 2011, Amazon dominates all other channels by far, with 61% as a purchase source in the US[32] and 66% in the UK (Global eBooks Monitor, 2012b).[33]

The arrival of the Apple iPad in 2010 changed the game, as the IT company set up its own sales platform iBooks (following the model of its iTunes), and proposed a different kind of contract (the so-called agency model[34]) to the publishers. PWC considers that 2010 was the turning point as regards penetration by eReaders into mainstream markets: eReader prices declined and spending rose by 51% (PWC, 2011). The market took off only recently. In 2012, for the French publishing house Lagardère Publishing (Hachette Livre), the sales of e-books amounted to 7.7% of the total turnover; however, although it reached 15% in the UK and up to 23% in the US, it remained under 2% in other markets (LivresHebdo, 2013).

Digital technologies were introduced upstream in the publishing value chain, but they were not used for the final product, but, rather, mostly for internal business processes.[35] The legacy players appeared reluctant to opt for this direction. The ability of this new nascent market to compensate for declining or stable sales is clearly a major issue for the industry. Revenues derived from this new channel are also lower than those from printed material.

The trade segment is still lagging behind, though STM publishing is already in digital format (90%). Already in 2007, about 90% of all science journals were available online, in many cases via a subscription (EC, 2007: 3).[36] In the trade segment, some specialized publishers speeded up the process so as to manage the shift, for instance, of the publisher Harlequin ('romance' fiction[37]) (Benhamou, 2012b).

Nevertheless, some major digital technological platforms,[38] bringing together several national companies, were launched in the EU in 2010: in Italy (Edigita by RCS, Mauri Spagnol and Feltrinelli), France (Eden by Flammarion, Gallimard and La Martinière) and Spain (Libranda by Planeta; Santillana and Random House Mondadori). In Germany, Bertelsman and Holtzbrinck set up a joint platform, Premium Vertriebs GmbH, for e-books to compete with the retailers' platform MVB[39] Plattform libreka! Another platform, Tolino, was launched in 2013, together with a specific reader, by a wider alliance (Hugendubel, Thalia[40], WeltBild, Bertelsmann Club, and Deutsche Telekom) (ActuaLitté, 2013). In the US, Cengage and Pearson have launched similar 'interactive' publishing platforms. Some new intermediaries are also appearing to supply services to publishers to enable the transition; for instance, in Spain Publidisa[41] provides service to some 700 publishers. In Italy, Simplicissimus Book Farm, an e-book distribution platform, offers services to publishers.

IDATE (2011) predicts that revenues from e-books for the period 2008–2014 will go from less than 1% of the total book market to around 17% in the US, from 2% to around 8% in Japan, and from less than 1% to nearly 9% in the EU5. Up until now, the European e-book market has been fragmented and diversified; fast-expanding markets and initiatives exist alongside very underdeveloped ones.

Toward new industry configurations?

Benhamou (2011, 2012) highlights that, although still perceived as a minor market and considered by publishers as a by-product rather than a newborn, despite its strong growth, digitization is at the core of the concerns of all actors in the book world, as it disrupts the whole book ecosystem. Some costs disappear with digitization (printing, physical transportation, storage),[42] some remain unaffected (creation, authors' advances, editorial process, marketing and sales), some are shifted (e.g. promotion, with the coming of blogs and other tools) and some new ones also appear – mostly on the software side of the equation (computer programmes, file conversion, cataloguing and permitting search of text and metadata, storing, security, rights management, etc.). The latter are, by and large, an unknown quantity, thereby making a proper assessment of the cost differential between the two formats very difficult to predict.[43] Not only is the cost structure changing, but the organization of the publishing firms is impacted (logistics, sales and promotion, book design and production).

On the demand side, usage patterns are difficult to predict. However, consumer surveys, carried out for different trade associations, usually indicate a global acceptance on the consumer side (Börsenverein des Deutschen Buchhandels, 2008; *Le livre sera-t-il numérique?* 2010; AIE, 2012b), with some exceptions: Global eBook Monitor (2012b) reports a lack of interest in France (no interest: 66%) and Japan (72%).

Customers may not know what to expect from an e-book. The consumer is facing a myriad of formats, with PDF and ePub being the most common,[44] and has to deal with several devices and numerous readers,[45] using different software. There is uncertainty about how consumers may move from the ownership of books toward the management of access to the relevant content, although readers are not unfamiliar with previous forms of access through loans from libraries or from friends and relatives. Indeed, two different notions of property are clashing: physical objects (books) as goods are sold and become the property of their buyers, but digital contents are 'licensed' and remained managed by the rights owner. There is uncertainty about the terminal as well, linked to the impact of tablets. For instance, in Korea, e-book terminals almost disappeared in 2011, and e-book sales were already slowing down in 2012. SNE (2013) notes a similar phenomenon for France with the growth of online sales.

Consumer willingness to pay appears linked to price reduction, according to a survey (between 2% and 15%, depending on the kind of books) (IPSOS-CNL, 2010). However, publishers are stressing the negative role of value added tax (VAT), pointing out that a 20% VAT on e-books is likely to eat up the cost reduction brought by digitization. Indeed, rates of VAT on e-books vary widely, and are usually much higher on e-books (classified as 'software') than on print books. According to an IPA 2010 survey on VAT on books and e-publications (88 countries: IPA, 2011a), a small number of countries (like France and Spain) have already adopted a real non-discriminatory, consistent tax regime for e-publications (reduced VAT rates remain the norm for printed books).

e-books can be offered for free (by Project Gutenberg, The Internet Archive or non-for-profit organizations) or sold. Prices vary across the

EU, but in some cases consumers can benefit from drastic discounts: in Italy, the average price of an e-book is around €11 (printed book around €20), in Spain (May 2012) €7.7 (printed book €17: an average discount of 55% over the physical price) (Badenes, 2012). So far, prices have not stabilized, not even for the eReader, as illustrated by the eReader price war in the US. Not only can the price vary, but also the way to monetize, directly or indirectly ('free' models)[46]: per unit or subunit (chapter, page), subscription, rental rather than sale (perennial), pay per view, a limited number of downloads, bundled sale, etc. These models and options are evolving toward the direction of books as service with specific contents (enhanced books) (Guiry et al., 2012: 13; OECD, 2012), an array of new (e)services from digital bookstores, digital bookshelves and digital libraries, a choice between purchase or rental of e-books, consultation of single works or collections, and full search of books on a platform.

The (new) players are following various strategies. Some are 'pure players' serving niche markets or communities. They usually strike favourable deals with authors (in France, Publie.net: grants 50% to the author: le MOTif, 2010). Others aim to achieve vertical integration and lock-in. Within this category, the strategy varies. Apple, under a mandate or agency contract, grants 70% of the revenues to the publisher and leaves the publisher free to set the retail price. Amazon initially sold new titles at a loss and imposed a 50/50 split of subsequent revenues on publishers. Publishers were opposed to prices they held to be too low, as Amazon was selling many new best-sellers at US$9.99 (bought from publishers at about US$13) to encourage consumers to buy its Kindle electronic readers. Pressure from the publishers, however, has resulted in a subsequent move to an agency contract like Apple's.

Taking into account the facts that bookshops remain the major channel of distribution and that they operate under very tight margins,[47] but that they are still the favourite source for customers, publishers should not be expected to further destabilize their main distribution channel. They may be cautious not to weaken this already weak link and may grant some time to the bookshops to adapt themselves to the new environment. The prevention of the side-effects of unregulated discounts was one of the rationales for the adoption of fixed price[48] in several countries, seen as a supply-side policy to avoid price competition and maintain a network of retailers. Nevertheless, there is no agreement about this policy; opponents to this measure, for example, Swedish publishers and booksellers, argue that any regulatory interference artificially increases the price of books.

Conclusions

In the book sector, the power struggle has changed scale. Companies described until recently as media giants (Bertelsmann, Hachette), often critically because of the concentration they achieved, are now competing with the world's largest market cap[49] companies: Apple, Amazon and Google. The publishers are threatened with losing their central role as the value chain is more and more dominated by these downstream players with an increased bargaining power: in 2012 Amazon revenues were over US$57 billion, comparable to the size of the entire US market (US$27 billion).

The digitization of book publishing generates a shift from the central role and domination of the book value chain by the publisher toward a downstream domination by the new entrants (distributors). However, the main difference from the music and newspaper industries, where a similar trend is taking place, is that the book industry has so far managed to control and manage its own assets, copyrighted works. The scientific and technical subsector has successfully introduced access licensing,[50] a new way to monetize its intellectual property rights. In any case, the shift illustrates that the two worlds (printed book/digital) operate under different logics: economics of production for the former, economics of distribution for the latter.

The EU book sector, at least its publishing segment, seems to be enjoying a rather good economic position, with leading global firms in spite of a fragmented EU market. This may leave some room for more balanced negotiations. US publishers won their legal case against Google in 2011 (Google Settlement, De Prato and Simon, 2012).[51] This landmark decision from the US Supreme Court will probably affect relationships and may send a signal of moderation to other IT players. The transition to the digital world is likely to take some time to unfold, as did the transition brought about by the invention of the printing press.

Notes

1. Latin *caudex* for tree trunk.
2. *Source*: Wikipedia 'Codex'. http://en.wikipedia.org/wiki/Codex.
3. In 1440, Johannes Gutenberg introduced a printing press, but the first movable types were made in China in 1045 AD.
4. For PWC, the market consists of retail spending by consumers on consumer books; spending by schools, government agencies and students on elementary, high school and college textbooks, including graduate school textbooks; and spending on books in electronic formats, or so-called electronic books or e-books. Spending includes library and institutional subscriptions

to electronic book databases. Print sales include audio books. Educational books do not include supplemental educational spending, administrative software or testing materials. Professional books are covered in another segment: the 'Business-to-Business' segment (trade magazines, professional books, business information, directory advertising). This segment amounted to nearly US$150 billion, global business information being the largest component: over 50% (PWC, 2012).

5. IPA(2012): €105.6 billion for 2011.
6. Bertelsmann holds 53% of the newly merged company, with Pearson controlling 47%. *Source*: Press release: http://www.us.penguingroup.com/static/pages/aboutus/pressrelease/penguin_random_house_102912.html.
7. A public company run by the Chinese Ministry of Education.
8. A subsidiary of the Grupo Abril involved in newspaper, audiovisual and e-commerce. The company launched a portal for educational content.
9. Quoting figures from BookStats 2013. BookStats uses several sources, including numbers from 1,500 publishers, economic analysis and estimate of the full sizing of the industry (extrapolation).
10. US publishers currently export, on average, 90% of their titles in print and/or e-formats and work with nearly 15,000 international retailers in 200 countries. More than 750 million people outside the US can read English (AAP, 2012b).
11. In 2011, 42% of readers of e-books said they consume their books on a computer, 41% of readers of e-books consume their books on an e-book reader such as an original Kindle or Nook, 29% of readers of e-books consume their books on their cell phones and 23% of readers of e-books consume their books on a tablet computer (Pew, 2012).
12. The large one year drop in about 1998 apparently reflects a change in data definitions in that year by the government. So although the revenues decline since then is unaffected, The author would like to thank D.Waterman for suggesting this footnote.
13. These figures are much lower than the ones provided by PWC, as they indicate the turnover of publishers, while PWC accounts for the global market: the sales. The EC Publishing Market Watch: Final Report (2005a: 40) indicated €26.6 billion in 2000, and for the EU15 Members States only (with 1999 data for Greece and Portugal).
14. FEP survey based on reports from the national book publishing associations, and on further analysis and refining of data, for the year 2011. FEP represents 28 national associations of publishers from the European Union and the European Economic Area Member States.
15. Publishers turnover: 2.804 billion Euros (SNE, 2013).
16. *Source*: Minidata, but 3,586 'enterprises' in the sector according to Eurostat in 2007 and around 10,000 according to SNE 2013, 5,000 with less than 10 titles.
17. Even if namely 7.590 are recorded.
18. VAT-based book publishers.
19. In Germany, in 2010, 22% of sales were concentrated in five large retail chains: Thalia Holding, DBH, Mayersche Buchhandlung, Pustet and Wittwer.
20. With a share of 14.8%.

21. Works councils, kiosks, stations, book fairs, etc.
22. Includes book clubs.
23. Bargain bookshops, schools, markets.
24. Elaboration on AIE 2010 data: covers instalment, mail, direct orders, book club and exports.
25. Bargain bookshops and other shops
26. Based on the number of ISBN.
27. Trade books only, not including educational and reference books. 5.4 percent share of total sales (Fischer, 2011) for 2011.
28. Amazon only.
29. For critical skills for publishers, see the FEP (2007: 5).
30. In France, Virgin filed for bankruptcy protection in January 2013.
31. A six-inch electrophoretic display.
32. Leaving number two, Barnes& Noble, far behind.
33. Respectively 63% and 75%, according to J. Badenes (2012), for the first semester 2012.
34. The contract includes 'most favoured nation' clauses; publishers are prevented from selling books to other buyers at a cheaper rate. Publishers set the final price of the books, and distributors, like Apple, get a fee from the publishers on every book sold (about 30%). Under the wholesale model (used by Amazon), the publisher sells books to the distributor at a set price (usually 50% of retail) and the distributor sells the books to the public at whatever price the distributor chooses.
35. See 'figure 12. "Use of online ICT technologies in media and printing" ' (EC, 2005b: 19).
36. In 2007, there were some 2,000 scientific journal publishers globally, producing about 1.4 million articles a year. Some 780 of these publishers are located in the EU, producing 49% of the total journal output. They employ some 36,000 persons directly in the EU and have a strong position in the world market. (EC, 2007: 3).
37. However, in 2012 a class action lawsuit was filed against Harlequin Enterprises over fraudulent licensed e-book publishing rights (NINC, 2010: 13).
38. A platform brings players together, in a loosely or tightly cooperative scheme, for the provision of services (usually on mobile) through a common set of hardware, software and techno-economic specifications. Each platform includes a number of 'gatekeeper' roles as a way to control the evolution of the platform and to secure the revenues (Ballon, 2009).
39. A subsidiary of German Publishers & Booksellers Association: 270,000 e-books available in 2013.
40. Thalia is one of the 5 large German retail chains.
41. A ten-year-old company which was involved in the first Spanish e-book project in 2001. www.publidisa.com/canales/red-librerios-afiliados.es.
42. According to industry sources (FEP), printing, storage and physical distribution accounted traditionally for less than one-sixth of the total.
43. Some indication of the costs in Le MOTif (2010).
44. Others are: Azurn International, BiblioLabs, E Ink, Ingram Content, LibreDigital, Lightning Source, Liquavista, Lulu, OverDrive. In 2013, the IPA endorsed ePub3 as a global publishing standard (IPA, 2013).

45. BeBook, Boox: Onyx International, Cybook, Elonex eBook, Foxit Reader, Hexaglot, iPad, jetBook, Kindle, Kobo, Letto, Libre, Netronix, Nook, Palm Reader, Pixelar MReader, Sony Reader.
46. Ex. Leroutard.com (a well-known French travel guide), advertisement-based, or the Spanish 24 Symbols. InLibro Veritas offers a free digital copy, but hard copies need to be ordered and paid for (Benhamou, 2012: 98).
47. Net result of 0.3% of the turnover of booksellers, according to the French Ministry of Culture in 2010 (DGMIC, 2012).
48. Austria (adopted in 2000), Denmark (2001), France (1981), Germany (de facto since 1887, but legally since 2002), Greece (1997), Italy (2005), Luxemburg, the Netherlands (2005), Norway, Portugal (1996), Spain (1975).
49. Market cap, simplification of market capitalization: total value of the tradable shares of a publicly traded company.
50. Even if the process has been painful for the companies with massive social plans, reinforced because of the 2008–2009 crisis.
51. Bringing to an end a 2005 class action initiated by the US Authors Guild, five US publishers and the American Association of Publishers.

6
The Television Industry

Esteve Sanz

When television first began, the verb 'to broadcast' was adopted to express the idea of scattered, undefined, anonymous dissemination of information on radio waves. In technological terms, 'broadcasting' evolved from prior technologies such as the telephone and wireless (radio), electro-mechanical then electronic television at the beginning of the 20th century. The Internet and the digital world are changing both dimensions of our understanding of television.

The television market, which remains one of the largest media markets, has a strong history of regulation that was generally justified on technological grounds. Frequency scarcity created the threat of over-crowded airwaves. Governments regulated the broadcasting spectrum by allocating frequencies and signal strength efficiently, intervening to restrict access to the medium and thus justifying their intervention on the grounds of service quality.

With the introduction of satellite and cable channels, the scarcity model of terrestrial television was called into question. The new channels of distribution promised channel abundance and opportunities for transnational services. In the US, the regulatory status of cable took some time to be established (over 40 years: Krasnouw et al., 1982; Simon, 1991), starting as an ancillary TV service[1] before morphing into a full-fledged and fast-growing industry in the 1980s. Cable is now the main distribution channel for broadcasting (Figure 2.1).

In the EU, the arrival of satellite and cable platforms in the 1980s made it difficult to justify on purely technological grounds the regulatory regimes that favoured a small number of nationally based public service broadcasters (PSB). At the EU level, the 'Television without Frontiers (TSF)' directive was designed to take into account new developments such as cable and pay TV, program sponsorship and teleshopping.[2] The directive was initially aimed at removing barriers to the free movement of television programming across national European boundaries (Art. 4 and 5). In the EU, with the widespread trend toward liberalization and privatization of broadcasting, the situation of public monopolies changed radically toward a dual system of commercial and public service television (Iosifidis et al., 2005: 192; Bignell and Fickers, 2008: 288; Sanz, 2012; Donders et al., 2013: 296).

By the late 1990s, the television industry was already involved in its second major turning point: the introduction of information and communication technologies (ICTs), especially the Internet, and digitization, together with the gradual emergence of an interactive, convergence culture (Jenkins, 2007) in the production and consumption of content. The digitization of cable and satellite television facilitated a trend of gradual replacement of analogue broadcasting, further amplifying the proliferation of channels and more or less open platforms. The falling costs of hardware and sophisticated software made the editing and publishing of content more accessible. This lowered the barriers of entry to production and distribution. The emergence of web delivery services and web-based standards, both in professional (Hulu in the US, iBBC in Europe) and amateur domains (user-generated content), became a major trend. The third age of European television is, then, a much more complex system than the previous dual system, where individuals, civil society players, increasingly concentrated private broadcasters, telecommunication and Internet companies, and public broadcasters are interconnected in variable geometries.

Moreover, at the core of the third age of television there is a detectable transformation of the audiovisual product. While the fragmentation of audiences is generally taken as a 'natural' trend of the third stage, the data indicates that relatively few television products, local or global, are capable of circulating massively through a diversity of distribution means. Audiences remain massive in almost every sense (Carpentier et al., 2013: 288), top channels remain top channels, but top, influential shows and their sociological signification have essentially changed from a relatively unproblematic consensual relation with the cultural codes of society toward a deeper, more critical position. Big audiovisual conglomerates and pay TV companies were among the first to realize the economic potential of certain new audiovisual products, but, once a series of shows and artists had been mainstreamed, spread and established, the foundational basis of the global television market transitioned toward what can be better described as a 'post-consensus' (Thorburn, 1987) media system.

The first section sums up the data available on the global market. It first gives an overview of regional markets, access technologies and the growing role of emerging economies (Brazil, India, China). Then it focuses on some elements for the EU markets specifically. The second section introduces the value network of the broadcasting industry, showing the evolving interaction between players. The second part deals with digitization and the new digital channels of distribution, then takes a look at online distribution and its revenues. The chapter closes with some elements on the evolution of viewership, the continuing role of legacy players and the central role of the US industry in the field.

The broadcasting markets

Broadcasting has continued to be a very profitable business worldwide, with combined global revenues (advertising, TV subscriptions and licence fees) of nearly US$400 billion in 2010 (PWC, 2011). In spite of the economic crisis, the audiovisual turnover of the ten leading audiovisual companies worldwide has been generally increasing since at least 2006.

At the global level, the European Audiovisual Observatory (EAO) has identified the leading audiovisual companies ranked in terms of audiovisual turnover (EAO, 2013). The 15 first companies are: Direct TV, Walt Disney, Time Warner, News Corporation, Comcast Corporation, NBC Universal, Sony, Vivendi Universal, Dish DBS Corporation, Viacom, CBS Corp., Microsoft, Gamestop Corporation, Apple Inc. and Liberty Interactive Corp. According to EAO, in 2006 62% of the global market was controlled by the leading audiovisual companies at that time. The percentage increased further, up to 68% in 2011, indicating growing concentration of ownership. Besides operating in oligopolistic conditions, these global companies hold privileged positions in their capacity to network with other global and regional players. They are involved in corporate strategies of vertical integration (Röder, 2007), characterized by extensive vertical links between as well as within the media industry value network segments. Within the first 15, only one is based in Europe: Vivendi Universal (France). The 16th leading audiovisual company was the BBC group,[3] with a turnover of US$81.25 billion in 2012.

Terrestrial TV is declining as an access channel and will continue to do so, reaching a share of roughly 23% of the global market by 2017 (according to IDATE's 2013 estimations). This would leave cable

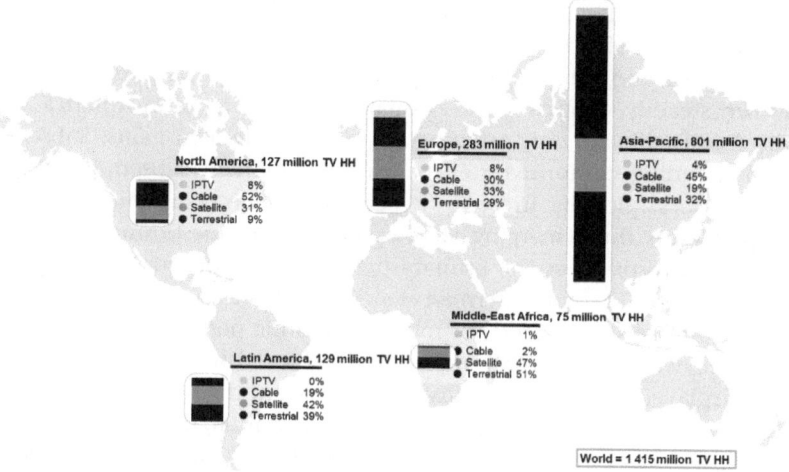

Figure 6.1   Breakdown of the globe's TV households by access technology
Source: IDATE (2013).

as the main access among traditional platforms in most of the regions. Terrestrial TV was still slightly dominant in 2012 in the Africa–Middle East region (Figure 6.1), with satellite ranking second.

Total television viewing seems to be growing worldwide and in Europe. The average daily television viewing time in Europe rose 19 minutes from 2000 until 2009, when Europeans were spending 222 minutes a day watching TV (EAO, 2011). According to Eurodata TV,[4] Europe had the strongest worldwide growth in viewing time in 2012, reaching a record 235 minutes a day. The US is nonetheless still leading the ranking, with 275 minutes per day, up to 34 hours per person per week (Waterman et al., 2012).

The global market

The total turnover for 2012 was US$333 billion (US$172 billion for pay and US$161 billion for advertising) (PWC, 2013). PWC (2013) highlighted as well the fast-growing Asia-Pacific and Latin American market (Brazil is the largest, with more than 45% of the Latin American market).

If one takes a look at the growth of the media segments (see Introduction), the TV markets are faring much better than most of the others, with the exception of the fast-growing video game industry (see Chapter 6). Although its advertising revenues have clearly been hit by the economic downturn, with a decrease of almost 8% in 2009, the broadcasting industry bounced back by 10% in 2010. The revenues from licence fees and subscriptions appeared resilient to the crisis and have grown steadily, though with regional variations, as Latin America and the Asia-Pacific are now catching up with double-digit gains. Subscription spending comprised 85% of the total market (subscriptions and licence fees) globally in 2011 (PWC, 2012). The economic centrality of pay TV is thus emerging at the global level, questioning the position of advertising as the primary means of funding for the industry. Waterman (2011) and Waterman et al. (2012) have analysed how pay TV has become a strong driver of robust economic performance in the US industry, where this trend is more appreciable. Historically this industry has displayed an amazing ability to benefit from the successive waves of technological innovation, as clearly illustrated in Figure 6.2.

In the Asia-Pacific region, mature markets like Japan are decreasing (in relative terms only), but emerging economies are taking over: IDATE predicts revenues of over US$11 billion as of 2013 for China (but over US$26 billion for Japan and nearly US$10 billion for the largest EU market, Germany, according to PWC, 2012) and nearly €7 billion for India. The size of the Indian market in 2012 was already US$6.9 billion (FICCI-KPMG, 2012). The pay TV market is still relatively small for a country the size of Brazil, with a penetration of 7.5 million subscribers in 2009

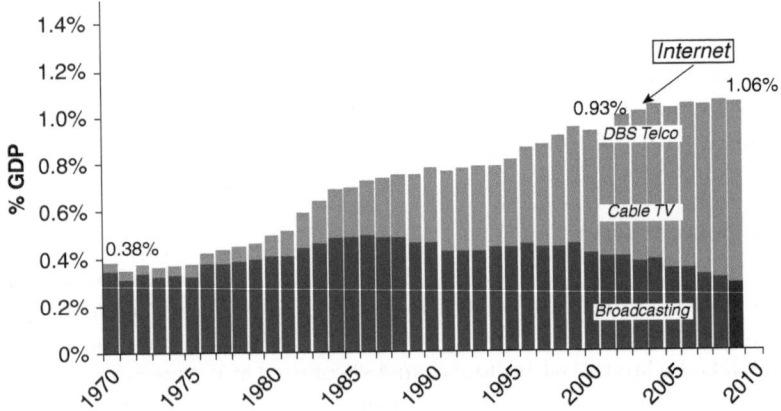

Figure 6.2 Television. Total revenue by category in the US as percentage of GDP, 1970–2009
Source: Waterman et al. (2012).

(from only 2.8 million a decade ago), a ratio of 3.61% (connections per 100 inhabitants, Business News America, 2009: 14).[5]

The EU market

Commercial television in Europe has suffered from the economic downturn; however, according to the Association of Commercial Television in Europe (ACT, 2011), TV advertising is now back above pre-recession levels in all large European markets. The economic crisis could indeed have influenced the decline of revenues from advertisements, but the changing structure of business models in television, such as, for example, the rise of pay TV, could also have affected the process. According to the EAO (2011), in the EU countries the total number of available television channels (including terrestrial, aerial broadcasting and satellite) grew from a few hundred at the beginning of the century to more than 9,800 in 2010, a tremendous increase.

Figure 6.3 gives an overview of the business models and revenue shares of European commercial television that displays a diversity of business models. The pay TV-based BSkyB ranks first in terms of revenues, but RTL follows closely with a different revenue stream. The following companies are advertising-based, and only the fifth (Canal Plus), the sixth (Prisa), the seventh (Modern Times) and the eighth

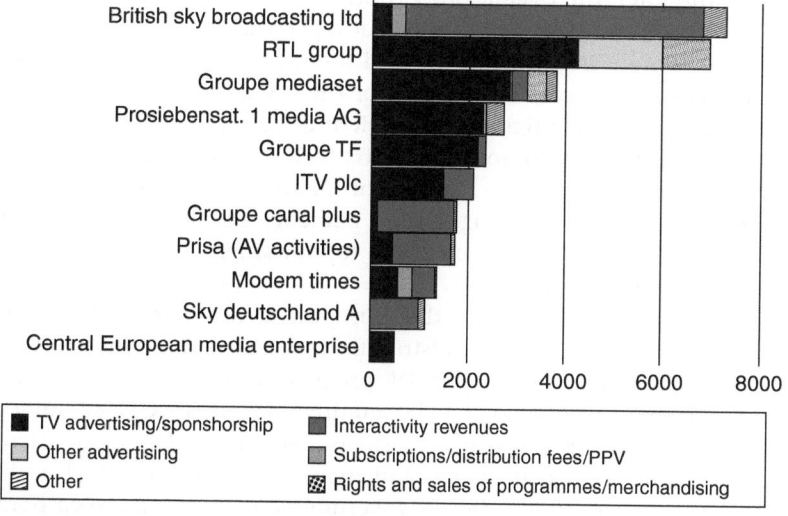

Figure 6.3 Breakdown of turnover by activity of leading European commercial television groups

(Premiere AG) have been able to establish a relatively strong leading position in the market through subscription fees.

Although there seem to be certain indications of change, it is interesting to note that, despite selling 'premium' content,[6] that is, shows that are perceived as 'better-quality' shows, the main European pay TV companies in 2010 still showed little interest in producing this content. Only RTL significantly produces and circulates content in the market.

In Europe, there are three clearly leading TV independent production groups with operating revenues above €1 billion: EDAM Acquisition Holding Cooperative (based in the Netherlands, but controlled by Mediaset), RTL Group (based in Germany and owned by Bertelsmann) and Imagina Media Audiovisual S.L. (based in Spain and born in 2006 from the integration of Grupo Arbol and Mediapro). The fourth is the British-based All3Media Holdings Limited, with operating revenues above €400 million. They own the great majority of the top 25 production companies. Endemol, the main company owned by the EDAM/Mediaset group, has subsidiaries in 23 countries, and specializes in relatively inexpensive game shows, which are appealing to broadcasters.

Apparently, the dominant position of American fiction of the 1970s and 1980s on European television (De Bens and Smaele, 2001) has not changed drastically in the context of the new media landscape. According to the EAO, the overall proportion of European content fell from 37.9% to 37% in 2009. Series and soap operas are the most abundant fictional content in European TV, and the most dominated by US productions, which account for 59.1% of the offer. Only 19.9% of these series are of national origin. Yet, this picture changes significantly if one takes into consideration not only the trade flows and the time the series are broadcast, but also the number of viewers and the time-range of such broadcasting. According to most audience studies, domestic series tend to outdo American series in the top rankings of both public and commercial channels.

What is less questionable is that European fiction has a much more limited global and European distribution than American fiction, with the very significant exception of UK productions (Chalaby, 2010; EAO, 2011). The BBC group had global operating revenues of €5.384 million in 2009, and 36 broadcasting channels, including BBC World News Channel, with one of the largest audiences of any news channel in the world. During the 1990s, the UK government encouraged the corporation to become a global multimedia player, capitalizing on its brands at home and abroad. 'Sherlock' was sold to over 170 countries; 'Misfits' to over 130 territories, becoming a hit for younger audiences; and 'Top Gear' to over 195 countries.

However, the global market for television format production was valued at €6.4 billion for the three-year period from 2002 to 2004, with an overall dominance of European companies. The production volume generated by traded formats grew to approximately €9.3 billion for the years 2006–2008, and, while European producers faced growing competition from others, particularly in the US, the UK, Netherlands, Sweden, Germany, Spain, France, Italy and Denmark remained top exporters (FRAPA, 2009).

A changing industry structure

Broadcasting and value generation

At the centre of the value-generation process of the new media landscape (see Chapters 1 and 7 for an analysis of the broadcasting value chain) there is a new type of experience, which is transforming the role of television as the central institution for modern storytelling (Fiske, 1987: 368; Silverstone, 1994; Thompson, 1995; Culik, 2013: 224). Around this experience, the value chain of the broadcasting industry is becoming very complex, with the digitization of the various segments at uneven speeds and different periods.

Within the different cultural industries, the core of the value chain remains the same: a large range of collective and individual agents, activities and technologies that create value cumulatively and in a mutually reinforcing way. Finance, pre-production, shoot, post-production, marketing and collective consumption are the fundamental processes related to such generation of value in both the film and the television industries (see Chapter 7). While the broadcast value network does not (yet) have a clear counterpart of the 'exhibition' equivalent in the television industry, it shares with the movie industry a production sector, which seeks funding to produce different sorts of programming.

This sector bears different (and economically crucial) forms of relationship with the entity in charge of 'distributing' programming: free-to-air broadcasters, pay TV companies, DVD and online rental companies, Internet platforms, and so on. Catalogues of content (under various forms of aggregation) are more and more available in a non-linear mode in services such as catch-up TV and Video-On-Demand (VOD), provided on IP broadband networks. Yet, TV markets are mostly two-sided markets: a TV aggregator bundles contents and advertising, the consumers will pay (or not) for the contents, the advertisers pay for the attention of the consumers. Attracting a customer on one side of the market allows the price to be raised on the other side of the market (e.g. advertisers), exhibiting the presence of cross-externalities between groups.

Collective and continued 'experiences' remain essential in the generation of value in the new media landscape, but these experiences are now more intense and more capable of de-fragmenting audiences emotionally than fragmenting them along the chosen technological platform. With its process of digitization, television has at the same time intensified its participatory and ritualistic character, in a process that has given the medium an unprecedented economic and cultural vigour. It is within this social process that the proliferation of closed (such as pay TV) and open digital platforms (open-access distribution websites such as YouTube) is playing its major role in the generation of new revenues for the industry (Sanz, 2012).

Going digital

Analogue television platforms are a dying breed, while the digital ones are proliferating worldwide, bringing more 'channels' of distribution and participation together with some qualitative features such as high definition (EC, 2003). Digital television can be received in four ways: online (generally through Internet-based technologies and platforms, but also through Internet Protocol Television (IPTV) and 'connected TVs'), through a satellite dish (digital satellite television), via a cable line (digital cable television), or by using an over-the-air transmission television set (digital terrestrial television (DTT)). The EU[7] (EC, 2005) and the US have adopted an agenda for the switch-off of analogue TV. In the EU, the proposed deadline for EU Member States to switch off analogue terrestrial broadcasting was January 1, 2012. In 2009, both regions were already leading the diffusion of the technology. Despite the different speeds at the national level, major markets such as France, Italy and the UK have almost completed the transition. In 2012, IPTV had been adopted as a primary television reception mode by 8% of the households in the EU and US (IDATE, 2013), and 2.4% of TV households worldwide.

IPTV is growing fast in the EU in terms of platforms, providers, viewers and company revenues, with France clearly leading in Asymmetric digital subscriber line (ADSL) distribution. With over 13 million subscribers in 2012, France was second only to China (respectively 20.6% and 23.3% of the global IPTV market) (Broadband TV News, 2013) accounting, in 2011, for 43% of IPTV European subscribers (EAO, 2013). Thus, France appears as a peculiar market, as most of the growth of the pay TV market comes from subscriptions to pay TV ADSL. The global IPTV subscriber base reached an estimated 65 million by the end of 2012, according too SNL Kagan (Broadband TV News, 2013). The consultancy predicted that the number of IPTV subscribers will reach 100.5 million as of 2017, from 40 million in 2010.

DTT and online platforms have, for the moment, a more limited spectrum capacity than cable and satellite. At the same time, DTT and online TV have proven to be much more successful in diffusing digital technology throughout society. Public administrations and PSBs have shown a strong preference for DTT (while large Internet companies such as Yahoo and Google continue to experiment with television manufacturers around the concept of 'connected TV' (or OTT[8] in the EU, OVD in the US), with an increasing diffusion in Europe). Moreover, German and French industry players have developed the 'Hybrid Broadcast Broadband Television' standard in order to harmonize the reach of HD broadcast and Internet multimedia content. Therefore, there is no clear division between actors' preferences around particular technologies – the changing television platform is a world under construction.

All sorts of TV-related platforms with a marginal audience in 2008 are experiencing a significant increase in recent years. Websites of series and TV programmes, together with websites of TV channels, are among the most visited websites in all European countries. In 2011, the Sky portal had 7.8 million visitors per month in the UK; in Germany, RTL attracted 14.8 million viewers to its website, and the Spanish public channel RTVE gathered 4.8 million visitors per month.

It is interesting to note that both sports and generalist newspapers have emerged as powerful competitors of traditional television in the provision of online video – although the opposite argument is also true: TV platforms now cover an informational space that is also based on the written word, and attracts massive audiences. Besides, it is also worth noting that YouTube is the current (and still rising) star of online video, by far the most visited online video website in Spain, Germany, France and elsewhere. While YouTube remains a mostly grass-roots form of online television, several audiovisual companies in the US and Europe have closed deals with the site not only to upload their copyrighted content in specifically customized websites, but also to broadcast part of their programming. Moreover, Google plans to organize a section of YouTube as a TV channel, including funding original content and providing live coverage of certain events.

The highly visited US-based platform Hulu also offers on-demand streaming video of TV shows, movies and 'webisodes' from major television networks and studios. This is one of the major creations of the American television industry (Hulu started as a joint venture between NBC and Fox in 2008, while CBS and Disney joined later), without any European equivalent.

Additionally, there are highly successful television-related online platforms that involve direct forms of payment by consumers. Good examples of this are online-based video rental and streaming services such as Netflix.[9] The US company started as a video rental mail service, and launched its online streaming service in 2007. The company is expanding in several European markets, together with its smaller national counterparts, such as Lovefilm (owned by Amazon) in the UK.

Mobile TV: Expectations never fulfilled

Mobile TV has benefited from strong and consistent standardization support since 2007 (DVB-H), especially in the EU, but is currently in 'limbo'.[10] Mobile TV had been expected to be a potential market of up to €20 billion by 2011, reaching 500 million customers worldwide. Despite attempting to use major events (the Olympics, football) for commercial launches, the output remains modest, with a limited response from EU markets (around five million users). Some modest success stories are to be found (Japan and Korea[11]), but also notorious failures. This 'impasse' situation stems from divergent technological options and standards (broadcasting vs. mobile communications), but also from a lack of perceived value and usefulness to users. The unexpected behaviour of users (at home, after prime-time, prolonged view, etc.) is another part of the explanation. As of December 2010, 63 mobile TV platforms were available in the EU.

Some pioneers are nevertheless to be found, such as the first mobile TV operator, the US MobiTV, born in 1999, reaching seven million subscribers in 2010, available from a variety of terminals (350) and networks (Sprint, ATT, TMobile), and charging US$9.99 per month for a premium package: ESPN Mobile TV, ABC Mobile, CBS, CNBC, Disney Channel and Fox Business. Customers have free access through an iPhone application to ABC News, NBC News, NBC Sports, MTV, etc. So far US telecom operators have been less successful. The explosion of smartphones and tablets may offer an opportunity for this market to take off, as broadcast operators seemed to believe in 2010 with the creation of a joint venture (Mobile Content Venture (MCV))[12] between 12 major broadcast groups to develop a national mobile content service.

The apps market

Indeed, the emergence of tablet computers, and the associated explosion of application stores, is another trend in the overall new media landscape that opens up the possibility of new forms of consumption (Chapter 3). Up to now it has been entirely dominated by American firms. Apple launched the App Store in 2008 with 500 apps, and the growth of downloads and paid content for the iPhone and the iPod Touch has been exponential[13]: within five years (July 2008–October 2013) the number of apps available for download in the Apple platform has grown from 500 to more than 1,000,000 with 60 billion downloads. The Android Market by Google, also launched in 2008, is currently available in 25 countries and holds a catalogue of nearly 697,000 applications at the end of 2013 (Appnation, 2013). Indeed, in the tablet app market the consumption of video (the fifth most frequent activity of tablet users in 2011, according to the Pew Institute, 2012[14]) is purposely mixed with social activity (sending and receiving mails and social networking are undertaken by more than 40% of tablet users).

Most of the major television companies have embraced this trend. Showtime, the second most popular pay TV channel in the US, launched in 2011 'Showtime Social', an application that aggregates content about its shows and facilitates synchronic online social interaction as its programmes air live.

The BBC application has recently inaugurated a subscription-based model that allows unlimited access to all its major TV shows, current and past (Brevini, 2013). By May 2010, the site was getting 123 million monthly play requests. BSkyB, Canal + France and Canal + Spain have all engaged in app creations which are available for free to their subscribers. All major Spanish public television channels, such as RTVE or the Catalan TV3, have dedicated applications for the iPad and Android, which allow the viewer to watch live programming (depending on location and copyright) and videos on demand, while commenting on them on social network sites. In the US, the Public Broadcasting Service offers an application for the iPad, where customers can preview forthcoming programmes and watch free full-length documentaries (programmes can also be watched from Europe). HBO Go allows HBO programming to be watched 'anywhere'. CNN's iPad app organizes its top stories in a tactile beehive, a stylistic switch that may indeed inaugurate the non-linear mass consumption of television news. Moreover, independent applications such as the highly successful Universal TV give access to hundreds of international channels available online.

Online distribution and revenues

Online video consumption and the revenues in the film, TV and video industry have increased significantly. Moreover, high definition is a very significant past and future asset for pay TV platforms. This is already being reflected in the data. In 2011, 40 million US households had Blu-Ray players, and the revenue from Blu-Ray discs was US$2 billion. In the US, the number of households with HD television sets increased from 25% during the 2007–2008 television season to 64% during the 2010–2011 television season (FCC, 2012: 4). According to EAO, at the end of 2011, 423 HD channels were available in the EU[15] against 274 in 2009, reaching almost 500 in 2011 (Hartman, 2011).[16] In broadcasting, sports channels seem to be overwhelmingly leading the trend toward HD, followed by film, generalist and documentary channels.

VOD services were first launched in 2001 in Italy and the UK (EAO, 2009). For the European Union, the EAO estimated that there were almost 2,458 VOD services as of April 2013 (Table 6.1). The largest number of VOD services were to be found in the UK (588), followed by France (358) and Germany (228). EAO estimates that there were 387 VOD services offering a catalogue of films as of April 2013, up from 142 in 2007.

Due to the relative lack of transparency of the industry, the VOD markets appear difficult to assess. EAO refers to Screen Digest,[17]

Table 6.1 Number of on-demand services by genre for the top ten countries and the whole EU (April 2013)

	Branded channels on open platforms	Catch-up TV services	VOD Films	VOD Films + TV Fiction	VOD TV Fiction	Other	Total
SE	3	58	32		2	15	110
NL	43	32	27			6	108
LU	8	3	82	3		14	110
IT	62	36	8		5	34	145
UK	232	144	39	1	40	132	588
FR	49	152	20	3	17	107	358
DE	48	91	23	10	20	36	228
CZ	6	15	5	19	1	51	97
BE	8	20	13		2	48	73
ES		60	16		6	11	93
Total EU	573	864	346	41	103	531	2458

Source: European audiovisual observatory (2013).

which reports that the consumers of the EU27 (except Bulgaria) spent €173 million in 2011 just for near video-on-demand film on pay TV. For the UK, the combined figures for consumer expenditure in digital video amounted to €137.7 million during the first quarter of 2013, 55.5% more than the previous year. The sustained increase in subscriptions to VOD services such as Lovefilm and Netflix together with the consumption of video on tablets are credited as key factors explaining this jump. In France, the revenues for VOD were €252 million in 2012; a 14.7% increase compared with 2011, while in Germany the VOD market was estimated to be €124 million in 2012, 59% more than in 2011.

Conclusion

This sector has been characterized by a continuing economic growth over the last 50 years (Waterman et al., 2012), stimulated by an enormous increase of channel capacities, improvement of picture quality with high definition and, most of all, a transformation in the type of audiovisual products, now more participatory and transformative than in previous eras.

Despite the obvious rise of pay TV and VOD, the industry is still finding its way among the proliferation of open and closed platforms. Online video streaming has become widespread, but its overall proportion of all TV viewing remained under 2% (Waterman et al., 2012: 15), with a revenue share of only 1.5% in 2010. Beyond the often quoted fragmentation of the audience, viewership remains concentrated on leading channels in the EU countries and the US. For instance, in Spain, TVE, Telecinco and Antena 3 maintain an overwhelming majority of the audience. In the USA, Disney, News Corp., NBC Universal, Time Warner Inc., CBS, Viacom and Discovery account for about 95% of all television viewing hours (FCC, 2012: 156). Digital television viewing seems to maintain a strong sociological character, whereby the decision of what, when and how to view a particular show is made at a collective level (for instance, see Dayan and Katz, 1992).

The predominant Anglo-American character of the global television trade flows seems to admit little contestation from the empirical point of view. The causes and consequences of this remain in question. Factors such as market size, including language segmentation (Lee et al., 2011), the American dominance in international cultural exchange, or institutional elements such as legal and commercial rules (Chalaby, 2012) have proven to be incomplete explanations, suggesting the need to bring autonomous cultural factors into the equation.

Optimists see the new media landscape as a source of potentially end-less expansion of choice for individuals, and as a liberating force from political and commercial control. Pessimists see a serious social problem in the proliferation of productions of poor quality, with only a few media conglomerates able to survive piracy, and the fragmentation of advertising revenues. For the most part, debates about digital television revolve around the idea of an 'uncertain' future for the medium and its industry, as the new media landscape appears to be dominated by an untraceable fragmentation, induced by the new technological wonders of production and distribution.

Yet, television watchers, more numerous and invested than ever, do not feel that way. The widespread perception that television is in a creative golden age, offering more original products and a much better experience than it used to, is not primarily related to technology and amplitude of choice: 'experience', to paraphrase a classic motto of the industry, continues to be king. For the time being, technological, economic, institutional and cultural factors have facilitated a shift in televisual content, still defined by its sense of continuity; that it may play a major role in Western cultural innovation, but that it is still unfolding, with no pre-determined direction.

Notes

1. Supposedly born in 1947 in Mahoney City (Pennsylvania) as community antenna television (CATV).
2. Directive 89/552/EC *Television without Frontiers* of October 3, 1989.
3. Not included in our calculation.
4. http://www.mediametrie.com/eurodatatv/communiques/one-tv-year-in-the-world-2012-or-the-multiple-tv-experience.php?id=831.
5. Serving 7% of households.
6. Broadly speaking, it also refers to website content that is available for a fee. Premium content can include e-books, articles or content that is offered to readers on a subscription basis.
7. As early as 1994, the EU Council adopted a resolution on a harmonized framework for a European policy on digital TV broadcasting.
8. OTT: Over-the-top television, OVD: online video distributors. The FCC distinguishes three strategic groups: multichannel video programming distributors ('MVPDs'), broadcast television stations, and online video distributors (FCC, 2012: 2). See chapters 7 and 10.
9. See appendix in De Vinck and Lindmark (2012).
10. Based on Feijoo (2011).
11. In 2005, South Korea became the first country in the world to have mobile TV when it started satellite DMB (S-DMB) and terrestrial DMB (T-DMB) service.

12. In 2012, a partnership was announced with Metro PCS Communications (FCC, 2012: 94).
13. *Source*: http://www.mobilebusinessbriefing.com/articles/distimo-us-losing-significance-in-global-app-store-market/24763.
14. More than four in ten American adults now own a smartphone. One in five owns a tablet.
15. Including Croatia and Turkey.
16. The video segment (VHS, DVD, Blu-Ray) of the European audiovisual market accounted for 8% in 2010. Blu-Ray so far has not compensated for the downturn of the TV market: a mere 0.5 million Euros in 2008.
17. www.screendigest.com.

7
The Film Industry

Sophie De Vinck and Sven Lindmark

This chapter delves into recent developments in the film industry (or sector) with specific attention to the evolution in a context of digital 'dematerialization'. We focus here on those companies involved in value-adding activities (from production, through distribution and marketing, to exhibition; see also below) with regard to feature films. These are typically defined as films with a runtime of more than one hour and intended for theatrical release[1] (see, for example, EAO, 2010: 8). This choice relates to our starting point, which is the traditional film sector as it developed historically, built around a theatrical release that has gradually expanded to include non-theatrical delivery channels. This chapter looks at the changes that digitization has brought for this traditional organizational model. We do recognize that, increasingly, the boundaries between the different types of content and their exhibition are blurring (e.g. when feature films are only very briefly theatrically released, when user-generated content (UGC) is programmed as 'alternative content' on a cinema screen, etc.).

Whether researching this sector from a global, US or European perspective, one of the main characteristics of this sector remains roughly the same: a global oligopoly in the core, with a fringe of smaller and medium-sized companies (Creton, 2008: 93). While the emphasis in this chapter is on Europe and how its competitive position in the global film market is potentially altered in a digital context, the discussions are thus inherently framed in a global perspective, in which US major firms form a continuous and dominant presence.

The first section introduces the film sector from a global perspective, in terms of output and major industry players. The second section explores the film sector's characteristics and its traditional value chain. The following section delves more deeply into production, distribution and exhibition of feature films. It assesses how ongoing digital transformations impact these prominent elements of the value network for feature films. In each of these subsections, specific strengths and weaknesses of the European sector are weighed in their relation to the US major players. These are then confronted with how digital evolutions and associated opportunities and threats affect the shape of the sector. The final section presents some conclusions about the future shape of the film markets.

The film markets

From a global perspective, the overwhelming presence of Hollywood in the film industry is clear. Yet, to understand this situation and the shape of contemporary Hollywood, it is necessary to take into account historical and complex evolutions. As such, shortly after the First World War, a group of US firms laid the basis of the so-called studio system that – through transformations and modifications – went on to dominate the film landscape. These firms combined a factory-based model of film production with the vertical integration of production, distribution and exhibition activities. Through expansion, mergers and acquisitions, a small group of companies evolved into an oligopoly that effectively controlled the industry (Schatz, 2008). The physical location of their major studios in Hollywood, California, thus became synonymous with something much larger.

Today, a small group of vertically integrated groups continues to dominate the production, distribution and exhibition of films from this location. The exact composition of this group of 'majors' has evolved over time through a succession of mergers and acquisitions. The introduction of television, changes in society lifestyles, and an anti-trust ruling in the US after the Second World War (the so-called 1948 'Paramount decision',[2] which prohibited the studio from having interests in the exhibition sector), moreover, induced fundamental changes to the studio model over time. It increasingly centred on control over distribution, with production and creativity decentralizing to include independent producers and other players. In the 1980s this trend became consolidated into a 'New Hollywood', focused on blockbuster franchises for which secondary markets (for example, home video) became increasingly important (Schatz, 2008). Nevertheless, as film studios are now part of global entertainment conglomerates, their names are still reminiscent of the heyday of the classic studio system. Today's members of the trade association Motion Picture Association of

America (MPAA) are Paramount Pictures, Sony Pictures, 20th Century Fox, Universal, Walt Disney and Warner Bros (MPAA, 2013).

Despite this situation, the numbers show that the world's largest film market in terms of production (i.e. number of film titles) is not the US. In 2010, India was the largest in this respect, with 1,274 titles produced, followed at a distance by the US with 795 titles. Global production in that year was estimated at 5,669 films (EAO, 2012: 13). Within Europe, France is the largest film market, whether one considers the number of films produced (261 in 2010), the total number of screens (5,478 in 2010) or the gross box office revenue generated in the country ($1.73 billion in 2010) (EAO, 2012: 11–12). The largest European film territories also include the UK, Germany, Italy and Spain (Baujard et al., 2009: 30).

The bulk of the European film community consists of nationally organized firms, many of which are relatively small and focused on one segment of the value chain. A few of Europe's top multimedia groups have motion picture departments, often linked to broadcasting activities. The French Canal + Group, encompassing Studio Canal, is the most prominent in terms of audiovisual turnover. Its parent company, Vivendi, sits in the top ten global media groups ranked according to this factor. Other European groups are active in several areas of the film value network (Pathé, Constantin Film, Kinepolis), but they remain a relative minority (EAO, 2011a).

The film sector's value chain and value network

The film sector is one of the core cultural industries, creating both economic and cultural value. In combination with its particularities as a high-risk, hit-driven, prototype industry (see, e.g., Hesmondhalgh, 2007), this fundamentally influences how it is approached by sector professionals and policy makers alike.

Several 'streams' engage in film-related value-adding activities. The resulting film value chain has traditionally been represented as a linear process. Starting with (1) the creation and production of films, it moves via (2) their distribution and marketing, to (3) delivery, through a variety of exhibition channels, to the end user for consumption (Figure 7.1).

One business actor can take several roles within this value chain. The Hollywood studios, for instance, are part of integrated groups that develop activities across all streams. On top of that, these and/or other players may engage in auxiliary film-related activities (merchandising, spin-offs and so on, not shown in the figure) (cf. Vickery and Hawkins, 2008). Increasingly, actors from other industries, such as the telecommunications industry, have become involved in the film sector's

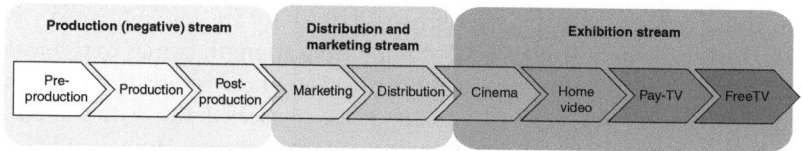

Figure 7.1   The traditional film sector value chain
Source: Adapted from De Vinck and Lindmark (2012) and Feijoo et al. (2013).

activities. As such, different industries, each with its own value chain, interact in a non-linear fashion and are nowadays part of what can be termed a 'value network'.

During the past three decades, digital technologies have been introduced in these three main streams (production, distribution, exhibition). The relatively rapid succession of change in all of them has, together, created an important disruptive impact on the traditional organization of the value chain and the actors' roles in it. All major activities within the film value chain are (in)directly affected to some extent (De Vinck and Lindmark, 2012).

Perhaps needless to say, digital technology is not an independent influencing factor in this equation. Technological inventions have historically and continuously interplayed with business environments, socio-cultural elements, policy frameworks, and so on. Moreover, the digital (r)evolution itself consists of several parallel evolutions (De Vinck, 2011), and it is only now, when the workflow has been almost fully digitized, that the impact of digital change in film landscape may fully come to the foreground (Finney, 2010).

Despite and throughout earlier periods of technological change of various levels of disruptiveness, Hollywood has so far been able to maintain a dominant position. In contrast, European films' and sector players' competitive weaknesses have been a source of concern for sector professionals and policy makers. For EU officials, the lack of European films' presence beyond their respective national borders has been a particular attention point in view of the realization of a single market for film (see, for example, Maggiore, 1990).

Going digital

Film production: The more, the merrier?

The production process or 'negative'[3] stream encompasses a variety of activities that can be categorized as being part of pre-production, actual production or post-production. This is the part of the film value chain in which Europe's creative strengths and diversity are arguably most visible, but also where Hollywood's competitive strength comes to the fore in a way that influences the potential position of the resulting European and US major film productions in other phases of the value chain, and, ultimately, the market power (im)balance between Hollywood and European film industries.

It is important to note that the US film production sector also comprises an important segment of smaller and more fragile independent players. Even if the boundaries between both worlds are not always easy to distinguish (Tzioumakis, 2006), the real distinction is, thus, perhaps between mainstream and non-mainstream film.

Nevertheless, in general, Europe seems to be falling short in terms of the presence of larger production players with sufficient resources and power, which is reflected in the development and financing stages. Data for 2008 show an average budget per film in Europe of $4.73 million, compared with $22.96 for North America. Within Europe, there are big discrepancies as well: that same year, the average budget in Western Europe amounted to $6.13 million, versus $0.67 million in Central and Eastern Europe (*Screen Digest*, 2009: 211). Moreover, the top 25 independent film production companies in Europe are mostly based in the larger markets (for example, Europacorp (France), Constantin Film (Germany), Pathé Production (France)) (EAO, 2011a). The bulk of the rest of the European sector is composed of small production companies, which lack a regular production rhythm, producing, on average, not even one film per year (Downey, 1999; Baujard et al., 2009). They are unable to invest as much (per film and in total) in film production.

European film production, therefore, is also very project-based, every film constituting a new intricate jigsaw of many different sources. Generally, sector players have difficulty in accessing private financing sources. A study by Baujard et al. (2009) has shown that European banks are averse to the risks involved in film financing. In order to fill this investment gap, the European production community has become largely dependent on public support. Over the years, an increasingly complex support framework has been created. Overall, some €2 billion are pumped into audiovisual support each year, mostly through national support schemes and funds, and usually targeted at production activities (EAO, 2011b).

Alongside public funds, financing risk for a film is usually spread among a further range of investors, including co-producers and various territory-based distributors and broadcasters. Often, the different players obtain part of the rights to the film in return for their investment,

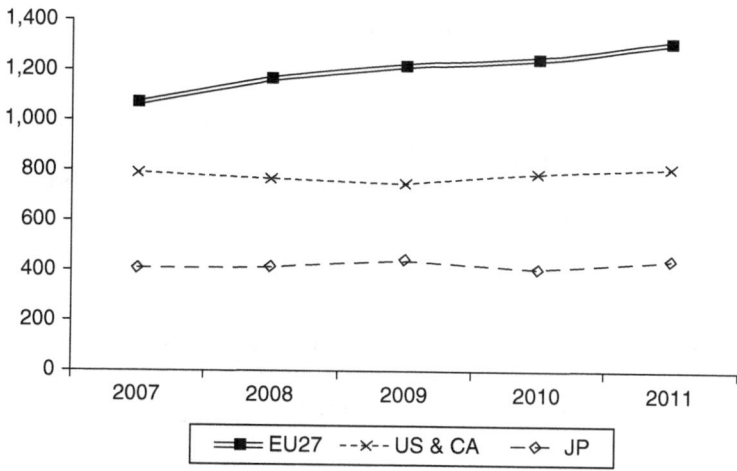

Figure 7.2 Number of feature films produced yearly in EU27, Japan and the US/Canada (2007–2011)
Source: EAO (2013a).

which contributes to the territory-based nature of film distribution and exhibition (Alberstat, 2004; Baujard et al., 2009; De Vinck, 2011).

At the same time, many talented players continue to make a large number of European films each year. As Figure 7.2 shows, the EU27 production output for 2011 stood at 1,321 films and shows an upward trend. While European film production is very much rooted in regional and national cultures, transnational production links are visible in the important role of co-productions in Europe (De Vinck, 2011). Moreover, the European film sector has generated a large number of directors with internationally recognized talent, and cultivates this 'auteur cinema' (Finney, 2010).

The general view of digitizing production has been positive (Eliashberg et al., 2006). Digital production comes with cost efficiencies, increased flexibility and quality improvements. It therefore becomes potentially easier for producers to connect with business partners as well as with the audience at the earliest stages of a film project. The set-up of intricate international co-production structures becomes more manageable, for instance, while crowd-funding platforms such as Kickstarter may offer new avenues for film financing (De Vinck, 2011).

As digital equipment becomes cheaper and more advanced, entry barriers are lowered to the extent that amateur or UGC producers become players to reckon with. As the fixed costs (for film stock or 35 mm camera rentals) go down, those films at the lower end of the budget scale find it easier to attain certain production standards.

At the same time, other elements in the production or post-production budget may increase, for instance when digital special effects are called upon (Vickery and Hawkins, 2008). In fact, budgets at the blockbuster end of the scale may go up further – the production costs for 'Avatar' (2009) are said to have been around $280 million (Keegan, 2009).

Moreover, the increasingly less linear organization of the production process may make the competition between, for example, the post-production industries of different countries fiercer. The lowering of market entry barriers at the production stage, meanwhile, tends to reinforce the trend toward over-production. Both trends may result in a more competitive environment for established and new players, including those in Europe.

Film distribution: Unlocking the gates?

With production levels high and (in Europe at least) on the rise, the crucial challenge is to effectively bring all these films to the audience. This is done in the distribution stream, when they are marketed and delivered to the various exhibition channels. Dally et al. (2002) distinguish between two typical distribution set-ups: one in which the distributor acts as the liaison between producer and exhibitors, and another that involves a sales agent as an additional intermediary between producers and local distributors. In Europe, relatively few sales agents are active (examples are The Match Factory (Germany) and Wild Bunch (France)).

Instead, the landscape in Europe, just as in the US, is dominated by distribution arms of the Hollywood studios, releasing their own films alongside a series of independent productions – sometimes through collective entities (for example, the United International Pictures structure set up by Paramount and Universal) or through cooperation with local distributors (Dally et al., 2002). Among the top distributors active in Europe, there are also some mid-sized or large, vertically integrated European companies (for example, Pathé Distribution), or companies that integrate different aspects of distribution (international sales, theatrical distribution, home entertainment, and so on). A number of European players are connected to television broadcasters, for example Medusa in Italy (EAO, 2011a). Yet many of the European distributors are relatively small, independent and generally territorially fragmented (*Screen Digest*, 2006), which impacts the competitive position of these players and the films they bring to market.

Distribution has become the central power node of the Hollywood system over time, and this is shown in the related budget. The last time the major film studios' trade association MPAA released 'print and advertising' (P&A) budget data (2007), the average major US film had an average advertising cost of $32.17 million, with an additional $3.7 million reserved for print costs (MPAA, 2008). Within a more risky business environment (non-mainstream and/or European films), large-scale and/or cross-border distribution and marketing campaigns are typically not an option. A study of the French theatrical market showed that a small 26-print release was accompanied by a promotion spend of €120,000, and a 100-print independent film by a spend of €400–500,000; but a blockbuster release included some €2 million in promotion and a much higher number of prints (*Screen Digest*, 2006: 262–263).

Film festivals, in which Europe has a strong tradition, offer an alternative, but limited, marketing route to the majors' marketing machine (cf. De Valck, 2007), in particular for the international circulation of non-mainstream (European) films.

In a digital context, new alternatives are coming to the fore, especially at the distribution level, with substantial cost savings. Digital files are easier to duplicate and cheaper to 'transport'. The theatrical 'digital print' or DCP (digital cinema package) is up to ten times less expensive than a 35 mm film print (Inglis, 2008; Mabillot, 2011). Digital, moreover, makes content customization (subtitles, dubbing) easier and less costly, which could prove to be an advantage for European films crossing borders (Media Consulting Group and Peacefulfish, 2007). The distributor can also work in a more flexible way and adjust supply to the uncertain demand level. Online and viral marketing strategies offer new and cost-efficient ways of targeting particular audience segments. This is useful for smaller films, as they rely on word-of-mouth more than mass marketing strategies. In an online context, so-called 'word-of-mouse' communities (Eliashberg et al., 2006) open up a new range of marketing possibilities by creating more emphasis on peer-to-peer information exchanges and recommendations (viral marketing). Social networks, micro-blogging applications, specialized aggregator review sites (for example, Metacritic, Rotten Tomatoes), recommendation mechanisms, and so on offer important tools in the creation of online communities. A potent mix of broad marketing and targeted niche actions thus offers a plethora of possibilities for film marketers (Vickery and Hawkins, 2008; KEA and Mines, 2010; Ulin, 2010). Not only may the risks of taking on a non-mainstream film title for release have been lowered, but the available tools to promote and position a film without a big marketing spend have increased.

While all of these trends are to the advantage of smaller European players, digitized distribution at the same time reinforces the competitive strengths of the big Hollywood majors. After all, the cost savings of working digitally have a bigger impact on large volumes of (theatrical) prints than on small, incremental releases of a few copies. In 2002, Bomsel and Le Blanc referred to estimated cost savings of around $1 billion for the US market alone. The triple trend of big opening weekends, short release lengths and a large number of film copies on release may thus be reinforced. Furthermore, in the face of an ever-increasing choice of leisure and audiovisual options, audiences will still need to find their way to non-mainstream films, both offline and online. Catching their attention in reality becomes more, rather than less, labour-intensive.

Film exhibition: Finding the right time, place and price for every audience

Historically, the exhibition of film has gradually expanded beyond the cinema theatre to include a variety of 'screens' (see Chapter 9) on which the audience can watch a film. Within each market, one can discern a competition between its main players (for example, various cinema theatres, television broadcasters, DVD retailers), as well as competition between individual titles. Moreover, each window competes with the others for the time and attention of the audience.

The release cycle is traditionally based on the idea of time holdbacks between each of the exhibition screens – the release windows system. In general, the sequence follows the order of highest marginal revenue generated over the least amount of time. Traditionally, this has meant that theatrical exhibition comes first, followed by video/DVD rental; video/DVD sales; pay-per-view; pay TV; and, at the very end, free television. This release pattern, based on different 'versions' of the film, allows price discrimination: in this way, the same product is sold at different prices to different consumers, according to their willingness to pay (Cichon, 2007). Every version is provided with exclusivity for a limited time period, supposedly improving the profitability of the film over its life span (Nikoltchev, 2008). It prevents consumers opting for a cheaper version of the film at the time of release in an earlier window, and thus cannibalizing, in particular, the theatrical revenue stream (Lehmann and Weinberg, 2000). While the concrete organization of systems varies between territories, the traditional sequence has long followed a 6–9–12–24 schedule, starting with a home video release approximately six months after the theatrical release (De Vinck, 2011).

In today's film market, the theatrical release for mainstream films mostly centres on bookings by large multiplexes, sometimes operating in circuits. In the US, in 2012, a large majority (81%) of the almost 40,000 screens were located at such venues with eight or more screens (MPAA, 2012: 22). In Europe, the percentage of multiplexes (compared with the total number of screens) is much lower, although the situation differs between countries: Media Salles (2011) data for 2010 (based on 17 European countries) range between 17% (Norway) and 67% (UK). These venues are typically seen as geared toward mainstream, mostly Hollywood blockbuster content.

Overall, the number of admissions realized in theatres has been dropping since shortly after World War II, as new leisure activities were introduced. In more recent years, admissions seem to have become more stable at around one billion, with a slight decrease noticed since 2009 (Forest, 2001; EAO, 2013a, 2013b). Nevertheless, the theatrical window is still considered to be the main showcase for films, determining the performance of films in subsequent exploitation markets (Vogel, 2007; Wolff, 2008).

Still, regardless of its importance, it is clearly difficult for the theatrical market to accommodate the 1,000 + European-produced films released each year. Today, moreover, a film's theatrical release is typically geared toward opening weekend performance and quick saturation (Gubbins, 2012). Such a hit-and-run environment is to the disadvantage of non-mainstream films, which European films often are (Lange and Newman-Baudais, 2007).

Clearly, US movies dominate not only their home market but also the European theatrical market with a 60–70% market share (Figure 7.3), with some individual countries nevertheless achieving relatively high market shares for national films (EAO, 2013a). The shared European film culture across borders is thus essentially a Hollywood one. The market share for European films outside Europe is typically marginal, circa 3–7% depending on the region (cf. European Commission, 2009: 14). In contrast, in most non-European markets, US films rake in the majority of admissions (notable exceptions are India and – to a lesser extent – South Korea) (Table 7.1).

Non-theatrical markets have become increasingly important in terms of revenue. In particular, the home video market has been a source of growth for the film sector since the 1980s. First VHS and then DVD have expanded this market substantially, making it the largest of the windows

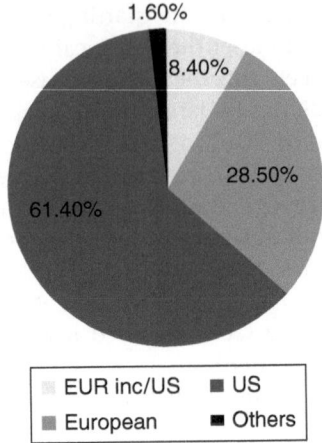

1.60%

8.40%

28.50%

61.40%

- EUR inc/US   ■ US
- ■ European   ■ Others

Figure 7.3   Admissions in the EU27 market according to the origin of films (2011 estimates)
Source: EAO (2012).

Table 7.1   Market share of European and US films in major third countries (2006)

Country	European films	US films
Mexico	3%	81%
Argentina	5.5%	82%
Brazil	3%	86%
South Korea	3%	47%
India	2%	10–12%
Japan	5–9%	50%
US	3.3%	94.5%

Source: European Commission (2009: 14).

in terms of revenues. In Europe, fiction forms an important part of the television schedule: in 2011, more than 200,000 program hours were filled with feature films (on a sample of 136 channels in 16 countries) (EAO, 2013a).

The home video and other non-theatrical markets also offer potential for non-mainstream (European) titles to reach an untapped audience that cannot be realized in the quickly rotating theatrical market. Yet the available data do not point to a stronger position of European films in non-theatrical markets, with mainstream Hollywood films dominating the whole cycle of exhibition. Detailed data for the French market, widely considered one of the strongest territories for domestic products, for instance, show a market share of French (theatrical) films in home video (sales) that is even lower than that in the theatrical market, achieving 23.7% of the market in 2012 (CNC, 2013). American films also dominate the television markets (EAO, 2013a and Chapter 2).

Digitization is affecting the delivery of films to the consumer in a number of ways. First, a new range of 'access screens' have been added to the exhibition cycle, including the computer and mobile screens – and a convergence trend is visible, both between these devices and between their underlying industries. Second, all windows for film have been digitized, with delivery and consumption of films largely happening digitally, in a dematerialized way. For each window, alternative 'on demand' offers have been developed. Third, and linked to this, the position of each exhibition window and its relation to the other windows is being reconfigured and is still in ongoing evolution. Last but not least, there is the factor of digitized illegal film delivery and consumption; that is, the circulation of copyright-infringed films, or, as commonly termed in industry and press, 'piracy'.

Indeed, illegal exhibition channels for film have also benefited from the digital transition, with copyright infringement becoming easier, less costly and less time-consuming. The potential economic impact of this evolution is still under debate, sometimes with doom and gloom prophecies, and exaggerations on both sides (Schermer and Wubben, 2011). What is clear is that copyright infringement poses a challenge, both in terms of direct economic loss and in a more indirect way, as current 'democratized piracy' menaces the basic premises of copyright in terms of audiences' willingness to pay. The profit-maximizing strategies behind the release window system enhance the attractiveness of non-authorized versions, which do not adhere to similar time holdbacks and can thus fulfil audience demand to view films before their official release in different markets (Currah, 2007 and Chapter 10).

Alongside defensive sector responses, centred on educational campaigns, technological protection, lawsuits and legislative lobbying, the need to develop an offensive strategy built on attractive legal alternatives has come to the fore. Most eyes are fixed on Video on Demand (VOD) as a new avenue for the relatively cheap and easy delivery of a film, whenever and wherever a consumer wants to watch it. However, the set-up of VOD services has been accompanied by contentious discussions on the length and position of various release windows. Already, the VOD window coincides with the DVD release in many cases (KEA and Mines, 2010). Moreover, the length of the exclusive theatrical window is being questioned, as experiments are being carried out with day-and-date, including premium VOD releases (alongside the theatrical release) and even so-called 'ultra' release models (where the VOD offer is launched before the theatrical release) (KEA and Mines, 2010; Miller, 2012). Significantly, even the French release window system, enshrined in legislation, shortened the theatrical-to-video window from six to four months in 2009 (Screen Digest, 2009).

While the VOD position in the exhibition stream is thus still evolving, it is clearly a growth market in which a large and growing number of (different) players (both old and new stakeholders: TV broadcasters, telecom and cable operators, content aggregators and rights holders, and, lastly, device manufacturers) are setting up an increasing number of VOD services. The modalities of these services differ in a number of ways: they make use of different platforms, offer films for downloading and/or streaming, and so on. All of these actors are trying out different business models, including free (ad-based), pay-per-unit or subscription models (Vickery and Hawkins, 2008; KEA and Mines, 2010; De Vinck, 2011). This market is still rather small, but growing rapidly. While not fully covered by statistics, the latest European data estimate total VOD and near-VOD film revenues (both online and on pay TV) at €845 million (for 2011). For the time being, however, growth in on-demand spend cannot yet compensate for the ongoing decline of physical home video (cf. EAO, 2011a, 2013a).

In terms of the VOD platforms on offer, the emerging nature of the market may be an opportunity for existing and new European players to capture a sizeable piece of the pie. At the same time, a number of US companies (Apple, Netflix, and so on) have already started to carve out what may turn out to be dominant positions on the platform side (KEA and Mines, 2010).

In terms of European films, opportunities for increased audience reach have been discerned. For instance, a more flexible application of release windows is said to offer potential for added marketing 'buzz' that can be created by more closely associating efforts across exhibition platforms – something that might offset the limited marketing budgets of European (theatrical) film distributors (cf. above). Within each window, moreover, the dematerialization of film delivery provides some further incentives for including European films in the digital offer. In the cinema theatre, for instance, after a sometimes difficult transition process, the deployment of digital cinema enables flexible programming and more interactive audience relationships (Ulin, 2010; De Vinck, 2011). Long-tail economics, centred on the notion that the digital economy increases the potential to render the offering of niche and catalogue content economically viable (Anderson, 2006), may, moreover, form an opportunity in terms of the presence of European films and more diverse content in general on VOD platforms.

However, language, culture, business practices and scattered rights continue to form barriers for European content to achieve wide(r) audiences, especially across borders. In the digital cinema theatrical environment, virtual print fees undo an important part of the digital cost savings on the distribution side and thus perpetuate existing bargaining power balances between distributors and exhibitors. This does not entice distributors to take digital chances (De Vinck, 2011). Moreover, with VOD being only an emerging market, VOD platforms not necessarily able and/or willing to invest in content production, and the sector reliant on pre-sales and other types of financing from other main stakeholders (for example (pay) television channels), film producers and distributors are not always tempted to experiment with new business and release models either (KEA and Mines, 2010).

According to the limited data at hand so far, the online market is not more diverse in terms of either supply or demand (Peacefulfish and Media Consulting Group, 2008; KEA and Mines, 2010). Crucially, customers still have to be given the tools to find their way to niche content. Social media, personalized recommendation and search technologies all have an impact on how the audience discovers and selects audiovisual works. Specialized search engines may play a role here (KEA and Mines, 2010).

Yet, even if the long tail brings about an expanded audience reach and consumption for European films, (revenue) fragmentation may be reinforced. In this scenario, it is the content aggregator, combining both hits and non-mainstream content in its offer, that reaps the economic benefits of the long tail.

Conclusions

Three main points come to the fore. First, many of the digital opportunities we outlined (cost efficiencies in production and distribution, flexibility, long-tail effects) form a good fit with the European film sector. We have seen that the global film marketplace is dominated by the strong presence of a Hollywood oligopoly, whose power manifests itself mostly in the distribution and exhibition streams of the film value network. European films and film players are diverse and manifold, but they are also small and fragmented – this makes it difficult to get access to structured market financing and strong marketing tools. Precisely in these phases, digital offers opportunities for European players to (re)connect with audiences, possibly increasingly across borders.

Second, however, digitization could also reinforce the competitive position of established and new consolidated, US-based players. They have the branding prowess and financial strength to back up a strong visibility in a context of digital abundance. So far, despite the potential, there are no strong signs of a substantially different market for European films across borders, in a digital context.

Third, and crucially, it is clear that the audience plays a vital role in determining the direction in which current, sometimes conflicting, trends will further evolve. In a context of copyright infringement, the further uptake of legal on-demand alternatives – which is so far relatively slow – will be crucial in order to arrive at a new balance between the different windows for film.

The main challenge for the film sector today, and more specifically for European stakeholders, is how to guarantee a diverse and accessible offer of films to European audiences, which is also sufficiently rewarding for the different incumbent and new stakeholders. This, in turn, will determine the shape and viability of the whole film sector ecosystem in the – inevitably digital – future.

Notes

1. This means that we do not focus on music videos, commercial advertisements, adult films or user-generated AV content published, for example, on YouTube. TV entertainment programming (including 'stock programming' such as filmed drama, comedies and documentaries) is not accounted for unless it consists of feature films that were originally intended for a theatrical release (i.e. no 'made-for-TV' films). Nor do we focus on supporting technical activities such as the manufacturing of production equipment, exhibition facilities or consumer electronics. However, when relevant, these supporting and complementary sectors are discussed.
2. The court held in this case that the existing distribution scheme was in violation of the anti-trust laws of the US, which prohibit certain exclusive dealing arrangements. *United States v. Paramount Pictures, Inc.*, 334 US 131 (1948).
3. That is, everything that happens before the film negative (or its digital equivalent) is made.

8
The Music Industry

Andra Leurdijk, Ottilie Nieuwenhuis and Martijn Poel

For centuries music used to be performed live by folk musicians and travelling troubadours or under patronage and supported by the aristocracy and churches. During the 19th century, modern, industrial work processes and technologies began to shape the music market, and music grew from a live performance practice into an industry. The music industry began as an industry of publishers who contracted composers and lyricists to produce songs that could be performed at concerts, vaudevilles, opera houses and music halls and whose sheet music could be edited and sold to private persons to be played at home.

This industry was totally transformed when, by the end of the 19th century, new recording techniques and the gramophone were invented and introduced to the market by Edison, Columbia and Victor. The music industry's core product changed from printed sheet music to shellac discs. First these were mainly used to promote the sale of gramophones, but gradually the manufacturing, recording and promotion of music itself became the industry's core product. The role of publishers changed to administering composers' and lyricists' copyrights and collecting royalties from the sales of records and other kinds of music licensing (Wikström, 2010; Hull et al., 2011).

Major changes in popular music followed from technological developments that made it possible to disseminate music to consumers on a larger scale or with better sound quality: sheet music, phonographs and jukeboxes followed by gramophones, recordings on LP, tape, compact disc (CD) and mp3. Digitization entered the music industry in the 1970s when digital technologies were introduced for producing and recording music. In the 1980s, with the introduction of the CD, these technologies extended to the field of distribution. In the 1990s and 2000s Internet technologies gained a major impact, by supporting all activities in the value chain, from talent scouting through production, promotion, distribution and consumption.

This chapter addresses the roles, strategies and position in the value chain of users, artists, record companies and providers of online music services in the past two decades. The first section sketches the major global market developments, while the second focuses on the European market and shows the economic meaning of the music industry in terms of employment, the number of firms and value added. The third section deals with the consequences of market developments for the value network and the reallocation of roles between main actors in the value network, stressing the role of new entrants. In the Conclusions, we try to assess which market players have gained or lost from market changes.

Market developments

The global market

Like most other media and content sectors, the music industry used to be characterized by high upfront investments, low marginal costs and high risks regarding commercial success. This led to a market structure that has been dominated by a small number of multinational, vertically integrated music firms on the one hand and a large number of SMEs on the other. Up until November 2011, four major labels (the Universal Music Group, Sony Music, the Warner Music Group and the EMI Group) accounted for 75% of the world market (Informa Telecoms & Media, 2012) and 80% of the US market (Nielsen Soundscan, 2013). In November 2011, Universal bought EMI Recorded Music,[1] responsible for the production of CDs, and Sony Music bought the publishing part, containing the exploitation of publishing rights. Since then, there are only three large music companies left.

In addition to these major companies, there are a large number of smaller record companies active in the market. These so-called 'independents' focus on specific genres, and/or on artists from specific countries. However, there are strong relations between majors and independents. Many independent labels have distribution deals with one of the major music companies. It is also common practice within the industry that the major record companies take over contracts or buy labels once artists look promising or have become successful. Often, independent labels that are bought by the major record companies continue to work under their own label and are granted a degree of independence in finding, selecting, developing and promoting talents in their particular niche markets.

Of the media and content industries, the music industry has been hit first and hardest by the changes brought about by digitization and the Internet. Infringements of copyright of illegally shared and downloaded music from P2P networks could take off on a large scale due to the digitization of music and the growth of the Internet. However, the growth in CD sales had already stopped by the end of the 1990s, as by then most consumers had replaced their vinyl collections with CDs (Rob and Waldfogel, 2004; Cooper, 2008; TNO, 2009). High prices for CDs might also have suppressed consumer demand (Cooper, 2008). In combination, these factors caused a large decline in the sales of physical music (including albums, single sound recordings and music videos). It has also led to the closure of many specialized physical music stores and has forced the record companies to change their traditional business models.

While consumer spending on physical music has been declining, revenues from live music and consumer spending on digital recorded music have been increasing. The latter consists of music distributed to (mobile) devices; music downloads from the Internet through licensed services and app stores like Apple's iTunes store; and subscription and advertiser-supported streaming services, such as Spotify and Last.fm. In 2008, physical music sales accounted for US$23.8 billion globally. In 2012, these physical sales declined to US$14.3 billion, a sharp decline. Digital music sales grew from €2.7 billion in 2005 to US$9 billion in 2010. These figures show that, although digital sales grew steadily, decline in physical sales was not yet compensated by an equal increase in digital sales. Physical sales are still declining, to approximately 58% (a substantial part of total revenues) of total sales in 2012 (IFPI, 2013).

In 2012, for the first time in many years, the combined revenues from digital and physical sales showed a small increase again. According to IFPI (2013), digital music consumption has become mainstream: two-thirds of the population aged 16–64 are now making use of some form of legitimate digital music service. This is also shown in the digital revenues of 2012: at US$5.6 billion, these revenues accounted for more than one-third of total revenues – an increase of 9% since 2011. In 2012, 70% of digital revenues came from download stores and approximately 10% from subscription services. In Europe the share of subscription services is significantly higher than the average: 20% (IFPI, 2013).

To gain a picture of the overall developments in revenue streams in the music industry, one needs not only to look at (changes in) sales of physical and digital music, but also to take into account revenues from other sources. Revenues from concerts and music festivals have increased substantially. Since 2010 these revenues have been higher than the revenues from recorded music (PWC, 2013).

The third largest source of revenues is music publishing and the collection of fees for the use of songs in recordings, live performances, radio broadcasts, film and TV, background music in restaurants, and so on. These revenues have been growing, also due to the increasing use of music on the Internet, on social networking sites and in video games (PwC and Wilkofsky Gruen Associates, 2010; Hull et al., 2011). In 2009, the global authors' rights total royalty collections of the Confederation of Societies of Authors and Composers (CISAC)[2] reached €7.152 billion (CISAC, 2011).[3]

The US market displays similar trends, with total revenues of the US music industry declining until 2010. Between 2009 and 2010, revenues declined from US$7.8 to 7.0 billion (RIAA, 2012). Between 2010 and 2012, the level of total revenues was stable. CD/DVD sales continued to decrease, but this was compensated by growth of other revenue streams. Revenues from online music services increased substantially.

Revenues from sales of digital music (e.g. iTunes) increased substantially. Between 2011 and 2012, revenues from digital sales increased from US$2.6 to US$2.9 billion (RIAA, 2012). This represents 41% of total US music industry revenues. The increase in so-called access models, whereby people pay for access to a large library of music, was particularly substantial. Collectively, they increased from just 3% of total industry revenues in 2007 to 15% in 2012, totalling over US$1 billion for the year. Part of the explanation for increased revenues from digital sales and online music services is their growing popularity with all age groups, not just youngsters (NPD, 2012).

In order to assess the overall effects of the Internet on the overall profitability of the industry, one should not only look at the revenues, but also take into account changes in costs. The cost structure is likely to have changed over the last decade, especially because the costs for manufacturing (of CDs), distribution and sales (in stores) of physical recorded music have dropped with the shift to online distribution. Marketing costs may have dropped as well, as online advertising and promotion are cheaper than most other forms of advertising. Moreover, social networks allow a greater share of self-promotion by artists, and enable consumers to contribute to music marketing by sharing and recommending music, at lower or no cost. It has to be taken into account, though, that online and social media marketing, if done professionally and on a large scale, still requires substantial time, expertise and labour costs. And there are, of course, also costs involved in digital sales and online music services (e.g. software, hosting, billing and helpdesk). But, overall, costs are likely to have shrunk.

The EU market

Developments in revenues are a main indicator of the economic relevance of a sector, but, in order to assess the economic relevance of a sector, one also needs to take into account developments in the number of firms and employees, and in the contribution of the sector to gross value added in the economy.[4]

Eurostat figures show that the number of firms in the music industry grew between 2005 and 2010 from 18,150 to 21,787, while the number of employees declined from 37,103 employees in 2005 to 35,900 in 2010. The decline in number of employees and simultaneous growth in the number of enterprises indicate that the average firm size in the industry has become smaller. A possible explanation for this development is that new digital production and distribution technologies (including the Internet and mobile applications) have made it easier for small companies to enter the music market.

The value added of the music industry has fluctuated over the years. Between 2005 and 2010, total added value rose from €1,800 million to €1,964 million. Growth of value added is remarkable because sales of physical records showed a sharp decline during that period, which was not compensated by the rise in digital sales. A possible explanation is that the costs decreased substantially. An additional explanation is that other revenue streams increased in this period, such as performance rights of music played on the radio, music used in films, video and games or from live performances. The six countries with the largest share in value added in 2010 were: Germany, the UK, France, Sweden, Italy and Spain. The UK and Germany had an almost equal share in the music sector, with 23.24% and 23.21% in value added, respectively, followed by France (21%), Sweden (5.1%), Italy (4.9%) and Spain (3.9%).

A changing market structure

The emerging value network

Figure 8.1 shows the different activities in the value network and the main actors in the value network in the music industry. It indicates how the main market actors try to bundle different activities in order to gain market power. Figure 8.1 is a simplified representation of a value network, and not all activities and actors are included. For instance, the activities of consumers are not included in this figure.

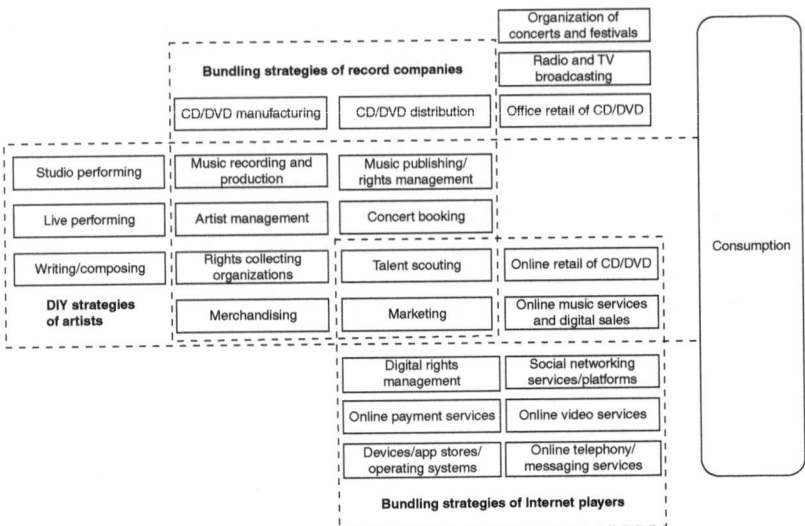

Figure 8.1   Value network for the music industry

While acknowledging that they have played a major role in disrupting legacy business models, by embracing P2P networks, sharing music and an active contribution to marketing and talent scouting, this figure focuses on the roles of the main business players in the value network.

The Internet has introduced new market players in the distribution, marketing and sales of recorded music, and made traditional market players take up new roles. Most importantly, in the new value network(s) in the music industry, record companies no longer orchestrate the activities of other actors. This has opened up the market for a whole set of companies that were traditionally not involved in the music industry.

The overlapping areas in Figure 8.1 point at value-adding activities in which the different market players compete with each other. For instance, music production is either done independently by artists, or controlled by record companies; for marketing and talent scouting all three market players are active. Marketing in this figure includes online and social media campaigns, as distinct from offering full social media services, which are listed as a separate activity of Internet players. In the following section the shifts in roles and market positions are discussed in more detail.

Reallocation of the roles in the digital music market

The Internet has brought *consumers* clear benefits, such as cheaper and more easily available digital music on different devices. Downloading music for free from legal and illegal file-sharing services still accounts for a large share of online music consumption. Increasingly, however, consumers show a willingness to pay for online music services; accept a certain amount of advertising; or pay for music indirectly when music services are part of (mobile) Internet access subscriptions. An additional benefit for consumers is the ability to integrate music consumption into their social media use and share and recommend music to their friends. Furthermore, consumers have increased possibilities to pay only for the songs they like most, instead of having to buy the full album as created by artists and promoted by record companies. These opportunities are accompanied by new constraints and switching costs: for example, consumers cannot easily transfer their playlists when switching from one online music service to another.

Traditionally *artists* earned their income from live music performances, but in addition, from the beginning of the 20th century, income from recordings came to play a major role. Like song writers, musicians were largely dependent on music publishers and record companies for access to the public as well as for sufficient funding to be able to create new music and songs.

Like record companies, artists have been affected by declining revenues from recorded music. At the same time, the Internet has also empowered them. For a range of activities, they can now opt for a Do-It-Yourself strategy or partner with specialized organizations, instead of handing over control to record companies. Music sharing over the Internet enables artists to gain wider reputations and consequently more opportunities for music sales and merchandising and also more live performances with larger audiences. They can achieve this without the help of record companies, by organizing their own marketing through social networks, online campaigns, music blogs and music video websites. This has also increased the opportunities for starting or niche artists to be heard (Kot, 2009).

Some artists even succeed in organizing their own funding through crowd-funding projects like Sellaband and Kickstarter. In this model, artists can retain complete copyright ownership. Since Sellaband started in 2006, fans have invested over €4,000,000 in individual bands, making it possible for 42 acts or artists to record an album (Sellaband, 2013). Nevertheless, the crowd-funding model has not so far become a real alternative for most artists.

Though the Internet offers artists many tools to develop a direct relationship with their fans, this does not necessarily mean that all artists become successful as Do-It-Yourself-ers. Building and maintaining a loyal (online) audience requires investment; however, not all individual artists can afford this, or possess the necessary skills. Being a DIY artist might be a good way to start one's career. It could also fit successful artists who are able to hire skilled people themselves, instead of having to rely on the upfront investments of record companies. But, for many artists, performing all these roles simultaneously might not be a very attractive option.

Previously, most artists transferred ownership of copyright to the record label. These days, transferring rights for a limited period of time is more common. After that the artist is again free to decide on licence deals. Artists can also individually sell their music through online services. To the extent that artists perform more activities themselves, they become less dependent on record companies, and the power balance shifts from the record company to the artist. A potential threat for artists (and record companies) is that the leading providers of online music services increase market shares and gain a controlling position in the value network similar to that once held by the record companies.

One Internet-driven opportunity for artists has not (yet?) materialized; the ability for small-country artists, and artists who are popular in niches and subcultures, to find new audiences and sell music across borders. In many music genres, language differences are less important than in other forms of popular entertainment. Even so, most local music is very popular in the country of origin, but hardly reaches foreign markets (except English-language music, particularly from the US and the UK) (IPTS, 2008). Some artists tour internationally and sell their albums in neighbouring countries, or in countries with a common language and cultural background. Other artists gain popularity among migrant communities and from there manage to reach wider audiences. Some genres – for instance, French *chansons* – have niche audiences across the world. But, overall, these remain exceptions.

Based on singles charts data from as many as 22 countries since 1960, Ferreira and Waldfogel (2010) find no evidence of changes in foreign success (export) of artists from the US and other regions. Instead, they find an increased bias toward domestic music. This suggests that Internet distribution has not caused major changes in music consumption patterns. Distance (geographic and cultural) and language continue to heavily influence music consumption and cross-border trade of music goods and services (Ferreira and Waldfogel, 2010).

Record companies were slow to respond to the opportunities and threats of increased Internet use and advanced equipment in private homes. But over the past few years the music industry has become more open to new business models. The complete demise of the music industry – as announced in many publications on the industry – does not seem imminent, and music companies are regaining some control over the new distribution and marketing channels for music. After a period in which record companies concentrated on fighting piracy and were reluctant to close deals with online music providers, they are increasingly signing contracts with online music providers and have also launched their own services or entered joint ventures. Consumers are getting used to paying for digital music, and more recently the market showed an increase in subscription and ad-supported models.

The coordination role that record companies used to perform no longer seems indispensable, as artists, users and smaller firms can now perform these roles as well, and, possibly, even more democratically. However, even though talent scouting and, to some extent, marketing are activities that record companies now share with consumers and artists, these activities still require a lot of skills, time and resources, which only bigger firms can offer.

Moreover, music firms have developed several strategies to face the challenges of the digital music market. First, record companies *diversified their revenue streams*, with, for instance, revenues from digital downloads, ringtones, the use of music in video games, film, TV and music video channels, and artist touring. Music companies have launched online music services or entered joint ventures, taken over online music services or concluded revenue-sharing deals with providers of online music services. Other examples to compensate for the loss in physical music sales are adding content like bonus tracks, behind-the-scenes-footage, positioning LPs (vinyl) as a luxury product and publishing digital magazines with lyrics, photographs, customizable posters and letters from the band (Capgemini, 2008). Record companies also support their artists to increase revenues from live performing (Thomas, 2013).

Ticket prices have – on average – risen, because artists are more dependent on income from live performances. If live performances were previously considered a way to promote the release of a new record, they now have to be profitable in themselves. This has also led to the stronger position of concert organizers/promoters like Live Nation and AEG Live.

Second, record companies now offer so-called *360 degrees deals* to artists. The company signs artists and subsequently manages their complete portfolio, from recordings, to live performances, merchandising and the rights for online services, radio plays, and use of the music in films, games and TV series. Concert promoters like Live Nation and AEG have also closed this type of 360 degree deals with artists. This strategy implies that music companies or concert promoters take on business risks in exchange for more control over the artists' creative process and business; the artists have to live up to their brand image in order to sustain the sponsorship deals and merchandising activities. This was already the case with most of the earlier deals between record companies and artists, but was less extreme. The tendency of record companies to evolve into companies that offer full-service deals leads to a more concentrated market structure with a small group of large companies (Johansson and Larsson, 2009).

A third response to the changing market conditions is that record companies reduce their artists' roster and *concentrate more on their successful artists*. Linked to this, record companies expect quick results and finish contracts when artists do not immediately become successful. Talent scouting and talent development (as part of artist management) are increasingly left to independent labels and artist management agencies. Only once an artist has built a fan base and is selling a significant number of records do major record companies contract the artist or take over the label. Wikström (2010) argues that record firms increasingly invest in well-established brands or build low-risk brands that are able to survive for decades. Some of the highest revenues in royalties come from artists who have already passed away (Elvis Presley, John Lennon, etc.). Their music is still used in many films and advertisements, played on radio, used in films or pop-idol contests and republished in anniversary editions of CDs and DVDs. Working with particular genres, such as Christmas carols or songs from the 1980s, or with artists from the immensely popular song contests such as Pop Idol, also proves to be successful.

Record companies thus try to sustain a central position in the value network by means of bundling a coherent set of services for artists and reclaiming a position in their contact with end users.

New market players

Technological developments enabled many new market players to enter the music market. Music distribution increasingly moved online when e-retailers (such as Amazon and BOL) entered the market for the distribution of physical – and later also digital – recorded music. After a phase in which music companies were merely fighting online piracy, in the early 2000s they slowly started to enter into deals with legal online music services such as Internet radio, personalized services (e.g. LastFM and Pandora), artist promotion websites (e.g. MySpace) and video websites (e.g. YouTube).

Apple's iTunes store was the first to break through in 2003. After closing deals with all major music companies, Apple managed to attract paying customers to its iTunes store, with its user-friendly interface, standard pricing and easy synchronization with Apple devices. In 2013 Apple welcomed over 500 million active subscribers to its iTunes store (Apple, 2013a). Amazon, which already sold CDs and DVDs, launched online music services soon after. Its overall number of customers is estimated to be around 180 million, of whom increasing numbers buy digital music (Thomas, 2013). Since then, many other new online services have been launched. After downloadable music, music streaming services like Spotify and Deezer became popular. Pandora reports over 200 million registered listeners to their Internet radio service (Pandora, 2013). As of March 2013, Spotify has 24 million subscribers, of whom six million are paying subscribers, which allowed the firm to become profitable (Spotify, 2013). Deezer has 30 million subscribers, of whom three million are paying subscribers (Hoek, 2013). Subsequently, Apple, Google, Microsoft and Amazon have expanded their music services with cloud-based services, making it possible to listen to one's music collection anytime and anywhere.

New market players also introduced new business models. The European online music provider Spotify was the first company to successfully introduce a subscription model on a large scale for its streaming services. In this model users do not pay for separate songs or albums, but they pay for access to a large music library, which they can access on their computer and other (mobile) devices for as long as their subscription lasts. In 2011 Spotify launched its service in the US market, where it immediately became popular. After many early failures, legal online music services have now gained a firm foothold in the market. They offer users a choice of models: free advertisement-based models, subscription models, or models in which users pay for pieces of content ('pay-per-transaction' model: songs, albums, etc.). Providers of online music services also try to bundle online music services with other services for consumers, for instance mobile telephony, storage, mail, messaging, search, and online sales of video, books and other products.

Social networks have become increasingly important for the marketing and sale of music (Preston and Rogers, 2011). They provide users with a means to share music and recommendations, and record companies with a platform for their online streaming services. Artists can now directly get in touch with their fans all over the world, not only when giving a concert. In addition, providers of online music services partner with social networking services/platforms like Facebook and Twitter. For example, Spotify users with a Facebook account can tell their friends what music they are listening to or share their favourite music and playlists with them. Music has thus changed from a physical product to a service that has become available anytime and anyplace without any boundaries.

A number of successful European companies have become the major company in their local markets, such as Spotify in Sweden, Soundcloud in Germany and Deezer in France. Some have also managed to enter other markets, including the US. Two possible explanations of these achievements are the balance – until recently – between Europe and the US in terms of major record companies (e.g. the former EMI and Polygram from Europe) and in terms of audio technology (e.g. leadership of European universities and research institutes in developing mp3, and involvement of European software experts in Vorbis audio compression technology, which is used by Spotify). Still, US-based online music services such as Amazon, YouTube and Apple's iTunes are dominant globally (Halliday, 2013). Part of the explanation lies in software expertise (Silicon Valley) and in a large home market that allows deals to be closed with the major record labels.

To exploit the opportunities that are created by the Internet, providers of online music services bundle their music services with other consumer services. For example, Apple's iTunes store sells music and videos. Likewise, Amazon sells music and offers streaming services, video and many other services and goods. Other examples are Microsoft, which is adding its Xbox Music service to its bundle of consumer services (Windows, Windows Phone, Skype, etc.) and Google, which is expanding its range of music services (e.g. YouTube, Google Play). Most providers of online music services (and other firms in the value network) are experimenting with different strategies and business models. It is still uncertain which strategies and business models will be sustainable, and which models can co-exist in the value network. Moreover, as specific new services prove to be highly profitable, major record companies, Google and other large firms are likely to acquire new entrants.

Conclusion

Digitization, and especially the Internet, has disrupted the business models of the record companies that used to dominate the music industry. After a period of sustained increases in sales and revenues following the introduction of the CD in the 1990s, the music industry faced substantial revenue losses in subsequent years. Although CD sales declined for other reasons as well, it is generally agreed that the Internet has fundamentally transformed the music industry. It has led to a shift in music distribution, sales and consumption, and has allowed new business models to be adopted by established and new actors.

Indeed, the value network of the music industry is changing, as revenues from CD/DVD sales decrease and revenues from online music services, live concerts and licensing increase. Users and artists benefit from the new and varied ways of communication and transaction that are enabled by the Internet. They also benefit from cost reductions that are inherent in the evolution from physical goods to online services. Consumers have gained greatly in ease of use, flexibility, added services and more variety in pay models. But at the same time they are paying for this with data about their identity, linked to their online behaviour and consumption patterns, and they risk being locked in (by switching costs) by some of the new services when they increasingly rely on one provider for a range of different services, including music, and switching to other services becomes increasingly complex. The Internet enables artists to pursue a DIY strategy and allows small firms to enter the market. However, so far, there is little evidence for more structural effects on the variety of available music or for a substantial strengthening of the market position of niche artists, or on consumption patterns. Artists may have concerns about the increased position of control in the value chain of providers of online music services. As such, the central role and bargaining power of the major record companies in the old value chain may be replaced by the substantial bargaining power of Apple, Google, Amazon, Facebook and/or Microsoft ('the big five').

Still, the role of record companies should not be underestimated. Their financial resources, music rights ownership and expertise allow them to extend their bundling strategy to the online domain. Acquisitions of successful online firms can be an element of this strategy. The position of the three major record companies (Sony, Universal, Warner) is still strong enough to negotiate partnerships with leading Internet players such as Apple and Google. The main challenge for providers of online music services is to increase user revenues and advertising revenues, without suppressing demand, triggering a comeback of piracy, or decreasing customer loyalty by neglecting privacy concerns and privacy laws. For new online music services, economies of scale still matter; firms with a large music catalogue and consumer base will still have a better chances of survival, and their success relies on the licence deals or joint ventures they manage to establish with all the major record companies.

As for the balance between the US, Europe and other regions, there are clear indications that US-based actors are becoming more important. The three major record companies are now from the US and Japan, although many of their labels – as well as independent labels – are from Europe and other regions. The world's largest concert and festival organizer/promoter – Live Nation – is also a US-based company. Like record companies, they have local units in Europe and other regions. The five main Internet players are from the US. From the perspective of diversity and chances for non-US market players, this is a reason for some concern.

Notes

1. Under certain obligations mandated by the DG Competition (EC, 2012).
2. 225 authors' societies. 100 entities: 44% are located in Europe.
3. Does not include the royalties collected directly by music publishers for song writers and composers.
4. Gross Value Added is usually taken to represent the true contribution that an industry makes to the national economy. This is the value of gross outputs minus the value of inputs from other industries. This added value of a particular industry is equivalent to the total staff costs plus profits before tax (KEA, 2006).

9
The Newspaper Industry

Andra Leurdijk, Ottilie Nieuwenhuis and Martijn Poel

In the late 19th and at the beginning of the 20th century, the newspaper market was dominated by a number of influential individual proprietors, like Lord Northcliffe in the UK and William Randolph Hearst in the US. These owners used newspapers as vehicles for political opinion and propaganda. No single newspaper was able to dominate the market. In the 1920s, the market concentrated. Fewer titles were published, and advertising developed as the main source of income for newspaper publishers (Hirst and Harrison, 2007). Newspapers started to cater to general interests and broad audiences in order to drive advertising income (Grueskin et al., 2011). Throughout the 20th century, the newspaper market was dominated by media conglomerates owning newspaper chains. In the second half of the 20th century, a process of increased concentration and consolidation in the international newspaper industry took place (Grisold, 1996). The newspaper sector grew into a mature sector, strongly linked to geographical location.

This chapter discusses the major changes in the newspaper publishing industry. The first section looks at the global market developments in terms of circulation, advertising revenues, employment, number of firms and gross value added of the newspaper publishing industry, with an emphasis on the EU markets. The second section reviews the value network for news production and follows the new opportunities brought by the digital shift for publishers, journalists and consumers. The third section analyses the changing positions in the value network of news provision and the strategies of the various players. The chapter concludes with an assessment of the evolving power relations in the value network and some reflections on the future of news(paper) publishing.

147

Market structure and market developments

Compared with other media industries, the level of concentration in the newspaper market is relatively low. There are a number of large newspaper publishers, some of which are part of multimedia companies, and many medium-sized and small publishers, especially at the regional and local level. Nevertheless, concentration of newspaper publishers is an ongoing development. Concentration took place in Europe in the 1980s and 1990s, partly in response to increasing competition from broadcasters. As newspaper publishers increasingly had trouble in sustaining their legacy business, they tried to gain efficiencies by merging with other newspaper publishers and combining regional titles. They also diversified their business, or they became part of larger media companies that are active in other sectors, such as commercial TV, radio, online (news) services, and magazine and book publishing. Newspaper markets tend to be more concentrated in small countries than in big countries, as the volume of the advertising market in small countries cannot sustain a large number of (independent) newspaper titles (ICRI et al., 2009). Some Scandinavian, German and Austrian publishers took advantage of the liberalization of the media market in Central and Eastern Europe after the fall of communism, when most state-owned media were privatized, to extend their business in these neighbouring markets.

The global market

After very profitable years, the newspaper industry in many countries has shown declining circulation and readership figures, as well as declining revenues from sales and advertising and declining employment figures (OECD, 2010; WAN-IFRA, 2012). Figures published yearly by trade organization WAN-IFRA show that, globally, growth in terms of turnover (i.e. revenues from advertising and sales) slowed down since 2004 and started to decline from 2006 in the US and more generally with the economic crisis in 2008 (WAN-IFRA). However, there are considerable differences between countries; for instance, in countries like India, China and South Africa, circulation is still rising, a likely result of increasing wealth and literacy.

Newspapers gain revenues from sales and advertising. Table 9.1 shows how the total newspaper revenues globally declined from US$187,479 million in 2008 to US$163,523 million in 2012, a decline of 10.3% in five years (PwC Global Entertainment and Media Outlook: 2013–2017, www.pwc.com/outlook). The decline can be fully attributed to a decline in advertising revenues, because revenues from sales still showed a slight increase. Of course figures can vary on a national level. The decline has been sharpest in the US, but as this is the largest newspaper market, it strongly affects the overall figures. Declines in Western Europe have eased somewhat in recent years (WAN-IFRA, 2012). Table 9.1 also shows how advertising income within the global newspaper publishing sector is divided between advertising in the newspapers' print and online editions. Table 9.1 shows how advertising income within the global newspaper publishing sector is divided between advertising in the newspapers' print and online editions. The figures show a decline in print advertising and an increase in digital advertising, except between 2008 and 2009, when digital advertising income decreased as well.

The newspapers' share of the total advertising market has shown a steady decline over the years, from covering almost 35% of the advertising market in 1997 to 19% in 2011, revealing a structural development (WAN-IFRA, 2012). Newspaper publishers have to some extent also benefited from the rise in Internet advertising through the revenues from advertising on their online publications. However, the losses in print advertising have been far greater than the gains in digital advertising for newspaper publishers, resulting in an overall negative growth in advertising income for newspaper publishers as illustrated by table 9.1.

Newspapers in most European countries and the US had already started to lose readers and advertisers to TV news (see Chapter 8) before the growth of the Internet, but the Internet contributed to another drop in readership and circulation. Most destructive, though, was the newspapers' loss of advertisers who turned to the Internet. This caused losses in revenues that, so far, have not been recovered by the advertising and sales revenues of newspapers' digital publications.

The decline in advertising revenues for newspapers can to a large part be attributed to their loss of classified advertising, which shifted to specialized online marketplaces, dating services, job recruitment and real estate websites. Especially search engines attract high volumes of advertising money. It is estimated that they have a share of approximately 50% of the total Internet advertising revenues (WAN-IFRA, 2012). New competitors like Google News also challenge newspapers by aggregating their online headlines and attracting large audiences and, subsequently, advertising income.

Despite declining newspaper readership, the demand for and instant access to news has never been higher. The available data seem to indicate that the online publications of legacy newspapers and broadcasters still attract a considerable share of the visits to online news sources, but that aggregators such as Google News, Yahoo News, Digg, NetVibes MSN

Table 9.1 Advertising and circulation revenues in the global newspaper publishing market (2008–2012)

	2008	2009	2010	2011	2012
Print advertising newspaper ($ millions)	102,181	83,848	82,617	80,524	78,411
% Change	–5,25	–17,94	–1,46	–2,53	–2.62
Digital advertising newspaper ($ millions)	6,591	5,722	6,406	7,017	7,637
% Change	23	–13,18	11,95	9,53	8,83
Circulation newspapers ($ millions)	78,707	77,825	77,637	77,237	77,475
% Change	13,63	–1,12	–0,24	0,51	0,30
Total newspaper ($ millions)	**187,479**	**167,395**	**166,661**	**164,777**	**163,523**
% Change	**2,74**	**–10,71**	**–0,43**	**–1,13**	**–0,76**

Source: PwC Global Entertainment and Media Outlook: 2013–2017, www.pwc.com/outlook.

and The Huffington Post attract increasing shares of online news readers (OECD, 2010: 30–31).

The European market(s)

Indicators for the economic strength of a sector are the developments in the number of firms and employees, and in gross value added.[1] Between 1995 and 2007 the number of firms in the European newspaper publishing industry increased from 7,251 to 9,006 and then dropped to 8,099 in 2010. At the same time, the number of employees showed a decline from 35,871 in 1995 to 30,230 in 2007, and then slightly grew again to 31,250 in 2010. Newspaper publishing showed a negative average growth rate for value added of –1.1% annually for the EU27, between 1995 and 2010, compared with an overall growth for the total economy of 2.6%.

In most EU Member States circulation figures have shown a steady decline since the mid-1990s. Only in some Eastern European countries has circulation been rising. The total average circulation of newspapers (paid for and free newspapers) per day in Europe declined from 13,011 billion on average in 2007 to 10,021 billion in 2011 (WAN-IFRA, 2012), a decline ranging from 0.1% to 10%.

There are considerable differences between countries in the state of the press, partly related to historical differences in circulation and readership. In Europe, the Nordic countries in particular are known for their high readership density, which means that a high percentage of the population read newspapers and also spend a considerable amount of time doing so, whereas in the UK relatively few people read newspapers and they spend little time on this (Elvestad and Blekesaune, 2008; OECD, 2010).

The crisis in newspaper publishing is felt more in some countries than in others. The French press, for instance, seems less able to respond to the challenges of new technologies and increasing competition due to its outdated and monopolistic production and distribution systems. In contrast, the German press is doing comparatively well. Germany is home to a number of well-established global publishing companies. As a whole, the European press is doing better than US newspaper publishers. The decline in circulation and employment in the EU27 is not as steep as in the US. This can be explained by several factors: a lower dependence of European newspapers on advertising revenues (50% versus 85%) (Pew, 2013)[2]; a higher newspaper readership, especially in the northern countries ; and the fact that quite a few European newspaper publishers are still family or privately owned businesses. The latter are often more resilient to economic recession than companies listed on the stock market, because maximizing profits is not their only or main goal.

Costs

In order to establish the overall effects of the Internet and digitization on the newspaper publishing industry, one needs to take into account not only the revenues but also the changes in costs. Traditionally, the costs for the editorial department have been estimated to be between 14% and 30% of overall costs, while production (printing and distribution) has varied between 20% and 50% of overall costs, depending on which distribution methods are used (home delivery, postal delivery or the sales of single copies) (OECD, 2010; Vogel, 2011). Because the 'first copy' costs are high, the sector used to depend on economies of scale. After the relatively high investment required for producing the first copy of a newspaper (in labour, printing presses, etc.), the costs for producing each extra newspaper are relatively low. The high fixed costs have meant high entry barriers.

For digital publishing and distribution, costs are substantially lower. A lot of initial costs, for example, the costs for investing in printing plants, are eliminated or decline to zero (Grueskin et al., 2011). This has lowered the barriers to entry, enabling many new competitors to enter the market. Scale, in the sense of a large audience reach, is still an important contributing factor to commercial success, especially for those news services that rely on advertising revenues, but, with lower upfront investments required, other models become feasible as well, like offering specialized news services, and producing for geographically dispersed niche audiences.

News gathering and the creation of content still depend to a large extent on the human labour of journalists and correspondents reporting on events, checking sources, interviewing, collecting evidence, writing news and background stories, as well as on photographers taking pictures, on editors reviewing stories and on people taking care of marketing and sales activities. Although some of these activities and processes can be done faster and more efficiently with the help of new technologies and input from readers, (professional) human labour is still a major cost factor. In this respect, online-only news providers have a competitive advantage, as they do not bear the costs of paper, printing and physical distribution. However, only a few online companies have succeeded in developing viable online business models for their news services, apart from the largest news aggregator services, which do not invest much in original news production, but mainly categorize, rank and personalize the news offered by other sources.

Most newspaper publishers have not completely turned to online news publications, and still also publish print newspapers. If newspapers were to drop their printed news and move completely online, this could save publishers significant investments in paper and printing plants. But this switch is not necessarily a solution for newspaper publishers. Thurman and Myllylhati (2009), for example, have shown that the Finnish financial newspaper *Tallousanomat* managed to cut costs by 50% by going online, but revenues dropped by 75%. Advertising and subscription income, in particular, showed a considerable decline. Therefore, for most newspaper publishers, completely terminating their print publications is no longer unthinkable, however not a decision that they foresee making in the near future.

The value network

The Internet and digitization have affected the different phases in the value chain of news production, aggregation, distribution and consumption in fundamental ways. Figure 9.1 introduces the value network for the news sector. It illustrates that the creation of value is not a straightforward, linear process from production to consumption, but

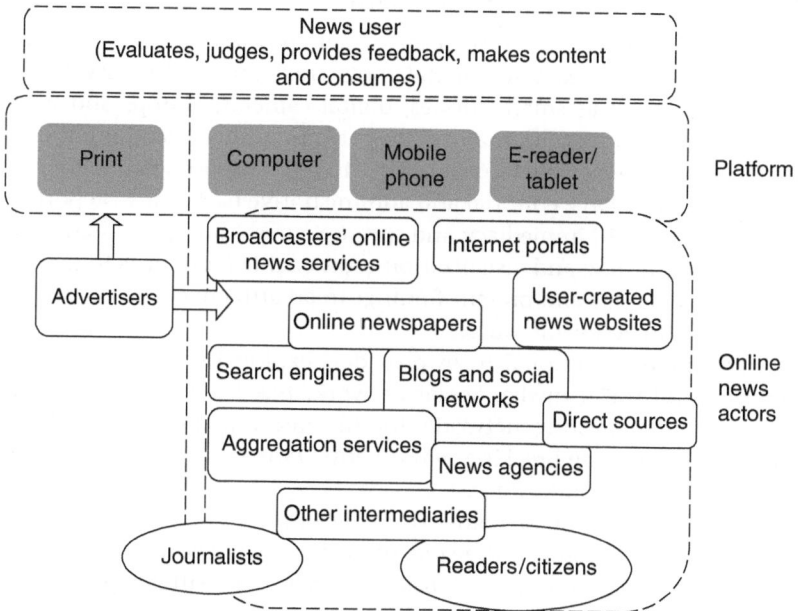

Figure 9.1 The news value network, based on OECD (2010)

that there are many players involved, which can have different (some-times combined) roles in different phases or aspects of value creation, and which can engage in a number of relationships, involving different cost and revenue streams. This model shows better than the traditional, linear value chain how news is published on more different platforms, with more options for advertisers to spend their advertising budgets and with more and different players involved in the market. The model also visualizes how users have gained different roles in the value chain, from being mere consumers to also producing, disseminating and responding to news.

The Internet offers news consumers a plethora of new sources for news and information, partly offered by the legacy newspaper publishers and partly by new players, varying from individual bloggers and user-generated content sites to large news aggregation sites like those of Google and Yahoo. In 1996, the *New York Times* and the *Wall Street Journal* were the first to offer their news online, and many newspapers followed. Since around 2008, users have also been able to access the World Wide Web via mobile devices like smartphones and eReaders (see Chapter 3). Tablet computers like the iPad, launched by Apple in 2010, are again causing changes in news publishing and news consumption.

New tools and platforms for journalists

The Internet offers journalists a lot of new possibilities to gather and produce their stories. With digital tools and lightweight, easy to use equipment, such as smart phones, digital cameras, laptops and voice recording equipment, journalists can perform an increasing number of activities themselves, instead of having to rely on photographers, technical staff and a large editorial and administrative back-office. Reporting has thus gained in immediacy and speed. Sources can be accessed more easily. Data-mining and visualization tools enable journalists to investigate large data sets and present findings in an attractive way, producing new stories in accessible ways.

Increasingly, traditional news providers exploit the potential of the Internet and social media. Social networks like Facebook and Twitter function as interesting networks for the dissemination of news and information. During breaking news events, Twitter has provided people the tools to communicate fast and easily. A lot of information, especially pictures and video, comes from eyewitnesses or victims, who are often faster and closer to the spot than the news reporters from traditional news publishers. Many journalists are using Twitter as a source of information and a means to contact sources.

The Internet has thus opened up a rich set of possibilities for journalists to collect, investigate and present stories. At the same time, if they want to keep track of developments, they also need to acquire a whole set of new skills. In addition, the participatory nature of the Internet means that they need to change their attitude toward their readers and instead of only sending information, they also need to enter into a dialogue with their readers and accept readers' contributions to their stories. Not all journalists welcome these changes, and some find it hard to adapt or even refuse to do so, especially those who consider the Internet a threat to core journalistic values, such as reliability and depth of news reporting.

Another effect of these changes is that it has increased the possibilities for journalists to be self-sufficient. It has become more common for some of the most outspoken among them to publish blogs on newspapers' websites, and to provide more personal news accounts. The use of Twitter and other social media by journalists contributes to this personal style. In a way, journalists have become brands themselves. This practice can be a potential source of conflicts of interest between the journalist and the newspaper, as some of the most popular journalists might choose to strengthen their own profile, rather than the newspaper's brand.

Users contributing to news production and distribution

Users take on increasingly active roles in producing or disseminating news through blogs and social networks. Traditional news providers are responding to this development by inviting users to respond to their content, but actual user participation options are often limited to filling in a survey, adding a comment or giving feedback to editors (Rebillard and Touboul, 2010). The addition of non-professional contributions into the main online news stream of legacy newspaper websites is (still) less common. However, interest in user participation is growing. Well-known examples where eyewitness participation has peaked are the bombings in the London Tube (2005), the post-election events in Iran (2010), the Arab Spring and revolutions in the Middle East (2011) and the earthquake and tsunami in Japan (2011). In all these instances citizens provided many pictures and stories that were used by newspapers, radio and TV news broadcasters. Alternatively, readers can also suggest subjects which they think journalists should go after, and put these up for funding. So far these seem to be more successful in the US, with well-known examples like SpotUS and ProPublica, than in European countries, possibly due to larger home markets and a longer tradition of private sponsorship than in Europe.

Tapping into the 'wisdom of the crowds' went one step further when newspapers started asking their readers to help them investigate certain issues (see Chapter 8). The 2010 publication of secret documents on the wars in Afghanistan and Iraq through the website Wikileaks, in collaboration with professional news media, is a prominent example of how citizens and professional journalists collaboratively produce news stories by examining huge amounts of open data (Benkler, 2011; Sifry, 2011). *The Guardian* is known for its innovative work in this field. The newspaper asked its readers to help examine the expenses of British MPs in the 2010 scandal around British MPs abusing public money for personal expenses, and in 2011 it investigated the cause of urban disturbances with the help of the public.

Going one step further, newspapers such as *The Guardian, USA Today* and *The New York Times* are experimenting with opening up their own data to the public, in order to enable others to develop new services or information based on these data: for instance, an app in which the newspaper's film reviews were combined with data from online film catalogues and services such as Netflix (Ingram, 2011).

Furthermore, supported by free and easy accessible online content management tools like Wordpress, the amount of user-generated websites and weblogs has expanded drastically. Some weblogs have grown into important players on the news market – for example, the US *Huffington Post* and the South Korean *OhMyNews*. European examples are *Agoravox, Baksheesh, Street 89* and *Mediapart* (France), *Readers Edition, Opinio* (Germany), *You Reporter* (Italy), *Nyhetsverket* (Sweden) and *Nu.jij* (part of Nu.nl, the Netherlands).

Sometimes user-generated news is considered as a way to fill in gaps that have emerged in news reporting due to the closure of print newspapers. In the US, in particular, local and hyperlocal online news production (i.e. news on neighbourhoods) is vibrant. Some of these sites even employ paid staff; AOL, for instance, has hired local reporters/editors for its local news service Patch in about 800 communities, and the *Huffington Post* (since 2011 owned by AOL) has numerous local editions. But, compared with the numbers of newspaper editors and journalists who have been laid off and the drop in editorial spending on newspapers, the overall increase in paid staff and earnings is minimal (Waldman, 2011).

There is criticism that many of the user-generated news platforms focus on entertainment, lifestyle and sports news and offer much less reporting on local public affairs. Some journalists and publishers fear that the growth of user-generated news will be at the expense of traditional journalism, as it offers news publishers cheaper content than professional journalists can offer. They also argue that amateurs providing news often violate journalistic standards, and they accuse bloggers of 'stealing' their news messages without proper compensation and/or reference. User contributions are assumed to be sometimes unreliable, and the quality of most blogs is, according to some critics, very low (Fuller, 2010). Often practical constraints and routines within newsrooms make the integration of user-created content in legacy news publishers' websites difficult.

Collaboration between journalists and audiences

Even though the Internet offers great potential for more participatory forms of journalism, many still see important roles for professional journalists. Charlie Beckett (2010), for instance, investigates the options of networked journalism and claims that a continuous interaction between citizen-contributors and professional journalists has, in cases such as the British 2010 elections, led to groundbreaking and influential new forms of journalism. Professional journalists took on different, but still indispensable, roles in moderating content, encouraging people to contribute, linking citizen contributions to background information, and checking facts.

Another perspective comes from Jay Rosen (2011), who introduced the concept of the pro-am (professional amateur), which refers to practices in which news publishers invite dedicated users to contribute to news stories on a regular basis. An example of this is the Public Insight Network, an organization that manages a database of over 100,000 people who have agreed to being used as a source for journalists in a chosen field of expertise. The database contains information on their expertise, networks and location, thereby enabling the professional journalists of associated news media to ask questions of the right people (http://www.publicinsightnetwork.org/).

The various ways in which users can contribute to news and investigative journalism are impressive and multifaceted. They have proven to be a valuable addition to and expansion of the work of professional journalists, and in some ways have turned the relationship between media and consumers around. Instead of only being the end users of stories crafted by journalists, consumers are now active co-producers of these stories. Journalists have to acknowledge that in some cases they even know more than the journalist, especially when the journalist can tap into their combined knowledge. At the same time, professionals still play an important role in selecting, moderating and filtering information and in offering a platform and the tools for news reporting (Helberger et al., 2010).

News aggregators

Compared with the legacy news publishers, online-only news publishers have the advantage of starting from scratch, not bearing the sunk costs of earlier investments in printing presses, staff and offices. This enabled Internet companies like Yahoo, Google and MSN to grow into important news aggregators. News aggregators provide links to the headlines of news from other sources, which can be ranked and categorized according to the users' preferences. In general, these companies do not invest in original news production[3]. On their news portals they provide the first few lines of the news message and a link to the full article on the source's website.

This practice has led to ongoing disagreements between legacy news publishers and online news aggregators. Newspaper publishers accuse Google of generating income on the back of their content, by placing advertisements next to the links to their news in search results, and by deep-linking to articles instead of guiding visitors through the newspapers' online front page. Newspapers claim that this has caused major losses in online revenues for newspaper publishers. Although Google offers the opportunity for newspapers to remove the links to their websites from Google News, this is not an attractive option for most newspaper publishers, as they also benefit from the traffic to their own websites generated by Google Search and Google News.

The debate about the use of newspaper publishers' content by Google News illustrates the tension between the news incumbents, on the one side, and the new online intermediaries, on the other. In 2013, some trade associations lobbied EU governments (France, Germany) to legislate (Google tax; see Chapter 10). Similar issues are likely to arise between traditional publishers and the new providers of applications like Flipboard, Pulse and Zite which offer customized selections of news from different third party sources.

News publishers' strategies for market share

Newspaper publishers have responded in a variety of ways to the changing market conditions of the last two decades. In the early 2000s, a number of publishers started to circulate free newspapers in an attempt to win back some of the readers (and advertisers), especially young people, whom they had lost in preceding years. They also innovated with their print products to make them more attractive for readers and advertisers, adding more separate sections or magazines to the newspaper. For advertisers, these additional sections offer extended advertising space in a more relevant context; for instance, advertisements for travel agencies in the travel magazine or fashion advertisements in the lifestyle section. Some newspaper publishers have also offered advertisers the possibility to write their own content (advertorials).

Other examples are the transfer from broadsheet to tabloid, the introduction of Sunday newspapers in countries where these were not already common, and the launch of newspapers especially aimed at young people, often linked to major newspapers, with which some of the content is shared. Successful examples of the latter are *Dein Spiegel* in Germany (launched in 2009) and *NRC Next* in the Netherlands (launched in 2006). Finally, newspaper publishers have tried to create a more loyal readership by offering extra services for readers and subscribers, such as reductions in the sale of books, records, wine, festival tickets and travel arrangements. These are all examples of integrating their journalistic profile more strongly into their commercial potential and strengthening the relation with both advertisers and readers.

Many newspapers have also attempted (and succeeded) to become major Internet players. This meant that, just like individual journalists, newsrooms and news publishers have had to change the organization of their work. Many newsrooms have integrated their print and online workflow and have implemented digital workflow management systems, which enable them to organize work processes in a more resource-efficient and cost-effective way (European Commission, 2005a). One example of the effects the Internet has had on working routines and end products is that news production is no longer limited to a 24-hour cycle, but can be produced permanently and made available 24/7. For online news sites there are few spatial limitations (in terms of the number of pages and inches available in the printed newspaper) and news can be constantly updated. In times of breaking news and crises, many news providers generate a constant news stream online.

New business models

Revenues from advertising on news sites are growing, but are still low compared with revenues from print advertising. One reason for this is that the prices for online advertising are relatively low. This can be explained by the abundance of advertising space available, the fragmentation of readership and the short time online readers spend on any particular webpage. In addition, established measurements for Internet news consumption, accepted by all stakeholders, are still lacking.

Successful pay models are scarce as well. Due to the abundance of news and information available on the Internet, few people are willing to pay for online news services. Some newspaper publishers left the paywall model after a short time of experimentation, as the revenues from digital sales and subscriptions could not compensate for the vast loss of advertising revenues due to the loss of readers after the introduction of a paywall. Lately new attempts have been made by newspaper publishers to reintroduce paywalls for premium content, for instance, by the *New York Times*, a number of Murdoch's newspapers, and German newspapers like *The Berliner Morgenpost, the Hamburger Abendblatt*, and the French *Le Figaro*. In other pay models subscription for print and digital editions is combined. In particular, the iPad, tablet computers and new generations of eReaders are currently welcomed by newspaper publishers as devices that make digital newspapers more attractive to read and will potentially unlock consumers' willingness to pay for digital content.

Most successful businesswise, so far, are aggregation services like Google News, or services which manage to engage large numbers of readers with low-cost user-generated news and blogs, such as the *Huffington Post*.

Most recent experiments with alternative ways of presenting the news and adding value, for which users are prepared to pay, are innovative ways of bundling news. Consumers may subscribe not to full newspapers but to individual news stories from a variety of newspapers, in different content categories (economy, foreign news, art and culture, etc.) or stories that are selected by their favourite opinion leaders and friends. These services come with user-friendly pay models, such as micro-payments, subscriptions or a pre-paid model that allows consumers to download a certain number of articles for a certain amount of money. These models can only work if a sufficient number of the major newspapers cooperate, and it is still too early to determine the success of these models.

Conclusion

The newspaper publishing sector is in transition. Its legacy business is declining, it is facing increased competition, and its new online and mobile services have in most cases not (yet) grown into a profitable business. Newspaper publishers are trying out various new models, none of which have so far compensated for the revenue losses of the print newspapers. Meanwhile, they have to bear the double costs of sustaining their offline print newspapers while at the same time investing in new online news services.

The decline in print newspapers is not likely to stop soon, and not all newspapers will be able to achieve a strong online position. Newspapers have not only lost part of their readership; they have also lost a large number of their advertisers, who can reach their audiences at lower costs and more effectively online through Google and Facebook, online marketplaces and other forms of online advertising. For many of these new providers of news, producing original news is not their core business. The overall decline in revenues for news publishers is, therefore, a serious threat to investments in original news production, especially in more vulnerable news genres, such as investigative journalism and sustained reporting on local governments.

Consumers benefit from the increased availability of 'free' news and the options to tailor news consumption according to one's own preferences. There is some concern, however, as to whether the market can also sustain the desired quality of the output, and the ability of some vulnerable news genres, such as investigative journalism, sustained reporting on local government and local politics, or foreign news reporting, to survive.

Beyond market developments, the sector is not only economically relevant but also of social and political importance; newspaper publishers do not only operate on the market for supply and demand of goods, but also contribute to informed citizenship. A decline in the number of news outlets, a reduction in revenues or increasing concentration might in the long run disadvantage consumers in terms of quality, number of viewpoints and availability of channels. Besides, it would also affect the quality of our democracies, as unrestricted access to high-quality information contributes to the functioning of civil society and democracy. Therefore, continuing innovation and experimentation with development in news services and business models is of the utmost importance.

Notes

1. See Chapter 8, note 302. Due to the way Eurostat categorizes economic activities, the figures provide a partial picture; they express all economic activities of companies whose main activity is the publishing of print newspapers,

including their online and other (media) activities. It excludes online-only news providers and news(paper) activities in companies whose main activity is something else.

2. The report shows that some US newspapers are increasing their circulation revenue share as a result of the introduction of digital paywalls.

3. Google provides some small-scale support to journalism in offering trainings to journalists in using their data analysis and visualization tools. The firm also invests US$5 million per year in technological/innovative journalism projects, through for instance the International Press Institute and the Knight Foundation.

10
The Video Games Industry

Giuditta De Prato

The video games industry is the youngest branch of the media and content industries. Born digital and global, this industry has developed from scratch over 40 years, from a by-product of computer scientists' in-lab activities, then often portrayed as some kind of male teenagers-only preserve, later to become an industry producing profits in the billions and reaching an ever-increasing base of customers across all demographics.

The consultancy Newzoo reported 880 million gamers worldwide as of 2012 (Warman, 2013).[1] In 2010, within 18 European countries covered by the IFSE survey (ISFE, 2010), there were 95.2 million adult video gamers: 31% of males and 20% of females are gamers. In 2012, an average of 48% of adults surveyed were gamers[2]: 54% of males and 43% of females (ISFE, 2012). In the US, in 2011, ESA (2012) reported an even higher percentage of gamers, with 72% of households playing computer or video games, and 29% of gamers over the age of 50. In 2012, in the US, 53% were male and 47% female (ESA, 2012). The average US household owned at least one dedicated game console, PC or smartphone, with 49% of US households owning a dedicated game console. In the UK, nine out of ten children live in a household with a fixed or portable games console (Ofcom, 2012b).

Potential audiences have grown, worldwide communities have been reached, and access platforms have been added (consoles, portals, mobile handsets, etc.). Indeed, the video games market has been growing, not only in value but also in audiences. The demand has changed under pressure from a variety of factors, such as technological ease, the emergence of social computing and communities, and the supply of simple and short games, capturing a previously unsatisfied demand across age categories, socio-economic classes and gender. In other words, this industry is becoming more and more mainstream,[3] developing into an established form of entertainment.

163

Box 10.1 A market difficult to gauge

Although more and more studies are trying to calculate the dimensions of the game industry, the lack of official data clearly constitutes a constraint to the appraisal of its potentials and to the understanding of its dynamics. The video games industry is not classified under media, although the gaming industry fits the OECD (2007) definition, as it has many activities in common with television and film production. The video games industry is categorized under software and computer programming[4] (OECD, 2009), as well as in the US NAICS 2002.

It is not easy to quantify economic activity in the software market, where production is not accurately represented in official statistics. Measuring and monitoring the evolution of the online (De Prato et al., 2012) and mobile (Feijoo and Gomez-Barroso, 2012) games segments are even less straightforward, due to the characteristics of the product itself and to the consequent lack of basic indicators suitable to frame in a single picture the complexity of the different subcategories and articulated typologies implied by online gaming. Usage statistics and download numbers are often the only available ways to integrate data in order to monitor the dimension of the online and mobile markets. This is especially true where free applications are concerned, as to account for subscribers and paying customers is not possible. In any case, a lot of companies in the growing online and mobile field may not be accurately accounted for, thereby making it difficult to get a precise view of the size of these growing segments.

Giving a global overview of the market is, indeed, a very difficult task because of the proliferation of numerous segments, each with its own dynamism and business models; usage patterns also differ between heavy users and casual gamers. To gauge the economic dimension of the industry, one has to combine official and non-official data; however, they use various definitions, making it problematic to go much beyond the data supplied by major consultancies (IDATE, PWC, iSupply, in-Stat, GfK,[5] etc.) or trade associations.

The industry produces entertainment hardware and software[6] for use on personal computers, video consoles, portable devices and mobile phones, often described as 'an interactive kind of mediated entertainment' (Jeroen and Martens, 2005). All of these games have one thing in common – they are essentially computer programs or software.

The first section sums up the data available on the global market. It first gives an overview of regional markets, stressing the rise of the Asia-Pacific region and the new role of China. To better account for the proliferation of numerous segments, it then moves to look at the distribution between platforms. The second section first introduces the value network of the video game industry, and shows an industry structure that is still fluid and is expected to keep evolving: the relative position of each player in the value chain is not stable (hardware producers, game developers, publishers, software producers). Next, it shows the major trends under which the industry is being reorganized, and introduces the innovative business models that accompany these changes.

The video game markets

In 2012 the global video games market was estimated at €53 billion (US$68 billion: Warman, 2013). The market is expected to reach US$86.9 billion in 2017, growing at a 6.5% compound annual rate (PWC, 2013), up from less than US$30 billion in 2004. Despite some turbulence in recent years due to changes in the business models (Le Diberder, 2012; see second section of this chapter) and declining segments (consoles and PCs), the market is a healthy one, with exceptional growth dynamics forecast.

The global video game market

US and Japanese companies are dominating the market (see Table 10.1), with nine out of 20 among the top companies for the US and seven for Japan. However, new companies are climbing up, reflecting changes in the global market. The entry of two Chinese companies (Tencent, NetEase) with very high growth rates (36% and 21%) is to be noted. The two companies were not even included in the top 20 in 2009 (De Prato et al. : 41[7]). In July 2012, Activision Blizzard (ranking 3) and Tencent Holdings Limited announced a strategic relationship to bring *Call of Duty Online* to Chinese game players.[8]

By the same token, the entry of Apple is noticeable, with a comparable growth rate, indicating the strength of its ecosystem. The iOS market (iPad, iPhone and iPod Touch) generates 89% of the

Table 10.1 Top 20 companies by game revenues (2012)

Company	Country	Revenues US$ million	Growth rate
Activision Blizzard	US	4.856	2%
Sony	US	4.589	−20%
Microsoft	US	4.557	−1%
Electronic Arts (EA)	US	3.956	2%
Tencent	China	3.627	**40%**
Nintendo	Japan	2.775	−27%
DeNa	Japan	1.841	7%
GREE	Japan	1.735	**36%**
Ubisoft	France	1.639	18%
Konami	Japan	1.404	−20%
Zynga	US	1.281	12%
Apple	US	1.262	**65%**
Nexon	South Korea	1.254	10%
NetEase	China	1.248	22%
Take Two Interactive	US	1.063	24%
Namco Bandai	Japan	1.021	−5%
Square Enix	Japan	878	0%
Disney	US	857	−6%
Facebook	US	810	**45%**
Capcom	Japan	780	12%

Source: Newzoo (2014). The data is based on analysis of annual and quarterly financial reports of the universe of relevant publicly listed companies. Revenues exclude hardware sales and other non-game sales where possible. Authors' emphasis.

revenues from mobile gaming[9] (Newzoo, 2012 quoted by SNJV, 2012a). In 2013, Google entered the ranking with an even higher rate: 250% (Newzoo, 2014). Zynga's position also reveals the strength of mobile and social networks. DeNa is a Japanese global leader in mobile Internet services.

High entry barriers still limit the competition in the handheld market to two big players: Nintendo, by means of the long-lasting sales success of the GameBoy, and, to a lesser extent, Sony. In the console market, led by Sony, Microsoft joins the two other giants of handheld device games. This industry is characterized by vertical integration; in particular, hardware manufacturers often also act as game publishers and have their own development studios.

Regional markets for video games: Asia rising

Developed regions such as Europe, the US and Japan were the main markets for video games until 2009: these regions accounted for over one half, or €26 billion, of the video games market (IDATE, 2011). The

EMEA,[10] once the biggest market for video games among the four major world regions, was overtaken by Asia-Pacific in 2010. The main engine of this growth is the online and mobile segment. Online gaming in the People's Republic of China represents one of the largest and fastest-growing Internet business sectors in the world (Radoff, 2009). If the US is still the leading market, the next three are located in the Asia-Pacific region: China, Japan and South Korea.[11] In 2012, Asia-Pacific accounted for 32.9% of the global market (US$22.2 billion of revenues, 298 million gamers) growing at a rate of 13%, followed by North America with 32.2% (21.8 billion, 169 million gamers) growing at a mere 1%, then Europe with 27.8% (18.8 billion, 274 million gamers) growing at 3% (Warman, 2013). 'Games' is the fastest-growing Internet category in India (McClelland, 2012).

The US market declined slightly from a peak of US$16.9 billion[12] in 2010, to US$14.8 billion in 2012 for software, and a total of US$20.77 billion in 2012 (hardware: US$4.04 billion, accessories: US$1.93 billion), and content US$14.8 billion) (ESA, 2013). The Latin American and Africa/Middle East markets are small, 5.6% (US$3.8 billion, 89 million gamers) and 1.5% (US$1 billion, 47 million gamers) respectively, and likely to remain modest even though growing fast: by 14% and 22%, respectively.

In 2009, the five main EU markets accounted for around 30% of the global market, with revenues of US$15.2 billion, but these leading markets have been losing revenues since.[13] The UK was leading with €3.79 billion in 2012[14] (Newzoo, 2013), followed by France with €3 billion in 2012 (SNJV, 2012b: €1.7 billion for software). The turnover for computer and video game software amounted to a total of €1.99 billion in Germany in 2011 (software only: BIU, 2012). In 2011, sales amounted to €980 million in Spain (software: 51%, hardware: 38%, accessories: 11%) (aDeSe, 2012), and in Italy they fell from over €1 billion in 2009 to €993 million (a 22% decrease: AESVI, 2011; Barca and Salvador, 2012). Despite this recent slowdown, the market is expected to grow, and not only in the main markets.

Market size by platform: Online and mobile games as engines of growth

There are some significant differences in the dynamics of individual segments in terms of platforms (PC video games, home consoles and handheld console games, online games and mobile games). Regions display specificities with the share of each platform.

Consoles and handheld game platforms are currently the best-known set of products in the video games industry, with console products such as the PlayStation (Sony), the Xbox (Microsoft), the Wii (Nintendo) and handheld devices such as the Nintendo DS (Dual Screen) and PlayStation Portable (PSP). Games sold for home consoles and hand-held devices still have the highest share in the total sales of video games: 49% in 2011 (IDATE, 2012: 6% for home consoles and 13% for handheld devices) but 70% in 2004 (PWC, 2009). North America remains the main market for this segment: in 2011 49% of US households owned a dedicated game console (ESA, 2012), increasing to 56% in 2012 (Nielsen, 2012). Western Europe and the Asia-Pacific regions followed respectively.

The next largest product segments are online and wireless video games,[15] reaching a 44% share (online games: 32%, mobile games: 12%) (IDATE, 2012), and characterized by double-digit growth rates for 2017 (PWC, 2013). Casual Connect predicts a 27.8% of the global games markets for mobile games in 2016, and estimated the 2013 share at 17.4% (Casual Connect, 2013). Since 2004, the online and wireless market has grown with remarkable rapidity, driven by the increase in the number of broadband subscribers, the innovation in available games, and the transition to handheld devices and the newest-generation consoles: for instance, Nintendo DS Wi-Fi Connection was launched in November 2005, and both Microsoft and Sony launched their online services for gaming consoles between late 2003 and early 2004.[16]

On mobile handsets (mobile phones) games started to appear about a decade ago (Nokia started installing Snake in 1997), and did not at first raise much interest. Another milestone was the release by Apple Inc. in 2007 of the of iPhone, which combined Apple's previous experience with the iPod with improved touchscreen technology and many conceptual and technological novelties, opening up a completely new perspective for mobile-based video gaming. Since then, increasing convergence of content and services and greater acceptance of online delivery of services have continued to develop. Tablets are bringing new opportunities as well.

Social networks such as Facebook contributed to popularizing the games on these platforms (e.g. *Farmville*), offering simple games, but based on servers allowing the kind of interaction offered by massively multiplayer online games (MMOGs[17]), fuelling audience and revenue growth in the online games segment. Social networks are providing another kind of platform, experiencing exponential growth since 2010, with US$5 billion globally in 2011 (Facebook: US$1.69 billion), and an expected US$6.2 billion in 2012 (a 30% growth) (Casual connect, 2012).

Tablets and smartphones are now being adopted as gaming devices for casual game players,[18] driving the demand for wireless games, and becoming in turn one of the most dynamic segments. Jupiter Research predicts sales for tablets of up to US$3.1 billion in 2014 (SNJV, 2012a). From a technological viewpoint, beyond this growing role of the latest portable devices, cloud computing is likely to open new avenues and strengthen the role of online distribution, growing the customer base (casual gamers). The game becomes a service supplied by leading companies such as Take Two, EA or Ubisoft. OnLive was the first company to offer such services, in June 2010, followed by Gakai. Connected TV is bringing similar opportunities (Michaud, 2011), with companies like OnLive and Playcast Media investing.

The market share of PC-based games grew steadily up to 2000. Then it started a slow but continuous decline. While PC video games accounted for 17% of the whole global video games market in 2004, by 2013 their share was expected to have dropped to around US$4 billion, or 6% of the overall video games market value. The decline of the PC video games market in the EMEA area is not yet as marked as it is in North America, although there are national differences. The PC business context reflects low entry barriers which are free from proprietary restriction and manufacturers' licensing fees, and benefit from lower development costs (no need for specific – and highly expensive – software development kits, very low costs of duplication and deployment).

Asia-Pacific is leading in online and mobile games and has been a pioneer in the field. The Asia-Pacific region is the biggest market for online and wireless video games, already accounting for 48% of the global mobile games revenues (Casual Connect, 2013). China has by far the world's largest online video game market, accounting for 35% of global spending on online video games; its share will continue to climb, according to PWC (2012).

A changing industry structure: The (changing) rules of the game

This section reviews the configuration of the video games software value network, and traces its evolution, dealing with the mutual relations between players and how they create the value chain dynamics. Figure 10.1 shows a simplified view of the value chain for video games. The product, from its creation to its consumption, goes through a series of intermediaries necessary to achieve its commercialization, each of the intermediaries exercising its specific role and aiming to optimize

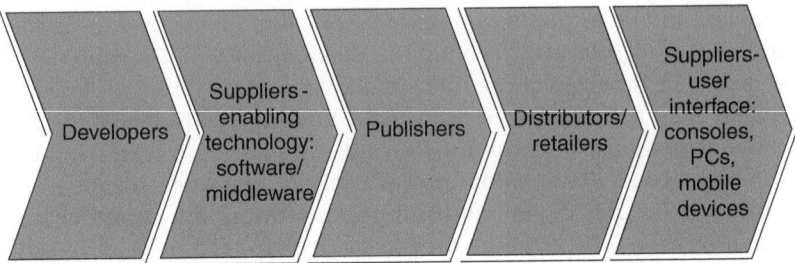

Figure 10.1 Video games traditional value chain
Source: Author elaboration on EGDF (2011).

its profit and position. Besides the significant role of manufacturers, the specificity of video games is linked to the role of developers who create and sell under licence their 'content' through the use of middleware so as to deliver software that can be published and distributed to consumers through a technological platform (Mateos-Garcia et al., 2008).

The second part sheds light on the potential transformations that this value chain might incur in the case of disruptive trends introduced with online and mobile distribution, new platforms and the changing role of the users.

Game developers

A video game developer is a company that invents and develops the necessary software to run the video game, which will be published and distributed to consumers through a technological platform (Mateos-Garcia et al., 2008). Development includes activities such as designing, prototyping, pre-producing, producing and testing games (Kerr, 2006). A video game developer may specialize, or may develop for a variety of platforms or different types of games. The game development role may be taken up either by independent third party developers or by internal teams of publishing companies (Kerr, 2006; Miles and Green, 2008).

The production of video games is characterized by the high fixed costs and low marginal costs of prototypes, as in the case of information, digital and creative content goods, due to extremely high initial financial investment to create the first 'copy'. Once it exists, additional copies can be (re)produced at almost zero cost. This need for an early investment affects the power relation in the value chain, and usually leads to the emergence of publishers for pre-financing. The heavy risk faced by independent developers involved in prototyping often forces them to look for other sources of funding, notably among venture capital funds.

Developers are usually studios, with multidisciplinary teams, as production and pre-production are complex activities requiring various players (Miles and Green, 2008). The production cost varies from some thousands of euros for simple games, to millions; and development time varies accordingly, from three to six months for mobile games to 24 months for last-generation MMOGs (Bakshi and Mateos-Garcia, 2010).

Since the segment started growing in the 1990s, a lot of companies have been acquired by international integrated publishers like Electronic Arts (EA). In the EU, a population of highly creative small development studios is found mainly in the UK, France, Germany, the Nordic countries and, to a lesser extent, in Spain. For instance, the UK has the biggest developer base in Europe, and is home to 48 of the world's top 100 development studios (Develop 100, 2010). UK has retained a large independent developer community, alongside companies owned by international publishers. However, independent companies (Indies) seem to be on the rise again in the US (GDC, 2013), a move[19] that may reflect the role of mobile platforms (including smartphones and tablets). SNJV (2012b) also stressed the role of 'garage' developers for 'original' creation. The Northern countries represent the largest 'developer' area, with 361 active companies in 2012 (Nordicgame.net, 2013) and firms like Funcom (a leading developer of MMO), DICE, CCP, Remedy, IO, Starbreeze and Rovio Mobile,[20] the Finnish firm which created the world success *Angry Birds*, aiming at a billion users.

Middleware development[21]

There are four layers of software modules. The first layer is the operating system (OS), the closest to the hardware. A second layer collects device drivers and application programming interfaces (APIs), which are tightly connected to the OS. A third layer consists of software development kits (SDKs), called 'engines', and, more generally, to the software intermediary applications commonly named middleware. The end-user applications are included in the fourth layer.

The middleware layer mainly refers to applications like engines, designed to provide higher-level applications with specific functionality. This additional layer is needed, first, to ensure the reduction in application development costs by allowing reuse of components, and, second, to improve the efficiency and effectiveness of the applications' development process, thus making it possible to develop cross-platform applications. Once a core game engine has been developed and used to power a successful game, other developers are likely to take advantage of the consolidated effectiveness of the tool to power their games.

The core game engine allows the higher-level application (the part of the game containing the content) to interact more easily with the lower layers, drivers and OS, and, as a consequence, with the hardware. The game engine is intended to be in charge of heavy and repeatedly accessed routines; for example, it deals with graphics rendering and with the 'intelligence' of the game. The first separated middleware modules appeared between the late 1980s and the early 1990s to handle the graphics in video games; further evolutionary steps led to today's highly modulized engines, integrating a wide range of tools, and the middleware environment is still changing rapidly. Successful companies are often bought by big studios or platform producers,[22] and then either integrated to work in-house or kept as dedicated satellites.

Publishers

A video games publisher is a large company with major marketing departments, which publishes video games that it either develops internally or has ordered from a video games developer. The publisher is responsible for licensing the rights and the concept on which the game is grounded, and for handling the marketing and, often, even the distribution. Publishers are often presented as the central economic actors in the video games value chain, ruling the overall organization of the market. The strong position of the publishers is due to their specific intermediary role in the value chain: they have the scale and skills to generate the relevant deal-flow, manage large budgets, develop global branding, and organize marketing and property rights. A new title was generally expected to reach break-even point in the first few months after release, when some hundreds of thousands of copies had been sold.

As a result of taking advantage of economies of scale and scope, during the 1990s, the global publishing industry consolidated around 10–20 major companies (such as EA, Nintendo, UbiSoft and Infogrames/Atari), while the 2000s saw a trend of vertical integration with developers (and distribution) (Kerr, 2006).

Publishers endeavour to reduce risks and the uncertainties of a prototype industry by adopting strategies familiar to other fields of publishing (book, films and music), creating portfolios, focusing on the most popular genres and building strong brands.

Distributors

Video games distributors usually market the games, handle the packaging and transport, organize the infrastructure for distribution and sometimes even provide user support. Together with the retailers, they cover the logistics of the chain. As large publishers are primarily interested in promoting their own games, independent game companies find small specialized distributors for their titles. Retailers are usually electronic chains, multimedia shops and specialist shops, but nowadays video games can be easily found in ordinary retail chains such as FNAC, Wal-Mart, the Metro group or Carrefour.

The distribution of revenues between the stakeholders is difficult to apprehend. According to the EU trade association of developers, EGDF (2011: 5), for boxed products the publisher will receive €26, the distributor €10 and the retailer another €10, leaving €4 out of the retail price of €50 for the developer.[23] With further digitalization and standardization, the balance of power between these actors could be affected. A growing number of new actors are therefore foreseen, which will position themselves in the video games value chain as video games go progressively online and mobile. For example, big retailers, such as Wal-Mart or FNAC, are increasingly playing the role of distributors and contacting video game publishers directly. On the other hand, the increased importance of online distributors like Amazon in many cases reduces the role of 'traditional' retailers. The same holds for social networks that act as exclusive distributors of the games, as is the case with the Zynga games on Facebook.

Online and mobile games: The coming of an era

Several trends are expected to affect the current and future dynamics of the video games software industry. For example, mobile games are challenging the dominant position of existing OS owners and are offering a new distribution channel to developers. Moreover, online games are offering users a new role, which could bypass the publishers and create different revenue streams.

Disintermediation/reintermediation

The progressive but impressively fast switch to online gaming introduced new distribution methods and started to rearrange the relative roles and interaction dynamics among the actors at the different levels in the supply chain. Logistics has lost relevance in the online games segment due to the fact that digital goods are reproduced and distributed over the network at low cost. One whole part of the former business – manufacturing boxes, printing electronic support (disks, etc.), the organization and the infrastructure of distribution, retail sales, inventory and returns – has disappeared. Online digital distribution has affected the value chain structure, resulting in a convergence of the roles of the distributor and of the retailer under the range of activities of the publisher.

The part of the core business involving publishers, distributors and retailers has basically disappeared, as there is no longer any need to duplicate physical products, because games can be distributed over the network. The publisher, in many cases, directly distributes games, without the need for a distributor to act as intermediary between the publisher and the retailer: 'disintermediation' is taking place, cutting out the role of the distributor. Publishers can also opt to distribute games through Internet service providers (ISPs). ISPs act as content aggregators and provide portals for game distribution which allow easier promotion and localization of new games by users; at the same time they attract advertising, which brings an added source to the mixed revenue models. The increasing importance of ISPs has triggered a process of 'reintermediation': ISPs are taking on the role previously played by distributors.

In past years, the distribution of online games has been progressively concentrated on some Internet portals serving the PC-based side (including, among many others, Valve's Steam Service and Manifesto Games), and on a few, very powerful, network platforms for console games, each controlled by the console's hardware provider.

Independent application stores are growing rapidly, providing PC users with access to online games together with the possibility to download not only games but also movies, music and additional content. In the same way, console-oriented gateways are also increasing their importance and audience by differentiating the type of content and services made accessible to users. Having started as gateways for accessing video games, and related contents and communities, they are more and more offering different kinds of digital contents and resources.

These changes to the value chain of online video games, as compared with that of 'traditional' video games, affect not only the interactions between the actors in the value creation process, but also the type and number of actors involved. Different types of games are affected to different extents. Though the characteristics of browser-based games have heavily reduced the need for distributors and retailers for logistic support, portals and dedicated sites with adequate visibility are required. In some cases, developers can afford to publish their browser-based games directly, shortcutting the next stages along the value chain. With direct sales a developer will receive the whole €5 paid by the consumer, instead of the €4 he was getting through the traditional value chain (out of €50 by the consumer). This is not necessarily true for client-based online games, particularly the complex and expensive games, which in many cases still rely on the more traditional chain to reach consumers.

With emerging opportunities, new companies might become essential intermediaries in the video games value chain, such as online portals (Google, Yahoo, pogo.com), ISPs, social networks (Facebook, MySpace) or even telecom operators (Orange, Telefonica, Vodafone) or handset equipment manufacturers companies (e.g. Apple, Nokia).

Innovative business models

Sources of revenues and business models are bound to change, and to keep evolving at the same pace as the underlying products, or services. The alternative business models which users face when entering the world of online games are actually rather different from those they were used to; the business models are under (re)construction (see Figure 8.1, Chapter 8). However, though consultancies are predicting a fast growth of digital sales, triggering new streams of revenues, the core of the revenues was still coming from the physical world in 2011: in the UK (IPSOS Media, 2012) packaged products still accounted for 78% of the sales, online 15%, and mobile 7%; in the US (ESA, 2012) 69% of the sales were in the physical format and 31% digital.

Online and mobile games are characterized by two major business models: pay (subscription usually the case for MMOGs) and freemium or free-to-play (F2P). The F2P model is built on economies of scale: Bigpoint (Roth, 2010), a German video games company, distributes free browser games to its customer base of 110 million users (as of March 2010), of whom 10% will buy some items for a small amount. It should be stressed that this model is introducing games as a service. Users are more confident and more willing to pay small sums for digital items offered to enhance their gaming experience, once they already know the game itself and enjoy playing it.

Advertising is a source of revenues, but its formats are changing to become more compatible with the new distribution approaches (in-game advertising, portal advertising, etc.). Virtual items and game extension sales are expected to account for the biggest revenue share in a market ruled by micro-transactions. The emerging revenue stream from selling virtual goods online, an innovation born in Asia with leading companies like Tencent for social networking and online gaming (SNOW: Wi, 2009; In-Stat, 2010a, b), is attracting a lot of attention in the online video games industry. The virtual items model allows gamers to buy individual digital components such as virtual currency (e.g. 'zcoins' from Zynga), items, characters and any in-game good. Basically, every item could be sold as a virtual item. The purchase of virtual items is generally associated with games providing persistent worlds and character-building capabilities; therefore MMOGs are the best category to exploit this monetization method. This model does not suit those MMOGs that still ask users to pay monthly fees, but, rather, those that allow free access (lite MMOGs).

The flexibility of this model is bound to be exploited by creative producers and publishers. Publishers are motivated to adopt the virtual items model by the huge difference in sales life span between virtual items and the games themselves. Virtual items have a much longer life in terms of sales, a major advantage for the seller. A single virtual item product could be sold online for years, while the 'productive' life of a standard game is some (or, more often, only a few) months.

Conclusion

Consumer behaviour has evolved over the past few years and has allowed the viral diffusion of online gaming to take place at an unexpected pace. Demand has been a driving force, pushing all multimedia content toward convergence. As noted above, video games process the data entered by players to explore the 'plot', this constitutes a major difference from other existing media like books or films. The latter are based on a 'willing suspension of disbelief' to follow the narrative; on the contrary, video games are based on the interaction, not the narrative. Such an evolution can pave the way for new content models such as immersive films/games (see Chapter 4).

The increasingly active role of users has been sustained by the interactive and social nature of the online gaming experience. User engagement has been largely driven by the social aspects of interaction in multiplayer games, where communities of users play a big role and communications among them are mandatory. This is seen as a first step for users toward interaction with the game itself, to the creation of content. Events in a game's virtual world are influenced instantaneously by each player's actions, and the game itself never stops, but is continuously changed by users' actions. Nevertheless, this trend could take time to establish itself, and one should be cautious about predicting the different paths it could follow and its potential impact on industry.

Online and wireless video games are expected to increase their importance in the video games market. Increased consumer awareness, growing Internet broadband penetration in households, and increased content development for online-specific and mobile-specific games sustained by exploitation of new technology are expected to be among the elements that will allow the revenue from the online and wireless gaming market to continue to grow. Smartphones and tablets are adding new screens to play and opening new opportunities.

The proliferation of devices is leading to an era of 'ubiquitous games'. The demand from users for a similar gaming experience will increase the need for developers and publishers to adopt a multiplatform strategy. Sony has already announced that it will allow users of its forthcoming PlayStation 4 to use iPhones, iPads or Android-based smartphones and tablets as a second screen for the games console.

Online games play a major role in the digital content convergence process. This phenomenon is affecting not only the video game industry, but also the movie, video, music and mobile communication industries and the whole publishing sector in general. The role of this industry is now spreading out from the media sector. Technology pioneered by games is now being put to use in various fields (*Economist*, 2011). Such services, mainly based on software development, are progressively invading other areas in the sector, such as casual games, advergames[24] or edutainment,[25] multiplying the supply-side actors. Evolving from mere entertainment into virtual worlds, the online game segment is providing a marketplace for online economic activities (Wi, 2009).

Notes

1. Although more and more studies are trying to calculate the dimensions of the game industry, the lack of official data clearly constitutes a constraint to the appraisal of its potentials and to the understanding of its dynamics. The video games industry is not accurately represented in official statistics, where it is categorized under software and computer programming (OECD, 2009) rather than under media, although having many activities in common with television and film production. Measuring and monitoring the evolution of the online (De Prato et al., 2012) and mobile (Feijoo and Gomez-Barroso, 2012) games segments is even less straightforward, due to the characteristics of the product itself and to the consequent lack of basic indicators. See Box 10.1.
2. The survey defines a gamer as anyone who has played a game on any of the listed devices and formats in the past 12 months.
3. *The Economist* (2011) traced the move from niche to mainstream back to the launch of the Sony PlayStation console on December 3, 1994.
4. Categorized under ISIC rev 4: 'The production (goods and services) of a candidate industry must primarily be intended to inform, educate and/or entertain humans through mass communication media. These industries are engaged in the production, publishing and/or the distribution of content

(information, cultural and entertainment products), where content corresponds to an organized message intended for human beings' (OECD, 2009).

5. Most of the media trade associations are relying on GfK, a German marketing institute with worldwide operations. See company website: http://www.gfk.com/Pages/default.aspx

6. There is ongoing debate over whether video games should be classified as a software or a cultural product; trade associations hold different views about this, see EGDF (http://www.egdf.eu) and ISFE (http://www.isfe-eu.org).

7. Top game publishers 2008, 2009: Nintendo, EA and Activision ranked 1, 2, and 3 in these two years.

8. *Source:*   http://www.tencent.com/en-us/content/at/2012/attachments/20120703.pdf.

9. Based on the revenues from the 200 most popular games in the iPad, iPhone/iPod App Store and Google PlayStore.

10. Europe–Middle East–Africa.

11. In this case public policies played a role after the start of the market (Wi, 2009; Simon, 2012).

12. Total consumer spend.

13. The Swedish market declined by 18.9% in 2011 (AESVI, 2011).

14. The UK trade association (UKIE, 2012) reported revenues for 2010, from the sale of all entertainment software, console hardware and console/PC gaming accessories, of £2.875 billion.

15. These kinds of games do not have the same technological features and are not in the same segment; however, it is easier to present them together as they differ from all former platforms.

16. It must be taken into account that figures on online games only refer to subscription fees, while retail purchases of games are accounted for in the relevant categories: PC, console or handheld.

17. Online video games can be divided into two main subcategories: single-user games and multiplayer games. The former are generally available as browser-based games (BBGs), not requiring additional software and offering cheap and easy 'casual' entertainment to the widest variety of users of basically all ages. Multiplayer games are instead often played in the form of 'client-based games', where the performance and elaborating power of the client machine are relevant and possibly installation of some kind of software program or engine is required. The availability of faster broadband and computing resources enabled massive interaction of a huge number of users: MMOGs are the most sophisticated video games, as interaction between many independent players adds a level of complexity. Different subclasses of MMOGs have been identified, according to their genre. *Source:* De Prato et al. (2010).

18. Casual games: easy-to-use games (to learn, to access and to play) spanning all genres.

19. Only 10% of the companies surveyed by GDC were still primarily publisher-funded.

20. The games have 263 million monthly active users as of December 2012, and its YouTube channel, which 'houses dozens of custom animations', has received more than one billion views.

21. This section draws on De Prato et al. (2010) and De Prato (2012b).

22. For a geographical distribution of firms, see GameMiddleWare.Org (2009), last consulted March 2013.
23. Wi (2009: 8): in the case of an offline game whose retail price is US$58, the retailer will keep US$18, the wholesaler US$10, and production cost will require another US$10, which leaves a profit of US$20 for the developer. Genvo and Solinski (2010) are offering the following break-up of a €55 euro retail price: game designer 14%, editor 29%, console manufacturer 22%, retail outlet 35%.
24. Advergames: a subset of the so-called serious games (i.e. allowing other uses than entertainment), sponsored and distributed for free to advertise a product or an organization.
25. Edutainment: games with educational outcomes targeted at specific groups of learners.

Conclusion

Giuditta De Prato, Esteve Sanz and Jean Paul Simon

This book has offered a journey through the evolving value networks of the different industries, pointing to the fast-changing relationships within these different elements of the value networks, following the way they interact in a mostly non-linear fashion. It explored the ways in which the different registers and technical layers (technological infrastructures, distribution and intermediation, and content) are being (re)articulated within a broader context. Each segment was born and grew with a specific chain of actors around specific technologies. Digitization brings a novel way to disrupt/modify and unify the entire value chain, from creation/production to consumption.

The economic dynamics at work appears to be designing a multicentre world, organized around numerous gravity centres (terminal, networks, contents and intermediation, among others) of its new ecosystem; an increasingly digital world will no longer be mainly organized around a single dominant player, but other forms of domination are emerging. The sector is giving birth to an array of strategies and bets on the evolution of the market, contributing to a multiplication of competing business models based on different, often clashing, business cultures.

The chapters have shown, globally and on a case-by-case basis, how traditional channels of communication and distribution have been supplemented by new opportunities. In turn, this has enabled producers to go beyond the physical and geographical constraints associated with the concept of the market and to serve a larger customer base at lower cost. The removal of geographical and physical constraints has opened up possibilities for development of economic activity in areas that would otherwise be deemed unfavourable due to low levels of demand or poor infrastructure. The evolution of digital media has also had a major influence on consumers. The increased and more diverse supply offers a greater variety of products and services at lower prices. Furthermore, it opens up possibilities of participation in all areas, including distribution and production (see the chapters on music, TV and video games).

The sectors are in transition, the changes are still going on, and changes of magnitude take some time to unfold. This concluding chapter sums up some of the major trends. The first section describes the shift of power that is taking place between creation and distribution. The second section concentrates on the new market structure and the emerging business models based upon new streams of revenues. It shows the delicate balance to be achieved between new, but uncertain, streams of revenues and legacy streams which are often declining. The third section notes the benefits brought to consumers and their progressive empowerment, but also the set of concerns that the move toward a five-screens world is bringing. The fourth section assesses the role of public intervention beyond the mere correction of imperfect markets and market failures, an even more complex task in a digital world. The sixth section revisits the trend toward globalization, noting the continuing dominance of US companies in some global markets, like the audiovisual (film, TV) and music industry; the strong role of European firms in others (book publishing); and the growing role of Asia. The chapter ends with more questions on the future of the media, but nevertheless indicates some possible ways forward.

The weight of the downstream: Competing business models, clashes of culture

Within the global ecosystem, the relative economic size of the media and content industries, although evolving over time, remains small compared with their industrial IT counterpart, the legacy telecom players (network operation and service, equipment) and the new players from the IT world (intermediation and IT services and software). This distribution of economic weight is not a new phenomenon (typically, telecom revenues are of another order of magnitude than audiovisual revenues). What is new, however, is the progressive intermingling of sectors that were previously separate. Additionally, within this ecosystem, each segment is now competing with all the others ('freewheeling' segments) for the final consumers (Chapter 3). Each segment now interacts vertically and horizontally with the others, pushing its own business model instead of working under the former linear chain of relationships that was once dominated by the publishing segment, thereby increasing the competition to become the primary gateway for content navigation and provision.

There are very different types of firms in this ecosystem, with varying performance: highly profitable IT companies, network providers with declining revenues, and media companies with often rather tight margins (though some are also highly profitable). This adds another clash of cultures: high-tech companies value the technical side and process over whatever content they may offer. The only notable exception is the video games industry, a fast-growing segment of the media and content industries that combines both kinds of creativity, bridging the two worlds.

In the 'old' world, each sector focused on its core business, managing its own assets accordingly. Typically, telecom providers provided services to all segments (residential and business), and media companies bought the services they needed to reach their final customers downstream and upstream (some production services, agents, wholesaling, logistics, transmission/distribution, retail). The new players act as disintermediation agents, and provide (or will provide) content aggregation and distribution or advertising management, as well as additional services. These services may compete with other services provided by legacy players to bring in the revenues used to subsidize the production of contents (for example, classified ads in newspapers).

On a global scale, the balance of power has shifted toward the downstream, away from the upstream, or from the 'production' side of the media toward the distribution side. In other words, there has been a collision between the economics of production of cultural goods and prototypes and the economics of distribution of digital goods and services. Downstream players not only circumvent the legacy players, managing direct relationships with the customers, but they introduce new skills to that end (data management) and benefit from major economies of scale and scope. Legacy players mostly lack these skills.

A greater control of the downstream is a feature of more mature markets, where marketing/distribution is taking backward control of production (engineers, artists). The emergence and domination of large retailers such as Carrefour since the late 1960s, and more recently the Wal-Mart phenomenon, serve as illustrations. Large retailers tend to impose their own conditions on their suppliers.

The new distributors have seen their sales exploding. Amazon, one of the fastest-growing IT companies since its foundation in 1995, had net sales of US$61 billion in 2012 (Amazon, 2013: 17), up from US$19 billion in 2008, while the total publishers' revenue from sales of books in the EU for that same year was around €22 billion (Chapter 1). Apple had net sales of US$156.5 billion (Apple, 2013c: 24), up from US$37 billion in 2008. Annual revenues for Universal Music Group, the largest music label, reached a mere €4.4 billion in 2010.

However, digitization is not new to any of the subsectors. They all underwent a transformation of their production processes (digital recording, computerized editing of films, desktop publishing) during a first phase of digitization, not to mention the transformation due to the introduction and development of computers within the firms (business processes). This phase varied in scope and scale across sectors; it was implemented with different agendas but apparently remained mostly upstream. The first digital innovations of the 1980s and 1990s did not have a disruptive character; they were sustaining innovations. This phase did not extend to distribution, and therefore did not directly affect customers and the management of the commercial relationship with them.

With digital goods, the entire value chain can be digitized. The value chain becomes homogeneous, with no physical disruption due to production, storage and distribution of goods. Online distribution, in a digital world characterized by huge economies of scale and scope and tremendous declines in cost, further strengthens the position of IT players, including the social networks. This evolution is ongoing within the cloud: for instance, server-based distribution of video services reduces the cost of making additional programmes available to customers, as compared with traditional multichannel video programming distribution (cable, satellite), because of lower storage costs.

It is often argued that this slow adoption of digitalization, common to all sectors, stemmed from concerns that the new products (which had insignificant revenues) would cannibalize existing products. However, the example of the introduction of videotape (to be replaced later by DVD) in the 1980s clearly proves this fear to be unfounded. DVDs now provide the main source of revenues, even though this took some time to stabilize. Nevertheless, legacy companies have to find ways to balance their vested interests and existing investments with their new investments. Companies are uncertain about how the new markets will develop, and the opportunities may not appear too financially attractive, as they have to face increased competition and lower margins, or to fund several distribution channels at the same time (newspaper: print and digital), unless companies manage to fully benefit from joint and common costs.

Changing market structures, new streams of revenues and innovative business models

The oligopolistic and vertically integrated market structure of the media industry is being challenged. This market structure allowed publishers not only to maintain a major influence on the distribution and retail segments, but also to manage their customer base as a major asset. They could sell additional services or products: for instance, newspapers could use their data bases for direct and indirect marketing. It also offered better protection of other assets, such as copyrighted content.

The world of edited media is moving toward another world of aggregation, keeping some dimensions of the earlier world(s), such as bundling/editing, but also adding others. In an online world, bundles increasingly include numerous services, bringing secondary and additional revenues. Some will be provided by new entrants and suppliers. App stores are offering brokerage services and indirect marketing (as newspapers used to do). New entrants such as telcos can offer billing services. Other services will be introduced by legacy players: for instance, the video games industry will sell virtual items such as avatars and others. Apps are companion services on BskyB's Sky Player. New players have appeared, such as Spotify, DailyMotion, Last.fm and Netflix, and new services and digital platforms have been launched by legacy players (ePresse, Kioskoymas, etc.).

During the first phases of online distribution, the 'natural' tendency was to duplicate the legacy business models from the analogue/physical world to the digital world. Even in the case of the video games industry, video games publishers tried to adapt the 'old' video games industry business models to their online and mobile distribution. Traditional media companies have been slow to adopt new business models, especially during the initial phase (Chapter 1). They have, therefore, found themselves under pressure from new entrants from other sectors or 'pure players' (YouTube, Netflix, Hulu).

The evolving business models are outputs of two simultaneous processes: the overall trend of transformation of digital products into services, and the processes of 'disintermediation' and 'reintermediation'. This two-pronged process increases the complexity of business models, bringing some to an end and opening up new ones. Online distribution offers a new channel for distribution, in much the same way as the cinema and broadcasting industries have benefited from each technological wave (cable, pay TV, DBS, home video and now the Internet), as illustrated by the data on the US market over 40 years. Studios are benefiting from online distribution, with increased margins compared with physical distribution.

As a result of disintermediation, direct sales from the producer/creator/developer have become possible, such as, for example, in the cases of video games and the film industry already mentioned. This opens up a window of opportunity for studios to directly distribute their contents on the market. Bloggers can find various ways to monetize (or not) their content. However, direct provision (DIY; see Chapter 8), though beneficial to some, may not be the ultimate solution for all. Smaller companies, or companies without strong brand names, are likely to find their marketing costs going up under increased competition.

However, 'reintermediation' through the new gatekeepers often means working under the conditions they impose on legacy players (e.g. under the agency model as offered by Apple, or wholesaling in the case of Amazon). Selling content wholesale, rather than distributing it directly to customers, creates tensions for the content industries no longer controlling retail. It is all the more uncertain as new entrants can also offer content, pushing their own product or service first, and even selling existing contents at a loss, as Amazon did with books, thereby reducing publishers' already narrow margins. Even though content is clearly a strategic asset for new entrants, it does not provide the bulk of their revenues. Apple's revenue from 'net sales of other music related products and services' accounted for a mere 6% of the company's 2011 net sales (FCC, 2012). For most of these players, content is just another important application within a more global strategy. These companies are introducing new forms of bundling that lead to the unbundling of legacy subsidies. For instance, the newspaper industry subsidized quality news with local news, classified ads and advertising. The new players are removing these funding sources.

Digital revenues do not appear to compensate for lost physical sales. Besides, net economic gains resulting from digitization, even if difficult to assess properly (Katz, 2012), do not translate into gain or improvements for every player, as the growth of online activity generates economic transfers from one set of players to another set of players: buying books and music online, as shown in chapters 5 and 7, can bring losses to part of the existing value chain, retailers (bookshops and music shops) in this case, even if the use of new devices like tablets has net positive effects on consumption (consumer surplus: Chapter 3). Some new streams of revenues are emerging, while former ones are resurfacing. Music is a typical case (Cameron and Bazelon, 2011) of an historical upturn whereby revenues are coming from performances[1] and related rights rather than from royalties redistributed by music companies. Online distribution of physical products is not the main distribution channel. Retailers (small and large) remain the main channels, typically for books.

Two-sided markets bring more flexibility. One can, for instance, contrast the music market (one-sided market) and the broadcasting market (two-sided market). However, what (still) works properly in the case of the broadcasting market does not seem to operate any more in the newspaper market. Previous ways of subsidizing edited news (the most expensive to produce) seem to have broken down, as customers do not appear to value it in the same way as they used to. Besides, the network effects brought by two-sided markets are highly beneficial for high-quality products with strong brands like the *NY Times*, but not for lower-quality products such as many of the US local newspapers. The online availability of a strong brand may be devastating for local online papers.

Two-sided markets allow very aggressive pricing strategies. For instance, games console manufacturers sell their consoles at a negative margin, anticipating the increased sales of games and other services, shifting the value toward the content they produce and not toward the device. This differs again from one-sided markets such as books and music, where, as mentioned, manufacturers and distributors (Apple, Amazon) are not betting on increased sales of content.

The other side of the equation to cope with declining revenues is the cost structure. Though the cost structure is obviously changing, the impact of the changes is not clear. Some costs disappear, some costs remain unaffected (creation/development, editorial process, marketing and sales), while others are shifted and new costs appear. Most of the involved legacy industries will argue that the savings are not big enough to drive prices significantly down, and that the bulk of the remaining costs, such as creation/development and the editorial process, remain important. Indeed, in the film sector, mainstream production costs are going up. Marketing expenses in a highly competitive environment of diversified sales channels are bound to increase. These industries are prototypes industries with fixed costs (from modest to very high), using over-production (see chapters 3 and 8) as a way to deal with uncertainty. The main gains (cost efficiency, flexibility and enhanced quality) come from some elements of the production function (with sector-specific variations) and, above all, from the distribution side, with tremendous decreases in the price of media distribution and information.

The rise of prosumerism: Consumers on steroids?

The increase of value brought by digitization seems to benefit more digital consumers. New forms of interpersonal communication (instant messaging, chatting, etc.) are emerging, and new kinds of content are being added to or are enriching legacy content. At the 'age of access'[2] (Rifkin, 2000), the status of ownership of a media product has been transformed toward the management of access rather than the ownership of the physical product. New ways of sharing are also emerging with social networks. New cross-media products and services, with numerous combinations, have become possible and enriched user experience (immersive media). Consumer consumption has a wider scope with the exponential growth of available content and access capacities.

Consumers are being empowered to interact with content in new ways: they can, for example, produce content (user-generated contents). This blurs the borders between professionals and amateurs in a new digital environment where the respective roles of producers and consumers tend to overlap, at least to some extent (co-creation, co-funding, 'crowdsourcing').

Besides, consumers are changing their patterns of consumption. Consumers are moving away from the physical product to its digital version, as they can now access the product as a service anywhere, anytime. The huge memory of portable devices (mobile, USB key, hard disk) and new connectivity and storage opportunities (cloud) enable consumers to plug into their 'playlist' wherever they go (at home, at work, travelling, etc.). As we move toward a five-screen world, screen-based media interactions become prevalent, leaving less and less room for non-screen-based interactions (radio, newspaper, magazines). This proliferation of devices generates more digital omnivores, but consumers with more choice may turn toward other sources than legacy players. Consumers are seeking and accessing customized items rather than a legacy bundle: an article rather than a newspaper, a tune rather than a DVD, a film rather than a cable network, catch-up TV rather than linear TV. However, brands matter, and legacy players remain popular (Chapter 1), at least for digital news.

At the same time, digital consumption offers a unique opportunity to observe, control and even capture consumers. It is a major asset for those companies that have direct access to the final consumer. It is also the object of considerable controversy as regards the legitimate use of automatically collected data and its exploitation, raising issues of privacy and data protection. Consumers may be confused and have concerns about several other aspects, from interoperability to legal functionalities. Therefore, this context of multidimensional demand, empowerment and enhanced consumer welfare (diversity, choice, pricing, etc.) is counterbalanced by consumer data collection, profiling and control. Future patterns of behaviour remain uncertain, and often customers' expectations (in terms of willingness to pay, tastes, ownership, privacy or data protection, for instance) may be at odds with those of the industry. So far, the industry has not found out how to monetize this new wave of consumption.

Brushing up public intervention?

Public intervention and policies are an historical feature of the media and entertainment industries (Chapter 4), the production of these merit goods being considered to generate further externalities for society at large (cultural, societal, etc.). An array of policies flourished to achieve various policy goals. The digital shift opens up new questions about such policies, about novel ways to implement them, and about their effectiveness in a digital world. At the same time, it creates space for policies which enable the transition toward these digital media world(s). The right policy balance between conflicting goals is difficult to achieve without opting for short-run benefits for consumers or propping up legacy players. The pending question is: do these new forms of distribution contribute to increased media production, more diversity and enhanced consumer and producer surplus? Extending public intervention beyond the mere correction of imperfect markets and market failures is a complex task.

Therefore, before considering any such intervention, a careful analysis of these digital markets is required. In a properly functioning market, the production of such goods should eventually find adequate financial resources. As noted, the debate on the funding of production or on cultural diversity is often confused and confusing, and plagued by entrenched positions. Measures to support the legacy players are often implemented through a tax levied (typically hardware-based levies) on some segments of the industry (the growing segment) to fund another one (a declining or more troubled segment), an approach likely to be distortive with new markets. The outputs of such measures remain difficult to assess properly: the EU copyright levies are still debated.

Besides, industrial policies meant to prop up legacy players have not had an impressive track record. The fixed price policy for books is allegedly considered to be a success for maintaining the network of retailers in the countries where it was implemented. Structural factors like the dominance of channels of distribution cannot be overlooked (bookshops in France or Germany and Spain). It does not follow that policies designed for the physical world will be effective in the digital world, as was been assumed when the same policies were designed for e-books. Distribution in the digital world is very different from physical distribution; these supply-side policies may reach their limits. In an emerging market, it would be unwise to freeze the market. When setting policies outside market mechanisms, policy makers should clearly identify market deficiencies first of all, and then select adequate remedies on a case-by-case basis, which is the standard position of competition authorities.

Global/multidomestic/local

The trend toward globalization has been going on for quite some time, and not only in digital markets. In some global markets, like the audiovisual (film, TV) and music industry, US companies dominate. Asia is now going forward with digital media (online games). In the publishing industries, however, EU legacy players have achieved a stronger position than US companies, with a small number of very large world leaders (Bertelsmann, Hachette, Pearson, Wolters Kluwer).

When the EU and US markets are compared, the former are fragmented, with language, culture, business practices and scattered rights acting as barriers to trade. Distance (cultural, geographical) and language still play a major role in a globalized world. Various studies have underlined the fact that there is low demand in national markets in the EU for TV or video originating from Member States (EC, 2011d, Enders, 2012, Plum, 2012). The proportion of European TV fiction broadcast by European TV channels was nearly 40%, and for films the single European market seems to work best for European subsidiaries of US firms. There is no single market as such, because either US or national films have the largest share of domestic markets: 'the common European film market remains Hollywood-oriented' (DeVinck et al., 2012). Most national films and TV series do not cross borders. By the same token, local music has an important share in each market, but does not cross borders either. Therefore, firms develop mixed strategies to suit domestic markets based on their local knowledge: for example, they use territorial rights, reformat content according to local conditions (DeVinck et al., 2012; Sanz, 2012) and set up local storefronts.

The cost savings enabled by digitization for distribution also seem to favour US companies on the content side, allowing Hollywood, for instance, to strengthen its economies of scale and blockbuster strategies. The same holds for the distribution side: digitization allows companies like Amazon to dominate in some segments, and raises concerns that this domination could be extended to other segments (for instance, the book industry in the EU).

The future of the media

With the digital shift, the media and content industries are facing the competing activities of an array of new entrants. They have lost much of their control over distribution and the final consumer. However, monetizing consumption and enabling content creation may call for collaborative schemes among all industrial players to define new business models and pricing, as well as to achieve a fair redistribution of revenues among all.

From an industrial viewpoint, there are limits to overlapping between different and heterogeneous activities, especially in terms of effectively integrating their management. We noted the zigs and the zags of telecom operators in the media sector. The new IT leaders may encounter similar issues. The demerging of the pioneer of convergence, AOL–Time Warner, tells a similar story of a lack of synergies. Stable relationships within a given 'world' or ecosystem are vital for the system to function well. There is a need to create a network of cooperation between the different players, to innovate to meet customers' requirements. New forms of 'coopetition' are likely to emerge between vertical ecosystems. Some partnerships are already being drafted: Disney–Netflix, Hachette–Google, *Wall Street Journal*–Facebook, and Yahoo–ABC. More will follow. Policy makers can help as brokers to facilitate both cooperation and fair competition.

Disruption takes place on the basis of some underlying continuity. However, it is always highly problematic to figure out the exact form of the continuity. The drastic transformations we have reviewed throughout this book are also somehow deeply rooted in other processes and part of an ever-evolving cultural process. Both are difficult to track, and changes of magnitude take some time to unfold.

Notes

1. In 2007, Madonna left Warner Music to sign a so-called '360 degree' deal with the live entertainment company Live Nation, sharing revenues from music sales, performances, merchandise and the right to her name (Cameron and Bazelon, 2011: 13).
2. According to Rifkin: 'In the new era, markets are making way for networks, and ownership is steadily being replaced by access... The exchange of property between buyers and sellers—the most important feature of the modern market system—gives way to access between servers and clients operating in a network relationship' (Rifkin, 2001).

References

The references are divided into two sections. Section 1 introduces the general references. Section 2 covers the specific literature devoted to the case studies; it also includes references to the case studies stemming from other chapters.

Section 1: General

Abbot, M. (2012), 'The Top 20 Global Operator Groups by Mobile Connections Q2 2012'. Available at: http://www.mobileworldlive.com/the-top-20-global-operator-groups-by-mobile-connections-q2-2012.

Ala-Mutka, K., (2008), 'Social Computing: Study on the Use and Impacts of Collaborative Content, IPTS', Available at: http://ipts.jrc.ec.europa.eu/publications/pub.cfm?id=1885

Amazon (2013), 'Annual Report 2012'. Available at: http://phx.corporate-ir.net/phoenix.zhtml?c=97664&p=irol-proxy.

Andersen, J. A. Danish Business Authority (2012), 'Presentation at the IIC Telecoms and Media Forum 2012'. Available at: http://www.iicom.org.

Andersen, J. A. Danish Business Authority (2013), 'Presentation at the EuroCPR 2013', Brussels, March. Available at: www.EuroCPR.org.

Apple (2013c), 'Annual Report 2012'. Available at: http://files.shareholder.com/downloads/AAPL/2471446692x0xS1193125-12-444068/320193/filing.pdf.

Appnation (2013), 'State of the App Economy Report'. Available at: http://appnationconference.com/main/research/

App Promo (2012), 'Survey: Developers Struggling to Sustain Business'. Available at: http://www.mobilebusinessbriefing.com/articles/survey-developers-struggling-to-sustain-business/23750?elq=59336ad8c9dc4c11851a1db913e79e19.

Arlandis, A. and Ciriani, S. (2010), 'How Firms Interact and Perform in the ICT Ecosystem?' *Communications & Strategies*, no. 79, pp. 121–141.

ATKearney, (2010), 'The Economics of the Internet', *The Vodafone Policy Paper Series*, no. 11, April 2010. Available at: http://www.vodafone.com/content/dam/vodafone/about/public_policy/policy_papers/public_policy_series_11.pdf

ATKearney, (2011), *A Viable Future Model for the Internet. Investment, Innovation and more Efficient Use of the Internet for the Benefit of all Sectors of the Value Chain*. Available at: http://www.atkearney.com/images/global/pdf/Viable_Future_Model_for_Internet.pdf

Auray, N. and Moreau, F. (Eds) (2012), *Industries culturelles et Internet. Les nouveaux instruments de la notoriété, Réseaux*, Vol. 5, no. 175, Paris, La Découverte.

Barnier, M. (2012), 'L'Europe au diapason des attentes des utilisateurs et des créateurs: pour un pacte numérique'. Available at: http://letsgoconnected.eu/files/SPEECH-12-354_FR_Michel_Barnier.pdf.

Becker, H. S. (1982), *Art Worlds*, Berkeley and Los Angeles, University of California Press.

Beckett, C. (2010), 'The Value of Networked Journalism', *Polis*, LES, p. 16. June 2010.

Benhamou, F. and Farchy, J. (2009), *Droit d'auteur et copyright*, Paris: La Découverte.

Benhamou, F. and Sagot-Duvauroux, D. (2007), *Économies des droits d'auteur* : *Synthèse V.* [CE 2007–8, décembre 2007], Paris: Ministry of Culture. Available at: http://www.culturecommunication.gouv.fr/Politiques-ministerie lles/Etudes-et-statistiques/Les-publications/Culture-etudes/V.-Economies-des-droits-d-auteur-Synthese-CE-2007-8-decembre-2007.

Benkler, Y. (2006), *The Wealth of Networks. How Social Production Transforms Markets and Freedom*, Yale: Yale University Press.

Benkler, Y. (2011), *The Penguin and the Leviathan: How Cooperation Triumphs over Self-Interest*, New York: Random House.

Biggam, R. (2011), 'Presentation at the ACT Conference', Brussels, November 9, 2011. Available at: www.act.be.

Bonneau,V. (2010), 'Internet Traffic and Economics', Presentation at the IDATE Digiworld Summit, Montpellier. Available at: www.idate.org.

Booz & Co. (2012), *The 2012 Value Shift Index. Change and Growth in the TMT Industries.* Available at: http://www.booz.com/media/file/BoozCo_The-2012-Value-Shift-Index.pdf.

Booz & Co. (2011a), *Value Shifts in the Telecom, Media and Technology Industries.* Available at: http://www.booz.com/media/file/BoozCo_The-2011-Value-Shift-Index.pdf.

Booz & Co. (2011b), *The Next Wave of Digitization Setting Your Direction, Building Your Capabilities.* Available at: http://www.booz.com/media/uploads/BoozCo-Next-Wave-of-Digitization.pdf.

Boston Consulting Group (BCG) (2011), 'The New Rules of Openness', *Liberty Global Policy Series*, January 2011. Available at: http://www.lgi.com/PDF/public-policy/New-Rules-of-Openness.pdf.

Bounie, D. and Bourreau, M. (2008), 'Les marchés à deux versants dans les médias', in Xavier Greffe and Nathalie Sonnac (Eds), *Culture Web*, Paris: Dalloz, Chapter 26, pp. 477–491.

Bourreau, M. and Davidovici-Nora, M. (2012), 'Les marchés à deux versants dans l'industrie des jeux vidéo', in Simon, J. P. and Zabban, V. (Eds), *Les formes ludiques du numérique. Marchés et pratiques du jeu vidéo, Réseaux*, Vol. 30, no. 173–174, Paris: La Découverte, pp. 97–135.

Bughin, J. (2010), 'TMT in Mutation', *Essays in Digital Transformation*, Volume 2, December 2010, McKinsey.

Bundesverband Deutscher Zeitungsverleger e.V. (BDZV) (2013), ,Verleger begrüßen Bundestagsbeschluss zum Leistungsschutzrecht'. Available at: http://www.bdzv.de/aktuell/pressemitteilungen/artikel/detail/verleger_begruessen_bundestagsbeschluss_zum_leistungsschutzrecht/.

Busson, A. and Evrard, Y. (2013), *Les Industries culturelles et créatives. Economie et stratégie*, Paris: Vuibert.

Busson, A. and Landau, O. (2011), 'La transformation de la chaîne de la valeur de l'audiovisuel', Presentation at the Médias 011 : Y a-t-il une Richesse des Réseaux? Aix Marseille University conference, December 2011.

Busson, A. and Pham. P. (2010), 'The French Media to the Year', *HEC-UDECAM*. Available at: http://www.udecam.fr.

Caillaud, B. and Jullien, B. (2003), 'Chicken & Egg: Competition among Intermediation Service Providers', *Rand Journal of Economics*, Vol. 34, pp. 309–328.

Cameron, L. and Bazelon, C. (2011), 'The Impact of Digitization on Business Models in Copyright Driven Industries: A Review of Economic Issues', Washington, Brattle Group paper prepared for the US National Research Council.

Charon, J. M. and Simon, J. P. (1989), *Histoire d'enfance. Les réseaux câblés audiovisuels en France*, Paris: La Documentation Française, Coll. Cnet/ Enst.

Cisco Visual Networking Index (2013), *Global Mobile Data Traffic Forecast Update, 2012–2017*. February 2013. Available at: http://www.cisco.com/en/US/solutions/collateral/ns341/ns525/ns537/ns705/ns827/white_paper_c11-52 0862.pdf.

Cohen-Tanugi, L. (1999), *Le nouvel ordre numérique*, Paris: Odile Jacob.

Coene, B. and Dumortier, J. (2012), *A Conceptual Framework for Copyright's Restricted Acts*. Presentation at the EuroCPR, 2012. Available at: http://www.future-internet.eu/uploads/media/2012-03-EurCPR-Programme.pdf

Confederation of Societies of Authors and Composers (CISAC) (2011), Patissier, F., 'Authors' Royalties in 2009: Return to Growth, Global Economic Survey of the Royalties Collected by the CISAC Member Authors' Societies in 2009', January 2011. Available at: http://www.cisac.org/CisacPortal/initConsultDoc.do?idDoc=20585. Previous reports on collections are available on the CISAC website: www.cisac.org.

Cooper, M. (2006), 'From Wifi to Wikis and Open Source: The Political Economy of Collaborative Production in the Digital Information Age', *Journal on Telecommunications & High Technology Law*, Vol. 1, no. 1. pp. 125–158.

Cooper, M. (2008), 'Round #1 of the Digital Intellectual Property Wars: Economic Fundamentals, not Piracy, Explain how Consumers and Artists Won in the Music Industry', Presentation at the TPRC 2008. Available at http://www.tprcweb.com/index.php?option=com_content&view=article&id=205& Itemid=65.

Costello, S. (2013a), 'Amazon Set for Virtual Currency Launch, Mobile World Live', April 16, 2013. Available at: http://www.mobileworldlive.com/amazon-set-for-virtual-currency-launch.

Costello, S. (2013b), 'IDC Increases Tablet Forecast'. Available at: http://www.mobileworldlive.com/idc-increases-tablet-forecast?elq=fd0d2f62759b4707bb29d9327a09900b.

Costello, S. (2013c), "Facebook Hits 750M Mobile Users, as ad Revenue on the Up", http://www.mobileworldlive.com/%EF%BB%BFfacebook-hits-750m-mobile-users-as-ad-revenue-on-the-up?utm_campaign=MWL_20130502% 20not%20US&utm_medium=email&utm_source=Eloqua&utm_campaign= MWL_20130502%20US%20only&utm_medium=email&utm_source=Eloqua& elq=79da5ce4e1bd48eeafd1f8e549f9efe4

Creative Economy Programme (2010), E-Newsletter, No. 12 (April 2010). 'Meeting of International Organizations on Cultural Statistics'. Available at: www.unctad.org.

CSA (2011), 'Actes du colloque sur les téléviseurs connectés', Paris. Available at: http://www.csa.fr/Etudes-et-publications/Les-colloques-du-CSA/Actes-du-colloque-sur-les-televiseurs-connectes-Musee-du-quai-Branly-28-avril-2011.

Decker, A. (2012), 'Looking for Business Models'. Presentation at the IPTS MCI Conference, Brussels, October 25–26, 2012. Available at: http://is.jrc.ec.europa.eu/pages/ISG/MCI/documents/DeckerArnaud.pdf.

Deloitte-Cisco (2012), *What is the Impact of Mobile Telephony on Economic Growth?* A Report for the GSM Association (GSMA). Available at: http://www.gsma.com/publicpolicy/wp-content/uploads/2012/11/gsma-deloitte-impact-mobile-telephony-economic-growth.pdf.

Department of Culture, Media and Sport (DCMS) (2001), *Creative Industries Mapping Document.* Available at: National Archives: http://webarchive.nationalarchives.gov.uk/+/http://www.culture.gov.uk/reference_library/publications/4632.aspx.

De Prato, G., Nepelski, D. and Simon, J. P. (Eds) (2013), *Asia in the Global ICT Innovation Network. Dancing with the Tigers*, Oxford: Chandos.

Donnat, O. and Lévy, F. (2007), 'Approches générationelles des pratiques culturelles et médiatiques', *Culture Prospective*, 2007–3, Paris: Ministère de la Culture.

Dutton, W. H. (2013), *China and the New Internet World*, Presentation at the IIC 2013 Annual conference. Available at: http://www.iicom.org/resources/annual-conference-resources/doc_details/399-annual-conference-2013-session-5-william-dutton-oxford-internet-institute.

European Commission (EC) (1989), Directive 89/552/EC *Television without Frontiers* of October 3, 1989. OJ L 298, 17/10/1989, p. 0023–0030

EC (1992), Directive, 92/100/EEC of November 19, 1992 on Rental Right and Lending Right and on Certain Rights Related to Copyright in the Field of Intellectual Property. OJ L 376, 27/12/2006, p. 28–35.

EC (1995), *Green Paper on Copyright and Related Rights in the Information Society*, Brussels, July 19, 1995, COM(95) 382 final.

EC (1996), Directive 96/9/EC of the European Parliament and of the Council of March 11, 1996 on the Legal Protection of Databases. OJ L 77, March 27, 1996, pp. 20–28.

EC (1997), Green Paper on the Convergence of the Telecommunications, Media and Information Technology Sectors, and the Implications for Regulation towards an Information Society Approach COM(97) 623, December 1997.

EC (2000), Directive 2000/31/EC of June 8, 2000 "on certain legal aspects of information society services, in particular electronic commerce in the Internal Market", OLJ 178, July 17, 2000, p.1.

EC (2001), Directive 2001/29/EC on the Harmonisation of Certain Aspects of Copyright and Related Rights in the Information Society (April 9, 2001). OJ L 167, June 22, 2001, p. 10.

EC (2007), Communication from the Commission to the European Parliament, the Council and the European Economic and Social Committee, on Scientific Information in the Digital Age: Access, Dissemination and Preservation {SEC(2007)181}, COM(2007) 56 final.

EC Working Paper (2007), *Media Pluralism in the Member States of the European Union*, SEC(2007).

EC (2010a), Commission Communication (COM(2010) 245) of May 19, 2010 on *a Digital Agenda for Europe*. Available at: http://ec.europa.eu/information_society/digital-agenda/index_en.htm.

EC (2010b), Green Paper, Unlocking the Potential of Cultural and Creative Industries, Brussels, COM(2010) 183.

EC (2011a), First Digital Agenda Scoreboard (SEC(2011) 708 of May 31, 2011. Available at: http://ec.europa.eu/information_society/digital-agenda/scoreboard/index_en.htm.

EC (2011b), 'Towards a Simpler, more Robust and Efficient VAT System Tailored to the Single Market', COM (2011) 851 final.

EC (2011c), Communication on a Single Market for Intellectual Property Rights (IPR). *A Single Market for Intellectual Property Rights. Boosting Creativity and Innovation to Provide Economic Growth, High Quality Jobs and First Class Products and Services in Europe.* COM(2011) 287 final.

EC (2011d), 'A Coherent Framework for Building Trust in the Digital Single Market for Ecommerce and Online Services', COM (2011) 942, http://ec.europa.eu/internal_market/ecommerce/docs/communication2012/COM2011_942_en.pdf

EC (2012a), Communication on 'Promoting Cultural and Creative Sectors for Growth and Jobs in the EU', Brussels, 26.9.2012, COM(2012) 537 final EC.

EC (2012b), Proposal for a Directive of the European Parliament and of the Council on Collective Rights Management of Copyright and Related Rights and Multi-Territorial Licensing of Rights in Musical Works for Online Uses in the Internal Market. COM(2012) 372 final.

EC (2013), *Green Paper on Preparing for a Fully Converged Audiovisual World: Growth, Creation and Values*, COM(2013) 231 final. Available at: https://ec.europa.eu/digital-agenda/sites/digital-agenda/files/convergence_green_paper_en_0.pdf.

Edelman, B. (2008), *La propriété littéraire et artistique*, Paris, PUF, coll. Que sais-je ? 1st edition, 1989.

Enders Analysis (2012), Digital Europe: Diversity and Opportunity, Report Commissioned for the 'Let's Go Connected' (www.letsgoconnected.eu) Event on May 8–10, 2012 in Brussels by Bertelsmann, NBC Universal and Vivendi.

Evans, D. S. and Schmalensee, R. (2013), The Antitrust Analysis of Multi-Sided Platform Businesses, Institute for Law and Economics working paper no 623 (2D SERIES), Chicago, The Law School of the University of Chicago, p. 73. Available at: http://www.law.uchicago.edu/Lawecon/index.html.

Federal Communications Commission (FCC) (2009), National Broadband Plan. Connecting America. Available at: http://www.broadband.gov/plan/executive-summary/.

Federal Communications Commission (FCC) (2010), Report and Order, December 21, 2010, FCC-10201.

Feijoo, C. (2011a), 'Mobile Media and Content Successes, Failures, Lessons Learnt and Challenges', Presentation at the 1stIPTS MCI workshop. Available at: http://is.jrc.ec.europa.eu/pages/ISG/documents.

Feijoo, C. (2011b), Presentation at the 2d IPTS MCI Workshop, Available at: http://is.jrc.ec.europa.eu/pages/ISG/MCI/documents/10.FeijoDiscussioneBooksv0.320111027cf.pdf.

Feijoo, C., Maghiros, I. and Gomez-Barroso, J. L. (2009), 'An Overview of Market, Institutional, and Social Drivers and Barriers for Content in the Mobile Platform', in Cunningham, P. and Cunningham, M. (Eds), *ICT-MobileSummit 2008 Conference Proceedings*, Dublin (Ireland): IIMC International Information Management Corporation Ltd; 2008, pp. 1–12.

Feintuck, M. and Varney, M. (2006), *Media Regulation, Public Interest and the Law*, Edinburgh: Edinburgh University Press.

Flichy, P. (2010), *Le sacre de l'amateur*, Paris, Le Seuil: La république des idées.

Forge, S. and Blackman, C. (2009), *OLEDs and E-PAPER: Their Disruptive Potential for the European Display Industry*, IPTS Report. Available at: http://ftp.jrc.es/EURdoc/JRC51739.pdf.

Fransman, M. (2010), *The New ICT Ecosystem. Implications for Europe*, Cambridge: Cambridge University Press.

Gabla, E. (2012), Presentation at the IIC Annual Conference, 'Trends in Global Communications: Devising Digital Policies for Tomorrow's Needs and Aspirations'. Singapore, October 8–9, 2012. Available at: http://www.iicom.org.

Gernet, J. (2002), *A History of Chinese Civilisation*, rev. 2nd edn, trans. J. R. Foster and C. Hartmann, Cambridge: Cambridge University Press.

Goody, J. (2010), *Renaissances. The One or the Many?* Cambridge: Cambridge University Press.

Google (2012), *The New Multiscreen World. Understanding Cross-Platform Consumer Behavior.* (August 2012). Available at: http://www.google.com/think/research-studies/the-new-multi-screen-world-study.html#.

Grance, T. and Mell, P. (2010), 'The NIST Definition of Cloud Computing, National Institute of Standards and Technology (NIST)'. Available at: http://www.nist.gov/manuscript-publication-search.cfm?pub_id=909616.

Handke, C. (2011), *Economic Effects of Copyright. The Empirical Evidence so Far*, Report prepared for the Committee on the Impact of Copyright Policy on Innovation in the Digital Era of the National Academies (USA), p. 51. Available at: http://sites.nationalacademies.org/xpedio/groups/pgasite/documents/webpage/pga_063399.pdf.

Hargreaves, I. (2011), *Digital Opportunity. A Review of Intellectual Property and Growth*, May 2011. Available at: http://www.ipo.gov.uk/ipreview-finalreport.pdf.

Helberger, N. and Guibault, L. (2012), 'Clash of Cultures: Integrating Copyright and Consumer Law', paper presented at the 27th EuroCPR 2012, Ghent, March 25–27. Available at: http://www.eurocpr.org/.

Hugenholtz, P. B., Guibault, L. and van Geffen, S. (2003), 'The Future of Levies in a Digital Environment', IVIR. Available at: http://www.ivir.nl/publications/other/DRM&levies-report.pdf.

Hurst, M. (2012), 'Fanfunding', *Yorokobu*, no. 35, pp. 27–28.

Hutchins, C. (2011), 'The Economics of MCI', presentation at the IPTS workshop. Available at: http://is.jrc.ec.europa.eu/pages/ISG/documents/ChrisHutchins-TheeconomicsofMCI-Sevilla30.5.2011.pdf.

ITU (2012), 'Measuring the Information Society 2012'. Available at: http://www.itu.int/ITU-D/ict/publications/idi/material/2012/MIS2012_without_Annex_4.pdf.

ITU (2013), 'The World in 2013. ICT Facts and Figures, International Telecommunication Union', Geneva, Switzerland. Available at: http://www.itu.int/en/ITU-D/Statistics/Pages/facts/default.aspx

Johns, A. (2009a), 'Piracy as a Business Force', *Culture Machine*, Vol. 10, pp. 44–63. Available at: http://culturemachine.net/index.php/cm/article/view/345/348.

Johns, A. (2009b), *Piracy: The Intellectual Property Wars from Gutenberg to Gates.* Chicago: University of Chicago Press.

Julien, B. (2011), 'Two-Sided Markets', Presentation at the first MCI Workshop IPTS Sevilla. Available at: http://is.jrc.ec.europa.eu/pages/ISG/documents/BrunoJullien-SevilleJune2011.pdf.

Jullien, F. (2012), *Entrer dans une pensée, ou, des possibles de l'esprit*, Paris, Gallimard: Bibliothèque des idées.

Katz, R. (2012), 'The Impact of Broadband on the Economy: Research to Date and Policy Issues'. International Telecommunication Union, The Impact of Broadband on the Economy, Broadband Series, Geneva, Switzerland. Available at: http://www.itu.int/ITU-D/treg/broadband/ITU-BB-Reports_Impact-of-Broadband-on-the-Economy.pdf.

Katz, R. (2013a), *The Latin American Path toward Digitization*, Presentation at the Acorn-Redecom Conference, Mexico, May 17–18, 2013. Available at: http://www.acorn-redecom.org/proceedings.html.

Katz, R. (2013b), Presentation at the IIC Brussels Forum, March 19–20, 2013. Available at: http://www.iicom.org.

Katz, R. and Koutroumpis, P. (2012), 'Measuring Socio-Economic Digitization: A Paradigm Shift', paper presented at the TPRC September 27–29, 2012. Available at: http://papers.ssrn.com/sol3/papers.cfm?abstract_id=2031531.

KEA (2006), *The Economy of Culture in Europe*. Study for the European Commission (Directorate General Education and Culture). Available at: http://www.keanet.eu/ecoculture/studynew.pdf

Kern European Affairs/Cerna (2010), *Multi-Territory Licensing of Audiovisual Works in the European Union*. Available at: http://www.keanet.eu/studies-and-contributions/multi-territory-licensing-of-audiovisual-works-in-the-european-union/

Korea Information Society Development Institute (KISDI) (2012), *2012 Media and Communication Outlook of Korea*, South Korea: Gyeonggi-do.

Lafrance, J. P. (2013), *La civilisation du CLIC. La vie moderne sous l'emprise des nouveaux médias*, Paris: L'Harmattan.

Landes, W. M. and Posner, R. A. (2003), *The Economic Structure of Intellectual Property Law*, Cambridge, MA: The Belknap Press of Harvard University Press.

Leborgne, F. (2010), 'Internet Traffic and Economics', Presentation at the IDATE Digiworld Summit, Montpellier. Available at: www.idate.org.

Lescure, J. (2013), *Culture-acte 2: 80 propositions sur les contenus culturels numériques*, Paris, Ministère de la Culture. Available at: http://www.culturecommunication.gouv.fr/Actualites/A-la-une/Culture-acte-2-80-propositions-sur-les-contenus-culturels-numeriques.

Lessig, L. (2004), *Free Culture: How Big Media Uses Technology and the Law to Lock Down Culture and Control Creativity*, New York, Penguin Press HC.

Leurdijk, A., de Munck, S., van den Broek, T., van der Plas, A., Manshanden., W. and Rietveld, E. (2012), *The Media and Content Industries. A Quantitative Overview. Statistical Report.* Available at: http://ipts.jrc.ec.europa.eu/publications/.

Lomas, N. (2013), 'Forrester: Tablet Ownership in Europe to Rise 4x in 5 Years – 55% of Region's Online Adults Will Own One by 2017, Up from 14% in 2012'. Available at: http://techcrunch.com/2013/02/20/forrester-tablet-ownership-in-europe-to-rise-4x-in-5-years-55-of-regions-online-adults-will-own-one-by-2017-up-from-14-in-2012/.

Lombard, D. (2011), *L'Irrésistible Ascension du numérique. Quand l'Europe s'éveillera*, Paris: Odile Jacob.

Marcus, S. and Elixmann, D. (2012), 'Re-Thinking the Digital Agenda for Europe *(DAE): A Richer Choice of Technologies'.* Available at: http://www.cable-europe. eu/policy-releases/lgi-report-re-thinking-the-digital-agenda-for-europe/

Marcus, S. and Elixmann, D. (2014), 'Build it!... But What if They Don't Come?', *Info*, Vol.18, no. 1, 2014, pp. 62–75.

Marsden, C. T. (2010), *Net Neutrality. Towards a Co-regulatory Solution*, London, Bloomsbury Academic.

Maxwell, W., J., 'A regulatory framework for dealing with online copyright infringement (OCI)', paper presented at the 40th TPRC, Washington, September, 21–23 2012. Available at: http://papers.ssrn.com/sol3/papers.cfm? abstract_id=2025332

McClelland, S. (2012), 'The Big Picture/The Rise of Asia', *Intermedia*, Vol. 40, no. 4, pp. 16–17.

Menger, P. M. (2003), *Portrait de l'artiste en travailleur, Métamorphoses du capitalisme*, Paris: La République des Idées /Seuil.

Menger, P. M. (2010), 'A quelles conditions peut-on créer?', *Critique*, Vol.10, no. 761, Octobre pp. 852–864.

Miège, B., Bouquillion, P. and Moeglin, P. (2013), *L'industrialisation des biens symboliques. Les industries créatives en regard des industries culturelles*, Grenoble: Presses Universitaires de Grenoble.

Minerva, L. (HSBC) (2010), Presentation at the IIC Annual Conference, Barcelona, 2010. Available at: http://www.iicom.org.

Mora, M. (2013), 'La entente de Google no es tan cordial', *El Pais*, February 9, 2013, pp. 34–35.

Nielsen (2013), Consumer Reports 2012. Available at: http://www.nielsen.com/ libs/cq/core/content/login.html?resource=%2Fcontent%2Fdam%2Fcorpor ate%2Fus%2Fen%2Freports-download%2F2013&$$login$$=%24%24login% 24%24.

Noam, E. (2005), Presentation at the TPRC 2005. Available at: http://www. tprcweb.com/.

Noam, E. (2010), Presentation at the IIC Annual Conference, Barcelona. Available at: http://www.iicom.org.

OECD (2005), *Guide to Measuring the Information Society, DSTI/ICCP/ IIS (2005)6/FINAL*. Paris.

OECD (2007), *Information Economy – Sector Definitions Based on the International Standard Industry Classification (ISIC 4), DSTI/ICCP/IIS (2006)2/FINAL.* Paris.

OECD (2009), *Guide to Measuring the Information Society*. Paris. http://www.oecd. org/science/sci-tech/43281062.pdf

Ofcom (2012a), Market-Data-Research. Available at: http://stakeholders.ofcom. org.uk/market-data-research/market-data/communications-market-reports/ cmr12/tv-audio-visual/.

Perrot, A., (2010), presentation at «Les modèles économiques du livre et le numérique», Conference, Innovation & Regulation Chair, Orange, Ecole Polytechnique, Telecom Paris,Paris, June 15, 2010. Available at : innovation-regulation.eu.

Perrot, A. (2011), 'Le numérique : Enjeux des questions de concurrence', Culture-médias & numérique: nouvelles questions de concurrence (s), *Concurrences* 3–2011.

Plant, A. (1934), 'The Economic Aspects of Copyright in Books', *Economica*, Vol. 1, no. 2, pp. 167–195.

Plum (2012), '*The Economic Potential of Cross-Border Pay-to-View and Listen Audiovisual media Services*'. Available at: http://ec.europa.eu/internal_market/media/docs/elecpay/plum_tns_final_en.pdf.

Preta, A. (2011), "Catching up with the Digital Impact", presentation at the IPTS workshop, May 30. Available at: http://is.jrc.ec.europa.eu/pages/ISG/documents/agcomtrendsmedia_content_preta_rev.pdf.

PriceWaterhouseCoopers (PWC) (2009), *Global Entertainment and Media Outlook 2009–2013*, 10th Annual Edition, PriceWaterhouseCoopers.

PriceWaterhouseCoopers. and Wilkofsky Gruen Associates (2010). *Global Entertainment and Media Outlook: 2010–2014*.

PriceWaterhouseCoopers (2011), *Global Entertainment and Media Outlook 2011–2015*.

PriceWaterhouseCoopers (2012), *Global Entertainment and Media Outlook: 2012–2016*. Available at: http://www.pwc.com/gx/en/global-entertainment-media-outlook/index.jhtml.

PricewaterhouseCoopers (PWC), (2013), *PwC Global Entertainment and Media Outlook: 2013–2017*, www.pwc.com/outlook

Punie, Y., Wainer Lusoli, Clara Centeno, Gianluca Misuraca and David Broster, (2009), The Impact of Social Computing on the EU Information Society and Economy, http://ipts.jrc.ec.europa.eu/publications/pub.cfm?id=2819

Ranjini Mei Hua, S. and Melissa, E. (2012), 'Investigating the Potential of Mobile Phones for E-Governance in Indonesia', Paper presented at the CPRAfrica2012/CPR7 conference, 'Connecting Africa & Asia: ICT Policy Research and Practice for the Global South'. Available at: www.cprsouth.org.

Rifkin, J. (2000), *The Age of Access: The New Culture of Hypercapitalism, Where all of Life is a Paid-For Experience*, New York: Penguin Putnam.

Salmon, K. (2013), *Créateurs, producteurs, distributeurs, consommateurs, pouvoirs publics…qui détient le pouvoir ?*. Available at: http://www.forum-avignon.org/sites/default/files/editeur/Etude_Kurt_Salmon_Qui_a_le_pouvoir_dans_la_chaine_de_valeurs_ICC_FA13_BD_.pdf

Sanz, E. (2012), 'The Economic Case of Copyright Policy in the Digital Age: A Cultural Economic Point of View', Paper presented at the VII International Conference on Cultural Policy Research Barcelona, July 9–12.

Savage, S. J., Waldman, D. M. and Hiller, S. (2012), *Market Structure and Media Diversity*, Time Warner Cable, Report Series, Fall 2012. Available at: www.twcresearchprogram.com.

Simon, J. P. (1991), *L'esprit des règles. Réseaux et réglementation aux Etats Unis: câble, électricité, télécommunications*, Paris: L'Harmattan, coll. Logiques juridiques.

Simon, J. P. (2010), 'From the "Broadband Ditch" to the Release of the 2010 US National Broadband Plan. A Short History of the Broadband Penetration Debate in the US', *Communications & Strategies*, no. 80, 4th Q. 2010, pp. 43–66.

Simon, J. P. (2011a), 'Are Telecom Services the Hidden Engine of Innovation in the ICT cosystem?', *Network Industries Quarterly Newsletter*, Vol. 13, no. 2, pp. 11–13.

Simon, J. P. (2011b), 'Long Term Dynamics in Telecom R&D Investments' at 47, in Nepelski D. and Stancik J. (Eds), *The Top World R&D-Investing Companies from the ICT Sector – A Company-Level Analysis*, PREDICT Series, forthcoming. Available at: http://is.jrc.ec.europa.eu/pages/ISG/PREDICT.html.

Simon, J. P. (2012a), *The Dynamics of the Media and Contents Sector*. A Synthesis Report. Available at: http://is.jrc.ec.europa.eu/pages/ISG/MCI.html.

Simon, J. P. (2012b), Changing Modes of Asset Management: IPR and Copyright in the Digital Age. Available at: http://is.jrc.ec.europa.eu/pages/ISG/MCI.html.

Stiglitz, J. E., (2008) 'The Economic Foundations of Intellectual Property', *Duke Law Journal*, 57 (6), pp. 1693–1724.

Thomas, D. (1967) *Copyright and the Creative Artist: The Protection of Intellectual Property with Special Reference to Music*. London: IEA.

UNCTAD (2008), *Creative Economy Report 2008 – The Challenge of Assessing the Creative Economy: Towards Informed Policymaking*. Geneva. Available at: http://www.unctad.org/creative-economy.

UNCTAD (2010), *Creative Economy Report 2010 – Creative Economy: A Feasible Development Option*. Geneva. Available at: http://unctad.org/en/Docs/ditctab20103_en.pdf.

UNCTAD (2013), Growth Rates of Creative Goods Export and Import, Annual 2002–2010. Available at: http://unctadstat.unctad.org/TableViewer/tableView.aspx?ReportId=716.

UNESCO (2005), *Convention on the Protection and Promotion of the Diversity of Cultural Expressions*. Available at: http://www.unesco.org/new/en/culture/themes/cultural-diversity/2005-convention.

United Nations (2007), *International Standard Industrial Classification of All Economic Activities (ISIC) – Revision 4*. New York. Available at: http://unstats.un.org/unsd/class/intercop/expertgroup/2007/AC124-6.PDF.

Verwaayen, B. and CEO Alcatel (2012), Presentation at the Idate 2012 Digiworld Game Changers: Mobile, cloud, big data, November 14–15, 2012. Available at: www.idate.org.

Waldfogel, J. (2011b), 'Describing Media Industries', Presentation at the IPTS workshop. Available at: http://is.jrc.ec.europa.eu/pages/ISG/documents/Waldfogeldescribingmediamarkets.pdf.

Waldman, S. (2011), '*The Information Needs of Communities. The Changing Media Landscape in a Broadband Age*'. Available at: www.fcc.gov/infoneedsreport.

Wallsten, S. (2010), 'The Future of Digital Communications Research Policy', in Laguarda, F. (Ed.), *The Future of Digital Communications Research Policy Perspectives*, Time Warner Cable, Essay Series, Fall 2010, pp. 28–35. Available at: www.twcresearchprogram.com.

Waterman, D., and S. Ji. (2012), 'Online vs. Offline in the U.S.: Are the Media Shrinking?' *The Information Society*, Vol. 28, No. 5, October–December.

Waterman, D. (2011), 'Digital Transition in the U.S.', Presentation at the IPTS workshop. Available at: http://is.jrc.ec.europa.eu/pages/ISG/documents/DavidWaterman_sevilla-digitalTV-2011-final.pdf.

Wauthy, X. (2011), 'Multi-Sided Multi-Platforms Markets', Presentation at the IPTS workshop. Available at: http://is.jrc.ec.europa.eu/pages/ISG/documents/XavierWauthy_MCIwsp.pdf.

Wildman, S. S. and Ting, C. (2009), 'Cost and Capability Drivers of Differences between Old and New Media', in *The Media as a Driver of the Information Society*.

Economics, Management, Policies and Technologies, Media XXI Formalpress, Lisbon: Universidade Catolica Editora.

Williamson, B. (2013), 'Over-the-top (OTT): Helping or Hindering Network Investment?' *Intermedia*, Vol. 41, no. 3, pp. 11–15.

WIPO (2012), Copyright + Creativity = Jobs and Economic Growth, *WIPO Studies on the Economic Contribution of the Copyright Industries*. Available at: http://www.wipo.int/export/sites/www/copyright/en/performance/pdf/economic_contribution_analysis_2012.pdf

http: //www.ip-watch.org/weblog/wp-content/uploads/2012/02/WIPO-Copy right-Economic-Contribution-Analysis-2012-FINAL-230-2.pdf.

Wireless Intelligence (2013 a), 'BRIC Markets Generating almost a Quarter of Global Mobile Sales'. Available at: https://wirelessintelligence.com/analysis/2013/02/bric-markets-generating-almost-a-quarter-of-global-mobile-sales/368/

Wireless Intelligence (2013b), 'Global and Regional Mobile Revenue Trends'.   Available   at: https://wirelessintelligence.com/analysis/2013/01/global-and-regional-mobile-revenue-trends/367/

Wireless Intelligence (2012a), 'Global Mobile Penetration – Subscribers versus Connections'. Available at: https://wirelessintelligence.com/analysis/2012/10/global-mobile-penetration-subscribers-versus-connections/354/

Wireless Intelligence (2012b), 'Half of All Mobile Connections Running on 3G/4G Networks by 2017'. Available at: https://wirelessintelligence.com/analysis/2012/11/half-of-all-mobile-connections-running-on-3g-4g-networks-by-2017/359/

World Economic Forum (WEF) (2011), INSEAD, comScore, and Oxford University, *The New Internet World. A Global Perspective on Freedom of Expression, Privacy, Trust and Security Online*. Available at: http://www3.weforum.org/docs/WEF_GITR_TheNewInternetWorld_Report_2011.pdf.

Wu, T. (2010), *The Master Switch. The Rise and Fall of Information Empires*, New York: Alfred A. Knopf.

Zelnick, P., Toubon, J., and Cerutti, G. (2010), *Création et Internet*, Paris, La Documentation française. Available at: http://www.ladocumentationfrancaise.fr/var/storage/rapports-publics/104000006/0000.pdf.

Section 2: Case Studies

Book industry

ActuaLitté (2013), 'Allemagne : Tolino, plateforme nationale autour du livre numérique'. Available at: http://www.actualitte.com/acteurs-numeriques/allemagne-tolino-plateforme-nationale-autour-du-livre-numerique-40712.htm

Association of American Publishers (AAP) (2012a), Press Release, Bookstats.

Association of American Publishers (AAP) (2012b), *US Publishers See Rapid Sales Growth Worldwide in Print end E-Formats.*

Association of American Publishers (AAP) (2012c), *BookStats Publishing Formats Highlights.*

Association of American Publishers (AAP) (2013), "Bookstats 2013 Now Available". Available from http://publishers.org/press/103/, last accessed May 2013.

Associazione Italian degli Editori (AIE) (2012a), *L'editoria italiana in cifre: 2010 > 2011*, October 2012. Available at http://www.aie.it/Portals/_default/ Skede/Allegati/Skeda10-1-2011.10.10/Sintesi_ottobre_2012.pdf?IDUNI= qc02xp1scdic43tbf2tvquwv183.

Associazione Italian degli Editori (AIE) (2012b), *Dentro all'e-book Le cifre dell'Ufficio studi AIE a giugno 2012*. Available at: http://www.aie.it/Portals/_default/Skede/ Allegati/Skeda10-50-2012.2.16/Dentro%20l'e-book%20giugno%202012.pdf? IDUNI=qc02xp1scdic43tbf2tvquwv3479.

Associazione Italian degli Editori (AIE) (2012c), *Rapporto sullo stato dell'editoria in Italia 2012*. Available at: http://www.giornaledellalibreria.it/Portals/3/ Convegni/Sintesi2012.pdf.

Badenes, J. (2012), *Value Creation through Changing Cost & Revenue Structures*. Presentation at the IPTS 'The Dynamics of the Media and Content Industries', Brussels, October 25–26, 2012. Available from: http://is.jrc.ec.europa.eu/pages/ ISG/MCI/documents/BadenesJesus.pdf.

Benhamou, F. (2011), Presentation at the IPTS MCI workshop May 2011. Available at: http://is.jrc.ec.europa.eu/pages/ISG/documents/.

Benhamou, F. (2012), 'Le livre et son double', *Le débat*, no. 170, May–August 2012.

Benhamou, F. and Guillon, O. (2010), 'Modèles économiques d'un marché naissant : le livre numérique', *Culture Prospective*, Vol. 1. Available at: http://www. culture.gouv.fr/nav/index-stat.html.

Benhamou, F. and Sagot-Duvauroux, D. (2007), *Économies des droits d'auteur : Synthèse V*. [CE 2007–8, décembre 2007], Paris, Ministry of Culture. Available at: http://www.culturecommunication.gouv.fr/Politiques-ministerielles/Etudes-et-statistiques/Les-publications/Culture-etudes/V.-Economies-des-droits-d-auteur-Synthese-CE-2007-8-decembre-2007.

Booksellers Association (2008), Bookselling: International Market Comparisons. A Benchmark Study of Profitability. A Report for The Booksellers Association of the UK and Ireland Bookselling. Sarah Charles and Tim Ingle, November 21, 2008. Available at: http://www.booksellers.org.uk/getmedia/abc0b80d-7de3-494a-bf01-e720302ab74f/Booksellers-International-Market-Comparisons-21-11-08

Börsenverein des Deutschen Buchhandels (2008), Buchkäufer und Leser – Profile, Motive, Wünsche (Band II). Available at: http://www.boersenverein.de/sixcms/ media.php/976/Buchkaeufer_und_Leser_2008_kurz.pdf.

Börsenverein des Deutschen Buchhandels (2012), Wirtschaftszahlen. Available at: http://www.boersenverein.de/de/158446/Wirtschaftszahlen/158286.

Confederación Española de Gremios y Asociaciones de Libreros (Cegal) (2010), *Sistema de Indicadores Estadísticos y de Gestión de la Librería en España*. Available at: http://www.cegal.es/2013/05/30/sistema-de-indicadores-2011/.Last accessed February 2013.

De Prato, G. and Simon, J. P. (2012), The Book Publishing Industry. Available at: http://is.jrc.ec.europa.eu/pages/ISG/MCI.html.

De Prato, G. and Simon, J. P. (2014), Public Policies and Government Interventions in the Book Publishing Industry, *Info*, forthcoming.

Diderot, D. (2012), *Lettre historique& politique adressée à un magistrat sur le commerce de la librairie*, Paris: Allia. 1st published in 1861, probably written in 1767.

Digital Millennium Copyright Act (DMCA) (1998), US Public Law 105–304—OCT. 28, 1998. Available at: http://frwebgate.access.gpo.gov/cgi-bin/getdoc. cgi?dbname=105_cong_public_laws&docid=f:publ304.105.pdf.

Direction générale des médias et des industries culturelles (DGMIC) (2012), *Le secteur du livre: chiffres-clés 2010–2011*. Available at: http://www.dgmic.culture. gouv.fr/IMG/pdf/Chiffres-cles_2010-2011.pdf.

EC (2005a), 'Publishing Market Watch: Final Report'. Available at: http://ec. europa.eu/information_society/media_taskforce/doc/pmw_20050127.pdf.

EC (2005b), Commission Staff Working Paper. Strengthening the Competitiveness of the EU Publishing Sector. The Role of Media Policy. *SEC(2005)1287*. Brussels. Available at: http://ec.europa.eu/information_ society/media_taskforce/doc/comm_pdf_sec_2005_1287_1_en.pdf.

EC (2011), Communication on a Single Market for Intellectual Property Rights (IPR). A Single Market for Intellectual Property Rights. Boosting Creativity and Innovation to Provide Economic Growth, High Quality Jobs and First Class Products and Services in Europe. COM(2011) 287 final.

Eisenstein, Elizabeth L. (1980), *The Printing Press as an Agent of Change*, Cambridge, Cambridge University Press.

Federación de Gremios de Editores de España (FGEE) (2011), Datos estadísticos. Available at: http://www.federacioneditores.org/SectorEdit/DatosEstadisticos. asp. Last accessed February 2013.

Federation of European Publishers (FEP) (2007), *The Whole World is Here. Books in the Digital Age*. Available from: www.fep-fee.eu.

Federation of European Publishers (FEP) (2012), *European Book Publishing Statistics, Brussels*. Available from: www.fep-fee.eu.

Fischer, E. (2011), *Publishing in Germany: An Overview*, Goethe-Institut, Internet-Redaktion. Available at: http://www.goethe.de/kue/lit/ein/en8331936.htm.

Forge, S., and Blackman, C. (2009), *OLEDs and E-PAPER: Their Disruptive Potential for the European Display Industry*, IPTS report. http://ftp.jrc.es/EURdoc/JRC51739.pdf.

Fowler, G. and Trachtenberg, J. (2010), ' "Vanity" Press Goes Digital'. Available at: http://online.wsj.com/article/SB10001424052748704912004575253132121412028.html.

Frugoni, C. (2011), *Le moyen age sur le bout du nez*, Paris: Les Belles Lettres. First published (2001), *Medioevo sul naso*, Roma-Bari, Gino Laterza & Figli.

Gaymard, H. (2009), *Situation du livre. Évaluation de la loi relative au prix du livre Et Questions prospectives*, Rapport à la Ministre de la Culture et de la Communication, Paris: Conseil du livre. Available at: http://www.culture.gouv.fr/culture/actualites/rapports/rapport_gaymard.pdf.

Global eBook Monitor (2012a), Available at: http://www.bookmarketing.co.uk/uploads/documents/global_ebook_monitor_order_form.pdf.

Global eBooks Monitor (2012b), Global EBooks Monitor Presention at BEA, June 2012. Available at: http://fr.slideshare.net/Jo_Henry/global-ebooks-monitor-presention-at-bea-june-2012.

Goody, J. (1977), *The Domestication of the Savage Mind*, Cambridge: Cambridge University Press.

Goody, J. (2010), *The Eurasian Miracle*, Cambridge: Polity.

Grafton, A. (2009), *Worlds Made by Words. Scholarship and Community in the Modern West*, Harvard: Harvard University Press.

Guiry, T., Horne, A., Skinner, B. and Spicer, M. (2012) 'Future of Publishing', Report NESTA. Available at: http://www.nesta.org.uk/publications/future-publishing

IDATE (2011), *E-Book Markets and Forecasts*, 3rd edition. Available at: www.idate.org/

International Publishers Association (IPA) (2011a), '*VAT/GST/Sales Tax Rate: Global Survey on Books and Electronic Publications*', Update 2011. Available at: http://www.internationalpublishers.org/images/stories/VAT/ipa_vat_2011print.pdf.

International Publishers Association (IPA) (2011b), Fixed Book Price. Pros and Cons. Available at: http://www.internationalpublishers.org/industry-policy-introduction/fixed-book-price/pros-cons

International Publishers Association (IPA) (2012), 'Drawing the Global Map of Publishing Markets'. Available at: http://www.internationalpublishers.org/images/stories/PR/2012/global_statistics.pdf.

International Publishers Association (IPA) (2013), 'Digital Publishing Is Now Truly Global: IPA Endorses EPUB 3 as Global Publishing Standard'. Available at: http://www.internationalpublishers.org/images/stories/PR/2013/epub3pr_final.pdf

IPSOS-CNL (March 2010), *Le livre sera-t-il numérique?* Paris: Centre national du Livre. Available at: http://www.centrenationaldulivre.fr/?Le-livre-sera-t-il-numerique.

Kamata, H. (2011), 'How Fear of Disruption Stalled Japan's E-book Development', *E-Book 2.0 Magazine*. Available at: http://publishingperspectives.com/2011/08/stalled-japan-ebook-development/.

Le MOTif, lemotiv.fr (2010), *Un livre numérique?* Available at: http://www.lemotif.fr/fichier/motif_fichier/151/fichier_fichier_coa.t.du.livre.numa.rique_syntha.se.pdf.

Le MOTif, lemotiv.fr (2012), *Le numérique en 2011*. Available at: http://www.lemotif.fr/fr/etudes-et-donnees/chiffres-cles/le-numerique-en-2012/bdd/article/1875

Le secteur du livre: Chiffres clés 2009–2010 (2011), Paris: Centre national du Livre.

LivresHebdo (2013), *Lagardère Publishing annonce une hausse de 1,9% en données brutes pour 2012*. Available at: http://www.livreshebdo.fr/

Martin, Henri-Jean (1997), *The Coming of the Book: The Impact of Printing 1450–1800*, London: Verso.

McDermott, J. P. (2006), *A Social History of the Chinese Book: Books and Literati Culture in Late Imperial China*, Hong Kong: Hong Kong University Press.

Minidata (2011), Ministère de la Culture. Available at: http://www.culturecommunication.gouv.fr/Disciplines-et-secteurs/Livre-et-lecture2/Documentation/Chiffres-et-statistiques.

Minidata (2012), Ministère de la Culture. Available at: http://www.culturecommunication.gouv.fr/Disciplines-et-secteurs/Livre-et-lecture2/Documentation/Chiffres-et-statistiques.

Novelists, Inc. (NINC) (2010), *The Future of Publishing*. Manhattan KS. Available at: http://www.ninc.com/conferences/2010/FutureofPublishing_NincRecap.pdf.

OECD (2012), 'E-books: Developments and Policy Considerations', OECD Digital Economy Papers No. 208.

Pew Internet (2012), *The Rise of E-Reading*. Available at: http://libraries. pewinternet.org/2012/04/04/the-rise-of-e-reading/.

Poort, J., Akker, I., van Eijk, N., van der Sloot, B. and Rutten, P. (2012), *Digitally Binding. Examining the Feasibility of Charging a Fixed Price for E-Books*, IVIR/SEO. Available at: http://www.ivir.nl/publications/vaneijk/Digitally_binding.pdf.

Publishers Association (PA) (2012), *The UK Book Publishing Industry in Statistics 2011*, Market Research and Statistics.

Publishers Weekly (2011), *Global Publishing: Staying Put*. Available at: http://www. publishersweekly.com/pw/by-topic/international/international-book-news/ article/47861-global-publishing-staying-put.html.

Publishers Weekly (2012), *The World's 54 Largest Book Publishers 2012*. Available at: http://www.publishersweekly.com/pw/by-topic/industry-news/finan cial-reporting/article/52677-the-world-s-54-largest-book-publishers-2012.html.

Robin, C. (2007), I. *Économies des droits d'auteur : le livre* [CE 2007–4, décembre 2007] Available at: http://www.culturecommunication.gouv.fr/Politiques-ministerielles/Etudes-et-statistiques/Les-publications/Culture-etudes/I.-Economies-des-droits-d-auteur-le-livre-CE-2007-4-decembre-2007.

Syndicat National de l'Edition (SNE) (2013), *Le livre en chiffres – 2012, données 2011*. Available at: http://www.sne.fr/dossiers-et-enjeux/economie.html. Last accessed April 2013.

Thomson, J. B. (2010), *Merchants of Culture. The Publishing Business in the Twenty-First Century*, Cambridge: Polity Press.

Tsien, T. H. (1962), *Written on Bamboo and Silk. The Beginnings of Chinese Books and Inscriptions*, 2nd edition 2004, Chicago: University of Chicago Press.

Waterman, D. (2011), 'Digital Transition in the U.S.', Presentation at the IPTS workshop. Available at: http://is.jrc.ec.europa.eu/pages/ISG/documents/ DavidWaterman_sevilla-digitalTV-2011-final.pdf.

Broadcasting

ACT Annual Conference (2011), available at: http://www.acte.be/EPUB/easnet. dll/execreq/page?eas:dat_im=026126&eas:template_im=025AE9.

Benhamou, F. and Peltier, S. (2007), III. *Économies des droits d'auteur : la télévision* [CE 2007–6, décembre 2007]. Available at: http://www.culturecommunication. gouv.fr/Politiques-ministerielles/Etudes-et-statistiques/Les-publications/ Culture-etudes/III.-Economies-des-droits-d-auteur-la-television-CE-2007-6-decembre-2007.

Bignell, J., and Fickers, A. (Eds). (2008). *A European Television History*. Hoboken, NJ: Wiley-Blackwell, p. 288.

Brevini, B. (2013). *Public Service Broadcasting Online: A Comparative European Policy Study of PSB 2.0 (Palgrave Global Media Policy and Business)*. Basingstoke Hampshire: Palgrave Macmillan, p. 224.

Burri, M. (2010), Implementing the UNESCO convention in the EU's Internal Policies.

Broadband TV News (2013), "Over 100m IPTV homes by 2017". April 25, 2013. Available at: http://www.broadbandtvnews.com/2013/04/25/over-100m-iptv-homes-by-2017/

Business News America (2009), *Statistics and Analysis, Latin American Telecommunications sector 2Q 2009*.

Carpentier, N., Schrøder, K. C. and Hallett, L. (2013), *Audience Transformations: Shifting Audience Positions in Late Modernity (Routledge Studies in European Communication Research and Education)*, London, Routledge.

Cawson, A. and Holmes, P. (1995), 'Technology Policy and Competition Issues in the Transition to Advanced Television Services in Europe', *Journal of European Public Policy*, Vol. 2, no. 4, pp. 650–671. Retrieved February 15, 2012 from: http://www.tandfonline.com/doi/abs/10.1080/13501769508407011.

Chalaby, J. K. (2010), 'The Rise of Britain's Super-Indies: Policy-Making in the Age of the Global Media Market', *International Communication Gazette*, Vol. 72, no. 8, pp. 675–693.

Chalaby, J. K. (2012), 'At the Origin of a Global Industry: The TV Format Trade as an Anglo-American Invention', *Media, Culture & Society*, Vol. 34, no. 1, pp. 36–52.

Charon, J. M. and Simon, J. P. (1989), *Histoire d'enfance. Les réseaux câblés audiovisuels en France*, Paris: La Documentation Française, Coll. Cnet/ Enst.

Coase, R. (1950), *British Broadcasting: A Study in Monopoly*, Cambridge, MA: Harvard University Press.

CSA (2011), Actes du colloque sur les téléviseurs connectés, Paris. Available at: http://www.csa.fr/Etudes-et-publications/Les-colloques-du-CSA/Actes-du-colloque-sur-les-televiseurs-connectes-Musee-du-quai-Branly-28-avril-2011

Culik, J. (Ed.) (2013), *National Mythologies in Central European TV Series: How JR Won the Cold War*, Eastbourne: Sussex Academic Press.

Dahlgren, P. (1995), *Television and the Public Sphere: Citizenship, Democracy and the Media*, London: Sage.

Dayan, D. and Katz, E. (1992), *Media Events: The Live Broadcasting of History*, Harvard: Harvard University Press.

De Bens, E. and Smaele, H. 'The Inflow of American Television Fiction on European Broadcasting Channels Revisited (2001)', *European Journal of Communication*, Vol. 16, no. 1, pp. 51–76.

De Sola Pool, I. (Ed.) (1973), *Talking Back: Citizen Feedback and Cable Technology*, Cambridge, MA: MIT Press.

Donders, D. K., Pauwels, C. and Loisen, J. (2013), *Private Television in Western Europe: Content, Markets, Policies (Palgrave Global Media Policy and Business)*, Basingstoke Hampshire: Palgrave Macmillan.

EC (2003), Communication on the Transition from Analogue to Digital Broadcasting (COM(2003) 541).

EC (2005), Communication on Accelerating the Transition from Analogue to Digital Broadcasting (COM(2005) 204).

EC (2008), First Report from the Commission to the European Parliament, the Council, the

European Economic and Social Committee and the Committee of the Regions on the application of Directive 2010/13/EU "Audiovisual Media Service Directive", Audiovisual Media Services and Connected Devices: Past and Future Perspectives", COM(2012) 203 final).

European Audiovisual Observatory (EAO) (2009), *Focus – World Film Market Trends*, Strasburg.

European Audiovisual Observatory (EAO) (2011), 'Yearbook Volume 2: Trends in European Television', Strasburg. Available at: http://www.obs.coe.int/.

Federal Communications Commission (FCC) (2012), *In the Matter of Annual Assessment of the Status of Competition in the Market for the Delivery of Video Programming.* MB Docket No. 07–269, released July 20, 2012. Available at: http://hraunfoss.fcc.gov/edocs_public/attachmatch/FCC-12-81A1.pdf.

Feijoo, C. (2011), 'Mobile Media and Content. Successes, Failures, Lessons Learnt and Challenges'. Presentation at the 2d IPTS MCI Workshop. Available at: http://is.jrc.ec.europa.eu/pages/ISG/documents/trends2feijooMobileContentApplicationsv0920110523cfipts.pdf.

FICCI-KPMG (2012), *Report on the Indian Media.* Published online: http://www.ficci.com/spdocument/20217/FICCI-KPMG-Report-13-FRAMES.pdf

Fiske, J. (1987), *Television Culture*, New York: Routledge.

FRAPA, (Format Recognition and Protection Association) (2009), *International TV Format. TV Formats to The World*, Available at: http://www.frapa.org/wp-content/uploads/2010/12/extract_frapa_report_2009.pdf

Harrison, J. and Woods, L. (2007), *European Broadcasting Law and Policy*, Cambridge: Cambridge University Press.

Hartmann, F. (2011), EAO, presentation at the IPTS MCI May 2011 workshop: http://is.jrc.ec.europa.eu/pages/ISG/documents/FHSEVILLA_2011_Digital_transition_final.pdf

IDATE (2010), '*TV Markets & Trends/ 2010 Facts & Figures'.* Available at: www.idate-research.com.

IDATE (2012), *Connected TV Markets.* Available at: www.idate.org.

IDATE (2013), *World TV Markets.* Available at: www.idate.org

Informa Telecom & Media Report (2013), OTT TV Viewers to Outnumber IPTV Viewers in 2013. Available at: http://www.informa.com/Media-centre/Press-releases–news/Latest-News/OTT-TV-viewers-to-outnumber-IPTV-viewers-in-2013-/.

Iosifidis, P., Steemers, J. and Wheeler, M. (2005), *European Television Industries (International Screen Industries)*, London: British Film Institute.

IT Media (2011), *Next-Generation Television. The Over-the-Top Challenge.* Available at: info@itmedia-consulting.com.

Jenkins, H. (2007), *Convergence Culture: Where Old and New Media Collide*, New York: New York University Press.

Krasnouw, E. G., Lonsley, L. D. and Terry, H. A. (1982), *The Politics of Broadcast Regulation*, New York: St Martin's Press.

Lafrance, J. P. (2009), *La télévision à l'ère d'Internet*, Québec: Septentrion.

Lee, S.Y., Wildman, S., and Jun Choi, Y. (2011). 'Why do large markets dominate? A new look at sources of the large home market advantage in the international film trade'. *Media Studies & Communication*, Porto, Portugal. July 07–10.

Missika, J. L. (2007), *La fin de la télévision*, Paris: Le Seuil, La république des idées.

Preta, A. (2013), *Televisione e mercati rilevanti*, Milano: Vita e Pensiero.

Röder, F. (2007), '*Strategic Benefits and Risks of Vertical Integration in International Media Conglomerates and Their Effect on Firm Performance'.* St Gallen, University of St Gallen.

Sanz, E. (2012), *European Television in the New Media Landscape.* Available at: http://is.jrc.ec.europa.eu/pages/ISG/MCI.html.

Silverstone, R. (1994), *Television and Everyday Life*, New York: Routledge.

Thompson, John B. (1995), *The Media and Modernity: A Social Theory of the Media*, Palo Alto: Stanford University Press.

Thorburn, D. (1987), 'Television as an Aesthetic Medium', *Critical Studies in Media Communication*, Vol. 4, no. 2, pp. 161–173.

Waterman, D. (2011a), 'Digital Transition in the U.S.', Presentation at the IPTS workshop. Available at: http://is.jrc.ec.europa.eu/pages/ISG/documents/DavidWaterman_sevilla-digitalTV-2011-final.pdf.

Waterman, D., Sherman, R. and Wook Ji, S. (2012), 'The Economics of Online Television: Revenue Models, Aggregation, and "TV Everywhere"', Paper presented at the TPRC 2012. Available at: http://ssrn.com/abstract=2032828.

Film

Alberstat, P. (2004), *The Insider's Guide to Film Finance*, Oxford: Focal Press.

Anderson, C. (2006), *The Long Tail. How Endless Choice is Creating Unlimited Demand*, London: Random House Business Books.

Baujard, T., Lauriac, M., Robert, M. and Cardio, S. (2009), *Study on the Role of Banks in the European Film Industry. Final Report (MEDIA Programme)*, Brussels: Peacefulfish.

BIPE (2002), *Final Evaluation of the MEDIA II Programme. Final Report. A BIPE Report for the European Commission*. Boulogne-Billancourt.

Bomsel, O. and Le Blanc, G. (2002), *Dernier tango argentique. Le cinéma face à la numérisation*, Paris: Ecole des mines de Paris.

Bonnell, R. (1978), *Le cinéma exploité*, Paris: Le Seuil.

Bonnell, R. (2011), Rencontre avec René Bonnell, le compte rendu. March 11, 2011. Available at: http://www.sacd.fr/Rencontre-avec-Rene-Bonnell-le-compte-rendu.2214.0.html.

Centre National de la Cinématographie (CNC) (2013), Le Marché de la Vidéo. *Les Dossiers du CNC*, mars 2013, no. 325, Paris: CNC.

Cichon, C. (2007), 'Licences and Media Windows', in Nikoltechev, S. (Ed.), *Iris Special: Legal Aspects of Video on Demand*, Strasbourg: European Audiovisual Observatory, pp. 51–62.

Creton, L. (2008), *L'économie du cinéma en 50 fiches (2e ed.)*, Paris: Armand Colin.

Currah, A. (2007), *The Internet Gift Economy. A Study of Socio-Technological Change in the US Film Industry*. Unpublished doctoral dissertation, Cambridge: University of Cambridge.

Dally, P., Durandez, A., Jiménez, L., Pasquale, A. and Vidal, C. (2002), *The Audiovisual Management Handbook. An In-Depth Look at the Film, Television and Multimedia Industry in Europe*, Madrid: Media Business School.

De Valck, M. (2007), *Film Festivals. From European Geopolitics to Global Cinephilia*, Amsterdam: Amsterdam University Press.

De Vinck, S. (2011), *Revolutionary Road? Looking Back at the Position of the European Film Sector and the Results of European-Level Film Support in View of their Digital Future. A Critical Assessment*, Unpublished doctoral dissertation. Brussel: Vrije Universiteit Brussel.

De Vinck, S. and Lindmark, S. (2012), *Statistical, Ecosystems and Competitiveness Analysis of the Media and Content Industries: The Film Sector*. JRC Technical Reports. Luxembourg: European Union. Available at: http://ipts.jrc.ec.europa.eu/publications/pub.cfm?id=5021.

Downey, M. (Ed.) (1999), *The Film Finance Handbook (Vol. 1)*, Madrid: Media Business School.

European Audiovisual Observatory (EAO) (2010), *Yearbook 2010. Film, Television and Video in Europe*. Strasbourg: European Audiovisual Observatory (consulted both in print form and online via http://www.obs.coe.int/oea_publ/yb/yb_premium.html).

European Audiovisual Observatory (EAO) (2011a), *Yearbook 2011. Online Premium Service*. Accessed online (April 29, 2013) at www.obs.coe.int.

European Audiovisual Observatory (EAO) (2011b), *Public Funding for Film and Audiovisual Works in Europe. 2011 Edition*. Strasbourg: European Audiovisual Observatory.

European Audiovisual Observatory (EAO) (2012), *Focus 2012. World Film Market Trends*, Cannes: Marché du Film.

European Audiovisual Observatory (EAO) (2013a), *Yearbook 2012. Online Premium Service*. Accessed online (April 29) at www.obs.coe.int.

European Audiovisual Observatory (EAO) (2013b), *Cinema Admissions in Europe Down Overall, but Some Countries Make Big Strides. Press Release of February 8, 2013*. Accessed online (April 30, 2013) at http://www.obs.coe.int/about/oea/pr/berlinale2013pdf.pdf.en.

EC (2003), *Report from the Commission to the Council, the European Parliament, the European Economic and Social Committee and the Committee of the Regions. Report on the implementation and the mid-term results of the MEDIA Plus and MEDIA Training programmes (2001–2005) and on the results of the preparatory action 'Growth and audiovisual: i2i audiovisual' (No. COM(2003) 725 final)*. Brussels: European Commission.

EC (2009), *Final Report on the Content Online Platform*, Brussels: European Commission.

Eliashberg, J., Elberse, A. and Leenders, M. A. A. M. (2006), 'The Motion Picture Industry: Critical Issues in Practice, Current Research, and New Research Directions', *Marketing Science*, Vol. 25, no. 6, pp. 638–661.

Feijoo, C., Lindmark, S., Pablo Villar, J., Tarin, C., Gelabert, J. and Matía, B. (2013), *Public and Commercial Models of Access in the Digital Era*, European Parliament, IP/B/CULT/IC/2012_18, PE 495.858. Available at: http://www.europarl.europa.eu/committees/en/studiesdownload.html?languageDocument=EN&file=93070.

Finney, A. (2010), *The International Film Business. A Market Guide beyond Hollywood*, London/New York: Routledge.

Forest, C. (2001), *Economies contemporaines du cinéma en Europe. L'improbable industrie*, Paris: CNRS Editions.

Gubbins, M. (2012), *Digital Revolution. The Active Audience: Reach – Experience – Engagement. A Cine-Regio Report in Collaboration with Shareplay*. s.l.: Cine-Regio.

Hesmondhalgh, D. (2007), *The Cultural Industries* (2nd ed.), London: Sage Publications.

Inglis, J. R. (2008), *Digital Cinema in Ireland. A Review of Current Possibilities*, Dublin/Galway: Arts Council/ Irish Film Board.

Keegan, R. (2009), How Much did *Avatar* Really Cost? *Vanity Fair*, December 22, Available at: http://www.vanityfair.com/online/oscars/2009/12/how-much-did-avatar-really-cost.html.

Lange, A. and Newman-Baudais, S. (2007), *Film Distribution Companies in Europe*. Strasbourg: European Audiovisual Observatory.

Lehmann, D. R. and Weinberg, C. B. (2000), 'Sales through Distribution Channels: An Application to Movies and Videos', *Journal of Marketing*, Vol. 64, pp. 18–33.

Mabillot, D. (2011), *La 'menace fantôme' ou la numérisation du cinéma*, Paris: OMIC.

Maggiore, M. (1990), *Audiovisual Production in the Single Market*. Luxembourg: Office for Official Publications of the European Communities.

Media Consulting Group & Peacefulfish (2007), *Study on Dubbing and Subtitling Needs and Practices in the European Audiovisual Industry. Final Report*, Paris/London: MCG/Peacefulfish.

Media Salles (2011), *European Cinema Yearbook 2011*. Accessed online on April 30, 2013 available at: http://www.mediasalles.it/ybk2011/index.html.

Miller, D. (2012), 'Sundance 2012: The Day-and-Date Success Story of "Margin Call"', *The Hollywood Reporter*.

Motion Picture Association of America (MPAA) (2008). *2007 Theatrical Market Statistics*. s.l.: MPAA.

MPAA (2012), *Theatrical Market Statistics 2012*. Last accessed on April 30, 2013 Available at: http://www.mpaa.org/policy/industry.

MPAA (2013), *About the MPAA*. Website. Last accessed on April 28, 2013 Available at: http://mpaa.org/faq.

Nikoltchev, S. (2008), Editorial. *IRIS plus. Legal Observations of the European Audiovisual Observatory (2008–4)*.

Peacefulfish and Media Consulting Group (2008). *Study on the role of SMEs and European audiovisual works in the context of the fast changing and converging home entertainment sector (PayTV, Homevideo, Video on Demand, video games, Internet, etc.)*. SMART 2007/0004. Final Report. s.l.: Peacefulfish/MCG.

Perrot, A., Leclerc, J. P., and Vérot, C. (2008), *Cinéma et Concurrence*, Paris, La Documentation Française. Available at: http://www.ladocumentationfrancaise.fr/var/storage/rapports-publics/084000189/0000.pdf.

Schatz, T. (2008), 'The Studio System and Conglomerate Hollywood', in McDonald, P. and Wasko, J. (Eds), *The Contemporary Hollywood Film Industry*, Malden: Blackwell Publishing, pp. 13–42.

Schermer, B. W. and Wubben, M. (2011), *Feiten om te delen. Digitale contentdistributie in Nederland*, Amsterdam: Considerati.

Screen Digest (2006), 'Independent Distribution in Europe', *Screen Digest*, no. 419, pp. 262–263.

Screen Digest (2009), 'French Video Windows Shortened', *Screen Digest*, no. 455, p. 229.

Segrave, T. (1997), *American Films Abroad: Domination of the World's Movie Screens from the 1890's to the Present*, Jefferson, NC: McFarland & Co. Inc.

Thompson, K. (1985), *Exporting Entertainment. America in the World Film Market 1907–34*, London: British Film Institute.

Tzioumakis, Y. (2006), *American Independent Cinema. An Introduction*, Edinburgh: Edinburgh University Press.

Ulin, J. C. (2010), *The Business of Media Distribution. Monetizing Film, TV and Video Content in an Online World*, Burlington/Oxford: Focal Press.

Vickery, G. and Hawkins, R. (2008), *Remaking the Movies. Digital Content and the Evolution of the Film and Video Industries*, Paris: OECD.

Vogel, H. L. (2007), *Entertainment Industry Economics. A Guide for Financial Analysis* (7th ed.), Cambridge: Cambridge University Press.

Waterman, D. (2005), *Hollywood's Road to Riches*, Cambridge: Harvard University Press.

Wolff, J.-P. (2008), Evaluation of the Report by Dr. Thorsten Hennig-Thurau et al. 'The Last Picture Show? Timing and Order of Movie Distribution Channels' (January 2007). Retrieved from http://www.filmonderzoek. nl/wp-content/uploads/2010/04/Onderzoek-windows-versie-september-08-Wolff.pdf.

Music

Apple (January 7, 2013a), *App Store Tops 40 Billion Downloads with Almost Half in 2012*. Retrieved April 2013, from: http://www.apple.com/pr/library/2013/01/07App-Store-Tops-40-Billion-Downloads-with-Almost-Half-in-2012.html.

Apple (February 6, 2013b), *iTunes Store Sets New Record with 25 Billion Songs Sold*. Retrieved April 2013, from: http://www.apple.com/pr/library/2013/02/06iTunes-Store-Sets-New-Record-with-25-Billion-Songs-Sold.html.

Aris, A. and Bughin, J. (2005), *Managing Media Companies: Harnessing Creative Value Book Description*, John Wiley & Sons.

Aris, A. and Bughin, J. (2009), *Managing Media Companies: Harnessing Creative Value*, 2nd edition, Chichester, West Sussex: John Wiley & Sons Ltd.

Bacache-Beauvallet, M., Bourreau, M. and Moreaux, F. (2011), *Portrait des musiciens à l'heure du numérique*, Paris: Editions rue d'Ulm.

Bastard, I., Bourreau, M., Maillard, S. and Moreau, F. (2012), 'De la visibilité à l'attention: les musiciens sur Internet', in Auray, N. and Moreau, F. (Eds) (2012), *Industries culturelles et Internet. Les nouveaux instruments de la notoriété, Réseaux*, Vol. 5, no. 175, Paris, La Découverte.

Bradshaw, T. (November 23, 2011), *Spotify Adds 500,000 New Subscribers*. Retrieved December 7, 2011, from: http://www.ft.com/intl/cms/s/0/da038766-15fa-11e1-b4b1-00144feabdc0.html#axzz1frYxwQcY.

Capgemini (2008), *Music Labels: Striking the Right Chord for Stimulating Revenues*.

Cimilluca, D. and Colchester, M. (November 12, 2011), *Universal, Sony Split Up EMI Group*. Retrieved April 2013, from: http://online.wsj.com/article/SB10001424052970204224604577031694160429400.html.

Clark-Dickson, P. (2013), 'OTT Threat: Top Strategies to Fight Smart', *Mobile Operator Guide 2013. The Evolution of Mobile Services: Challenges, Strategies, Opportunities*. SAP Mobile Services, pp. 148–155. Available at: www.sap.com/contactsap.

Confederation of Societies of Authors and Composers (CISAC) (2011), Patissier, F., 'Authors' Royalties in 2009: Return to Growth, Global Economic Survey of the Royalties Collected by the CISAC Member Authors' Societies in 2009', January 2011. Available at: http://www.cisac.org/CisacPortal/initConsultDoc. do?idDoc=20585. Previous reports on collections are available on the CISAC website: www.cisac.org.

EC (September 21, 2012), Mergers: Commission clears Universal's acquisition of EMI's recorded music business, subject to conditions. *IP/12/999*. Retrieved from: http://europa.eu/rapid/press-release_IP-12-999_en.htm.

Elberse, A. (2010), 'Bye-Bye Bundles: The Unbundling of Music in Digital Channels', *The Journal of Marketing*, May 2010.

Ferreira, F. and Waldfogel, J. (2010), 'Pop Internationalism. Has Half a Century of World Music Trade Displaced Local Culture?' Working Paper 15964. Cambridge MA: National Bureau of Economic Research.

Hadida, A. L. and Ryan, J. (2010), 'One Way to Save the Music Industry', *Bloomberg Business Week*, July 29, 2010. Available at: http://www.businessweek.com/technology/content/jul2010/tc20100729_564014.htm.

Halliday, J. (February 27, 2013), *Google Music Streaming Would Boost Industry, Says Universal Executive*. Retrieved March 27, 2013, from: http://www.guardian.co.uk/technology/2013/feb/27/google-music-.streaming-universal-digital.

Hoek, C. V. (March 12, 2013), *Nu.nl*. Spotify werft 1 mlijoen nieuwe betalende abonnees in 3 maanden. Retrieved January 3, 2013 from: http://www.nu.nl/internet/3367011/spotify-werft-1-miljoen-nieuwe-betalende-abonnees-in-3-maanden.html.

Hull, G., Hutchinson, T. and Strasser, R. (2011), *The Music Business and Recording Industry* (Vol. 3rd edition), New York: Routledge.

International Federation of the Phonographic Industry (IFPI) (2013), *IFPI Digital Music Report 2013: Engine of a Digital World*.

IFPI RIN (2011), *Recording Industry in Numbers*. Available at: http://www.ifpi.org/content/section_resources/dmr2011.html.

Informa Telecoms & Media (May 2, 2012), *The Adele Effect Hits Major Record Company Market Shares in 2011*. Retrieved April 2013, from: http://musicandcopyright.wordpress.com/2012/05/02/the-adele-effect-hits-major-record-company-market-shares-in-2011/.

IPTS (2008), *The Future Evolution of the Creative Content – Three Discussion Papers*, Luxembourg: EC/JRC.

Johansson, D. and Larsson, M. (December 2009), *The Swedish Music Industry in Graphs: Economic Development Report 2000–2008*. Retrieved April 2011, from: http://www.trendmaze.com/media/1038/swedish_music_industry_2000-2008.pdf.

Kot, G. (May 21, 2009). 'How The Internet Changed Music'. *Time Entertainment*. Retrieved December 2013, from: http://content.time.com/time/arts/article/0,8599,1900054,00.html

Lemelson Center for the Study of Invention and Innovation (2013), *The Invention of the Electric Guitar*. Washington, Smithsonian, last consulted February 2013: http://invention.smithsonian.org/centerpieces/electricguitar/index.htm.

Leurdjik, A. and Nieuwenhuis, O. (2012), 'The Music Industry'. Available at: http://ipts.jrc.ec.europa.eu/publications/pub.cfm?id=5022.

Lunden, I. (February 25, 2013), *Spotify Inks Its First In-Car Deal, Will Stream Music To Ford Via SYNC AppLink*. Retrieved March 27, 2013, from: http://techcrunch.com/2013/02/25/spotify-inks-its-first-in-car-deal-will-stream-music-to-ford-via-sync-applink/.

Nielsen Soundscan & Nielsen BDS (2013), The Nielsen Company & Billboard's 2012 Music Industry Report. Retrieved December 2013, from: http://www.businesswire.com/news/home/20130104005149/en/Nielsen-Company-Billboard's-2012-Music-Industry-Report.

Pandora (April 12, 2013), What Our 200 Million Registrered Listeners Can Mean for Under-theRadar Musicians. Press release. Retrieved May 2, 2013, from: http://blog.pandora.com/category/the-pandora-story/.

Preston, P. and Rogers, J. (2011), EuroCPR. Online Content: Policy and Regulation for a Global Market. *Social Networks, Legal Innovations and the 'New' Music Industry.* Belgium: Ghent.

Ranavoson, H., Iglesias, M. and Vondracek, A. (2013), "How to Decrease Transaction Costs Related to On-Line Music Licensing in Europe?". Paper presented at the EuroCPR 2013. Available at: www.eurocpr.org.

Rego, D. P. (March 6, 2013), *Spotify is Now Available in Volvo Cars.* Retrieved March 27, 2013, from: https://www.spotify.com/us/blog/archives/2013/03/06/spotify-now-available-in-volvo-cars/.

Rob, R. and Waldfogel, J. (2004), 'Piracy on the High C's: Music Downloading, Sales Displacement, and Social Welfare in a Sample of College Students'. Cambridge: NBER. Working paper 10874.

Sellaband (2013), *About Sellaband.* Retrieved March 2013, from https://www.sellaband.nl/en/pages/about_us.

Spotify (November 23, 2011), *Spotify Reaches 2.5 Million Paying Subscribers.* Retrieved December 7, 2011, from: http://www.spotify.com/us/blog/archives/2011/11/23/spotify-reaches-two-and-a-half-million-paying-subscribers/.

Spotify (March 19, 2013), *Spotify Fast Facts.* Retrieved March 27, 2013, from: http://press.spotify.com/nl/information/.

Thomas, D. (March 3, 2013), *Europe is HoT ticket for Live Nation.* Retrieved March 2013, from: http://www.ft.com/intl/cms/s/0/cf8730ca-840e-11e2-b700-00144feabdc0.html?ftcamp=crm/email/201334/nbe/MediaInternet/product#axzz2OveTpt8w.

Thomas, O. (March 11, 2013), *Amazon Has An Estimated 10 Million Members For Its Surprisingly Profitable Prime Club.* Retrieved April 2013, from: http://www.businessinsider.com/amazon-prime-10-million-members-morningstar-2013-3.

TNO (2009), *Ups and Downs,* Delft: TNO.

Tsukayama, H. (November 18, 2011), *Spotify, Other Streaming Services Lose More than 200 Labels.* Retrieved December 6, 2011, from: http://www.washingtonpost.com/business/technology/spotify-other-streaming-services-lose-more-than-200-labels/2011/11/18/gIQA1i7KZN_story.html.

Waldfogel, J. (2011a), 'Music for a Song: An Empirical Look at Uniform Song Pricing and its Alternatives', Presentation at the IPTS workshop. Available at: http://is.jrc.ec.europa.eu/pages/ISG/documents/JoelWaldfogel_MusicforaSong_EU_MCI.pdf.

Waldfogel, J. (2011c), 'Is the Sky Falling? The Quality of New Recorded Music since Napster'. Available at vox (http://www.voxeu.org/), November.

Wikström, P. (2010), *The Music Industry. Music in the Cloud. Digital Media and Society Series,* Cambridge: Polity Press.

Newspaper

Charon, J. M. (1991), *La presse en France de 1945 à nos jours,* Paris: Le Seuil.

Eimeren, B. V. and Vrees, B. (2011), 'Drei von vier Deutschen im Netz – ein Ende des digitalen Grabens in Sicht? Ergebnisse der ARD/ZDF Online Studie 2011', *Media Perspektiven,* pp. 334–349.

Elvestad, E. and Blekesaune, A. (2008), 'Newspaper Readers in Europe: A Multilevel Study of Individual and National Differences', *European Journal of Communication,* Vol. 23, no. 4, pp. 425–447.

ENPA (2010/2011), *Monthly Review. December/January 2010/2011.* Retrieved May 2011 from ENPA: http://www.enpa.be/uploads/Monthly%20Review/DecJan2010/monthly_review_december_january_2010_en.pdf.

Filloux, F. (2011), 'The ePresse Digital Kiosk: First Lessons', July 10, 2011. Available at: http://www.mondaynote.com.

Huysmans, F. and de Haan, J. (2010), *Alle kanalen staan open. De digitalisering van mediagebruik. Het culturele draagvlak deel 10*, Den Haag: Sociaal Cultureel Planbureau.

ICRI et al. (2009), *Independent Study on Indicators for Media Pluralism in the Member States – Towards a Risk Based Approach – the Country Reports*, Leuven: K.U. Leuven.

Iosifides, P. (1997), 'Methods of Measuring Media Concentration', *Media Culture & Society*, Vol. 19, no. 4, pp. 643–663.

Karp, S. (2007), *Newspaper Online vs. Print Ad Revenue: The 10% Problem.* Retrieved May 2011 from Publishing 2.0 blog. Available at: http://publishing2.com/2007/07/17/newspaper-online-vs-print-ad-revenue-the-10-problem/.

Katz, J. E. (2011), 'Communication Perspectives on Social Networking and Citizen Journalism Challenges to Traditional Newspaper', Paper presented at the ITS regional conference, Budapest, September 19. Available at: www.itsworld.org/ý.

Lee, A. M. and Delli Carpini, M. X. (2010), *News Consumption Revisited: Examining the Power of Habits in the 21st Century*, Texas: 11th Online Symposium on Online Journalism.

Pew (2009), *The State of the News Media – An Annual Report on American Journalism.* Available at: http://stateofthemedia.org/2009/.

Pew (2012a), *The State of the News Media 2012.* Available at: http://stateofthemedia.org/.

Pew (2012b), 'The Search for a New Business Model. How Newspapers are Faring Trying to Build Digital Revenue'. Available at: http://www.journalism.org/2012/03/05/search-new-business-model/.

Pew (2013a), *The State of the News Media 2013.* Available at: http://stateofthemedia.org/2013/.

Pew (2013b), 'Newspaper Turning Ideas into Dollars. Four Revenue Success Stories', February 11, 2013. Available at: http://www.journalism.org/analysis_report/newspapers_turning_ideas_dollars.

Pew Project for Excellence in Journalism (2010), *The State of the News Media. An Annual Report on American Journalism.* Available at: http://stateofthemedia.org/.

Pew Research Center (2010), *Americans Spending More Time Following the News.* Retrieved February 2011 from Pew Research Center for the People and the Press: http://people-press.org/reports/pdf/652.pdf.

Picard, R. (1988), 'Measures of Concentration in the Daily Newspaper Industry', *Journal of Media Economics*, Vol. 1, no. 1, pp. 59–77.

Picard, R. (2002), *The Economics and Financing of Media Companies*, New York: Fordham University Press.

PriceWaterhouseCoopers (PWC) (2013), *PwC Global Entertainment and Media Outlook: 2013–2017*, Available at: www.pwc.com/outlook

PriceWaterhouseCoopers (PWC) (2009), *Moving into Multiple Business Models. Outlook for Newspaper Publishing in the Digital Age.*

Quesada, J. D. (2013), 'El boom digital de Latinoamérica', *El Pais*, March 2, pp. 32–33.

Ramonet, I. (2011), *L'explosion du journalisme. Des médias de masse à la masse des médias*, Paris: Galilée.

Rosen, J. (June 7, 2011), *From 'Write us a Post' to 'Fill out this Form': Progress in Pro-Am Journalism*. Retrieved July 25, 2011 from PressThink: http://pressthink. org/2011/06/from-write-us-a-post-to-fill-out-this-form-progress-in-pro-am-journalism/.

Schrøder, K. C. and Kobbernagel, C. (2010), 'Towards a Typology of Cross-Media News Consumption: A Qualitative-Quantative Synthesis', *Northern Lights*, Vol. 8, pp. 115–137.

Schrøder, K. C. and Larsen, B. S. (2010), 'The Shifting Cross-Media News Landscape', *Journalism Studies*, Vol. 11, no. 4, pp. 524–534.

Slot, M. and Munniks de Jongh Luchsinger, F. (2011a), *To Read or Not to Read. Designing the Daily Digital Project*.

Slot, M., Ruhe, L. and Frissen, V. (2011b), *Nieuws Online. Designing the Daily Digital Project*.

Thurman, N. and Myllylhati, M. (2009), 'Taking the Paper Out of News', *Journalism Studies*, Vol. 10, no. 5, pp. 691–708.

Varian, H. (2010), 'Newspaper Economics: Online and Offline', Presentation by Hal Varian, Chief Economist, Google, and Professor, Univ. of California, Berkeley, FTC Workshop, 'From Town Criers to Bloggers: How Will Journalism Survive The Internet Age?' (March 9, 2010). Available at: http://www.niemanlab.org/2010/03/googles-hal-varian-to-newspapers-at-ftc-confab-experiment-experiment-experiment/. A summary is available on the Google Public Policy Blog: http://googlepublicpolicy.blogspot.com.es/2010/03/newspaper-economics-online-and-offline.html

Ward, D. (2004), *A Mapping Study of Media Concentration and Ownership in Ten European Countries*, Hilversum: Dutch Media Authority.

Wunsch-Vincent, S. (2010), *The Evolution of News and the Internet*, Paris: OECD.

Zenith Optimedia (2009), *Advertising Expenditure Forecasts*. Opgeroepen op May 20, 2011, van Zenith Optimedia: http://www.zenithoptimedia.nl/index. php?option=com_content&task=view&id=53&Itemid=67.

Videogames

Asociación Española de Distribuidores y Editores de Software de Entretenimiento (aDeSe) (2012), *El videojuego en España*. Available at: http://www.adese.es/la-industria-del-videojuego/en-espana. Last consulted February 2013.

Association for UK Interactive Entertainment (UKIE) (2012), *UKIE Fact Sheet Q1 2011*. Available at: http://ukie.info/sites/default/files/documents/UKIE_Fact_Sheet.pdf. Last consulted February 2013.

Associazione Editori Sviluppatori Videogiocchi Italiani (AESVI) (2011), *Rapporto annuale sullo stato dell industria videoludica in Italia 2011*. Available at: http://www.aesvi.it/index.php. Last consulted February 2013.

Bakhshi, H. and Mateos-Garcia, J. (2010), *The Money Game. Project Finance and Videogames Development in the UK*, London, Nesta. Available at: http://www. nesta.org.uk/publications/money-game-project-finance-and-video-games-development-uk

Barca, F. and Salvador, M. (2012), 'Il lento camino dell'industria videoludica Italiana', *I Videogiocchi nel mercato del contenuti, Economia della Cultura*, Anno XXII, no. 2, Bologna, Il Mulino.

Bourreau, M. and Davidovici-Nora, M. 'Les marchés à deux versants dans l'industrie des jeux vidéo', in Simon, J. P. and Zabban, V. Les formes ludiques du numérique. Marchés et pratiques du jeu vidéo, *Réseaux*, Vol. 30, no. 173–174, pp. 97–135, Paris, La Découverte.

Bundesverband Interaktive Unterhaltungssoftware (BIU) (2012),'Market figures'. Available at: http://www.biu-online.de/en/facts/market-figures.html. Last consulted February 2013.

Casual Connect Association (2013), *Smartphones and Tablets Games. Casual Games Sector Report*. Available at: http://casualconnect.org/research-reports/

Casual Games Association (2012), *Social Network Games 2012. Casual Games Sector Report*. Available at: http://casualconnect.org/research-reports/

De Prato, G. (2012a), 'Les jeux en ligne: un laboratoire de modèles d'affaires', in Simon, J. P. and Zabban, V. Les formes ludiques du numérique. Marchés et pratiques du jeu vidéo, *Réseaux*, Vol. 30, no. 173–174, pp. 54–75, Paris, La Découverte.

De Prato, G. (2012b), '*La production des softwares et des middlewares et la place des développeurs européens*', in 'Les jeux vidéo : quand jouer, c'est communiquer'. Paris: *Hermes*, no. 62, pp. 101–107.

De Prato, G., Feijóo, C., Nepelski, D., Bogdanowicz, M. and Simon, J. P. (2010), *Born Digital/ Grown Digital. Assessing the Future Competitiveness of the EU Video Games Software Industry*, JRC Scientific and Technical Report, 24555 EN. Available at: http://ipts.jrc.ec.europa.eu/publications/pub.cfm?id=3759

De Prato, G., Lindmark, S. and Simon, J. P. (2012), 'The Evolving Videogames Ecosystem', in Zackariasson, P. and Wilson, T. L. (Eds), *The Videogame Industry: Formation, Present State, and Future*, London: Routledge.

Develop 100 (2010), available at: http://issuu.com/develop/docs/develop100_2010.

Donovan, T. (2012), *Replay the History of Video Games*, Lewes: Yellow Ant.

Entertainment Software Association (ESA) (2013), *Essential Facts about the Computer and Video Game Industry*, Available at: http://www.isfe.eu/sites/isfe.eu/files/attachments/esa_ef_2013.pdf

Entertainment Software Association (ESA) (2012), *Essential Facts about the Computer and Video Game Industry*. Available at: http://www.isfe.eu/sites/isfe.eu/files/attachments/esa_ef_2012_0.pdf.

European Games Developer Federation (EGDF) (2011), *Game Development and Digital Growth*. Available at: www.egdf.eu.

Feijoo, C. and Gomez-Barroso, J. L. (2012), 'Jeux sur mobile: les développeurs et le rôle des plates-formes de logiciels', in Simon, J. P. and Zabban, V. (Eds), Les formes ludiques du numérique. Marchés et pratiques du jeu vidéo, *Réseaux*, Vol. 30, no. 173–174, pp. 76–95, Paris, La Découverte.

Game Developers Conference GDC (2013), Available at: gdconf.com.

Gamesindustryblog (2013), 'Prosiebensat 1 games and Kabam partner to bring-free-to-playgames across Europe'. Available at: http://www.gamesindustryblog.com/2013/02/prosiebensat-1-games-and-kabam-partner-to-bring-free-to-play-games-across-europe/.

GameMiddleWare.org. Available at: http://www.gamemiddleware.org/. Last accessed: March 2013.

GDC (2013), GDC State of the Industry Survey. Available at: gdconf.com.

Genvo S., & Solinski B. (2010), 'The video game: a cultural asset?'. *INA Global*, Available at: http://www.inaglobal.fr/en/video-games/article/video-games-cultural-asset

IDATE (2011), *World Video Game Market.* Available at: www.idate.org.

IDATE (2012), *World Video Game Market.* Available at: www.idate.org.

IDATE (2013), *World Video Game Market.* Available at: www.idate.org.

In-Stat (2010a), *The Digital Entertainment Revolution*, White Paper, IN1004828WHT, February 2010. Available at: www.in-stat.com (last accessed: March 12, 2010).

In-Stat (2010b), Virtual Goods in Social Networking and Online Gaming. Available at: www.in-stat.com (last accessed: March 12, 2010).

IPSOS Media (2012), *Next Level Observations on the UK Gaming Market. Bite Sized Thought Piece.* Available at: http://www.isfe.eu/sites/isfe.eu/files/attachments/ipsos_thoughtpiece_nextlevel.pdf.

ISFE (2010), *Video Gamers in Europe*, prepared by Gamevision Europe Nielsen for the ISFE. Available at: http://www.isfe-eu.org/index.php?PHPSESSID=uq9cthglq7iob2bggo1d2jj9b7&oidit=T001:662b16536388a7260921599321365911.

ISFE (2012), *Videogames in Europe: Consumer Study*, European Summary Report, November 2012. Available at: http://www.isfe.eu/sites/isfe.eu/files/attachments/euro_summary_-_isfe_consumer_study.pdf.

Jeroen, J. and Martens, L. (2005), 'Gaming at a LAN Event: The Social Context of Playing Video Games', *New Media & Society*, Vol. 7, no. 3, pp. 333–355, London: Sage Publications.

Kent, S. (2001), *The Ultimate History of Video Games*, New York: Three Rivers.

Kerr, A. (2006) *The Business and Culture of Video Games, Gamework/Gameplay*, Sage: London.

Le Diberder, A. (2012), 'Le modèle économique des jeux vidéo, un colosse en péril', in Lafrance, J. P. (Ed.), Les jeux vidéo. Quand jouer c'est communiquer, *Hermes*, no. 62, pp. 136–143, Paris: CNRS.

Mateos-Garcia, J., Geuna, A. and Steinmueller, W. E. (2008), 'The Future Evolution of the Creative Content Industries- Three Discussion Papers', in Abadie, F., Maghiros, I. and Pascu, C. (Eds), *IPTS*, Seville, Spain, pp. 16–17. Available at: http://ipts.jrc.ec.europa.eu/publications/pub.cfm?id=1920.

Michaud, L. (2011), 'World Video Games Market', *Communications & Strategies*, no. 83, pp. 137–144.

Miles, I. and Green, L. (2008), *Hidden Innovation in the Creative Industries*, NESTA Research Report: July 2008. Available online at http://www.nesta.org.uk/publications/assets/features/hidden_innovation_in_the_creative_industries.

Newzoo (2014), *Top 25 Companies by Game Revenues, 2013.* Available at: http://www.newzoo.com/free/rankings/top-25-companies-by-game-revenues/

Newzoo (2013), available at: http://www.newzoo.com/free/rankings/top-25-companies-by-game-revenues/#bubkvLzRXq5XPlSD.99.

Nielsen (2012), *Trends In U.S. Video Gaming – The Rise Of Cross-Platform.* Available at: http://www.nielsen.com/us/en/newswire/2012/the-latest-trends-in-us-video-gaming.html

Nordicgame.net (2013), *Game Development*. Available at: http://www.nordicgame. net/index.php.

NPD Group (2013), *New Physical Video Game Sales Make Up Less Than 50% of American Market*. Available at: http://www.gamesindustry.com/new-physical-video-game-sales-make-up-less-than-50-of-american-market/

Ofcom (2012b), *Children and Parents: Media Use and Attitudes Report*. Available at: http://stakeholders.ofcom.org.uk/binaries/research/media-literacy/oct2012/ main.pdf.

Radoff (2009). "chinese-online-game-market-roundup". Available at: http:// radoff.com/blog/2009/11/26/chinese-online-game-market-roundup-q3-2009/

Roth, B. (Bigpoint) (2010), 'On-Line Segment', Presentation at the IPTS Video Games Validation Workshop, Brussels, June 2010. Available at: http://is.jrc.ec. europa.eu/pages/ISG/PREDICT/games/documents/8BRothBigPointOnline.pdf.

Simon, J. P. (2012), 'Les politiques de soutien à l'industrie vidéoludique', in *Les jeux vidéo: quand jouer, c'est communiquer*. *Hermes*, no. 62, pp. 143–151, Paris, CNRS.

Syndicat National du Jeu Vidéo (SNJV) (2012a), *Les chiffres des marchés du jeu vidéo dans le monde et en France*. Available at: http://www.snjv.org/fr/industrie-francaise-jeu-video/. Last consulted February 2013.

Syndicat National du Jeu Vidéo (SNJV) (2012b), *Le jeu vidéo en France en 2012*. Available at http://www.snjv.org/data/document/livre-blanc.pdf. Last consulted February 2013.

The Economist (2011), *All the World's a Game, Special Report*, December 10, 2011. Available at: http://www.economist.com/node/21541164.

Tiga (2013), *Making Games in the UK Today: A Census of the UK Developer and Digital Publishing Sector*. Available at: http://www.tiga.org/about-us-and-uk-games/uk-video-games-industrycarbon in nature as the industry moves towards digital distribution.??

Tricot, M. (2012), 'Jouer au laboratoire. Le jeu vidéo à l'université', in Simon, J. P. and Zabban, V. (Eds), *Les Formes Ludiques du Numérique. Marchés et Pratiques du Jeu Vidéo. Réseaux*. May – July 2012, pp. 177–205, La Découverte, Paris.

Warman, P. (2013), 'Consumers v. Metrics', Presentation at the Mobile Games Forum, 2013. Available at: http://www.newzoo.com/keynotes/ mobile-games-forum-2013-single-screen-metrics-in-a-multi-screen-world-following-consumers-in-changing-old-habits/.

Wi, J. H. (2009), *Innovation and Strategy of Online Games*, London: Imperial College Press.

Zynga US Securities and Exchange Commission, file (July 2011), available at: http://sec.gov/Archives/edgar/data/1439404/000119312511180285/ds1.htm.

Index